P- J

The "Creda"
Housecraft Manual

The "Creda" Housecraft Manual

A TREASURY OF USEFUL RECIPES AND HOUSEHOLD INFORMATION

★

Contributors

MARGUERITE PATTEN

AMBROSE HEATH

CONSTANCE SPRY

ANN SMITH

KAY PENNETT

D. S. PANISSET

JOAN WHITGIFT

SIMPLEX ELECTRIC COMPANY LIMITED

STOKE-ON-TRENT, STAFFS

Published by Odhams Press Limited
for the
Simplex Electric Company Limited
Stoke-on-Trent, Staffs

© Simplex Electric Co., Ltd., 1958

Made and printed in Great Britain by
Odhams (Watford) Limited
Watford, Herts

Contents

Illustrations

COLOUR PHOTOGRAPHS

BY JOHN COWDEROY A.R.P.S., F.R.S.A.

BLACK AND WHITE PHOTOGRAPHS

Electricity in the Home

BY D. S. PANISSET

ELECTRICITY in the home—we take it for granted now, of course. And rightly so, because it is the essential service operating most of the labour-saving and comfort-creating equipment which, during the last 30 years, has changed housework from a drudgery into a pleasant occupation. But one does not need to be more than middle-aged to remember the days when the majority of houses had no supply, when light came from a hissing gas-burner and the carpet was swept with a broom. Then, electric appliances were regarded as a luxury, admittedly convenient and clean but so expensive to buy and to use that only the very well-to-do could afford them. To-day, there is a very wide range of modern electric equipment for the home, with models priced within the reach of all, economical in use and designed to do their work more effectively than can be achieved by any other means.

COST OF ELECTRICITY

For most of us, cost is a very important factor. You can see the price tag on the cooker or washing machine in the showroom before you buy—but what about the running cost? How much does it cost to use a spin dryer or to warm a room or have constant hot water by electricity? The answers to these questions come in two parts: firstly, the cost of electricity; secondly, the amount each type of appliance consumes.

You pay for electricity by the ' unit.' This is one kilo-watt hour — 1,000 watts for one hour. Inquire at your local Electricity Service Centre for the price of a unit in your own area because it does vary a bit in different parts of the country. In most places it comes down to about a penny-farthing a unit if you use more than a few hundred units a year, but, for the sake of simplicity, we will base our examples on a price of one penny a unit. In some areas you can buy electricity more cheaply if you use it only at night— off-peak as it is called—when there is spare generating capacity. This is of interest to those who are thinking of having floor-warming installed in a new house, so providing the cleanest and most convenient form of central heating. You should ask about this at your local showrooms, too, or your architect will find out about it for you.

But for the majority of uses—lighting, cooking, home laundry, water heating, cleaning and so on—we are not concerned with the off-peak tariff because the appliances will be used at any time of the day and so we need only consider the ordinary price which we will assume to be a penny a unit.

Since a unit is one kilo-watt hour (1,000 watts for an hour), an appliance that uses one kilo-watt will consume one unit if it is kept running continuously for an hour: a 100-watt lamp bulb will use one unit in 10 hours.

9

Every appliance carries a rating plate on which its loading is shown. For example, a two-bar fire will have a rating plate marked '2 kW' or '2,000 watts'; with both bars on it will use two units an hour—switch one bar off and it will use one unit an hour.

Vacuum cleaners, unheated washing machines and spin-dryers use so little electricity that you don't need to worry about it. For example, the Debonair is rated at 250 watts which means it uses only a quarter of a unit if you run it continuously for an hour. But to spin a load of washing (6 lbs. dry weight) takes only 4 mins., so you can spin fifteen loads in one hour's running time—or sixty loads for one unit! Suppose you spin a dozen loads a week, you will use one unit in five weeks—less than one shilling a year to get your clothes ironing dry.

Similarly, with a vacuum cleaner. Though you may use it every day the actual running time of the motor in each room is only a few minutes, and you probably consume less than half a unit a week. Floor polishers, food mixers and unheated washing machines—if you work out the running time in hours per week or year and multiply by the loading in kilowatts marked on the rating plate you will find the consumption is too small to worry about.

The consumption of refrigerators depends on their size and how they are used—how many times a day you open the door, how much you use the freezing compartment, how much food you put in, the temperature of the room in which it is installed, and so on. But a family-sized refrigerator of the compressor type (that is, one driven by an electric motor—not the absorption type which uses rather more electricity) uses about one unit a day as an average, costing about thirty shillings a year at one penny a unit. Heating appliances use much more electricity. If you have a heated washing machine or washboiler you will find the rating plate shows a loading of two or three kilowatts. To boil eight gallons of cold water in a washboiler and keep it boiling gently for half an hour will use about five or six units—if you fill it with warm water from the tap it will use less, of course. If you have an electric kettle, it will boil three pints of cold water six or seven times for one unit.

An ordinary two-bar fire uses a unit in half an hour with both bars on. If you use it in the bedroom for half an hour a day for six months in the year it will use 180 units, costing you fifteen shillings at a penny a unit—little enough to pay for the comfort it provides. Convectors and heating panels are usually rated from 750 watts to 3 kw., according to their size, using from three-quarters of a unit to three units an hour if they are running continuously at full load.

Electricity will provide constant hot water wherever you want it and one unit provides three gallons scalding hot. A good hot bath takes four or five units. Electric water heaters are thermostatically controlled which means they heat the water up to the temperature they are set at and keep it there until you use it—then they heat up some more. It is very important that they are correctly installed, otherwise you may waste as much electricity as you use; so if you have an electric immersion heater fitted in your hot water tank or a self-contained storage heater installed be sure this is done by your local Electricity Service or electrical contractor, who will see that the tank is properly lagged and the pipe runs are correct to avoid secondary circulation.

Electric cooking is far and away the cleanest, quickest, easiest and cheapest and it doesn't overheat the kitchen in summer. How much does it cost ? Well, of course, it depends on how much cooking you do. Do you cook two hot meals a day—do you bake your own bread—do you make cakes four or five times a week—do you make jam and bottle fruit ? Families vary so much it is dangerous to generalise on the cost of their cooking. A traditional ' Sunday dinner ' takes about three units; to cook a batch of scones uses about one unit. Experience shows that the average family of four uses about 1,500 units a year for cooking—say, about half-a-crown a week—but if you do a lot of cooking, it may cost you three shillings and sixpence or four shillings.

The cost of electricity to provide complete central heating in your home cannot be worked out simply from the rating plates on heating panels or convectors. It requires expert knowledge to calculate the heat loss from the house and this depends not only on its size and the temperatures you want to maintain in its various rooms but also on its position and construction. If you are having a house built it is well worthwhile considering the installation of the modern floor warming system which provides a wonderful degree of comfort without any visible heaters in the rooms. It saves on building cost because chimneys and fireplaces are eliminated and, of course, it is the cleanest and most convenient form of heating you can imagine. Consult your architect about it, he will be able to advise you on the saving in building cost and on the running cost.

WIRING AND INSTALLATION OF APPLIANCES

So much for the cost of using electric appliances in the home. Now what about house wiring and the installation of appliances.

Electricity is brought into your home by a service cable which may come underground or overhead (mostly in country districts) or by a rising main in a block of flats. The service cable terminates in a pair of main fuses which are sealed by the Electricity Authority and must not be disturbed by anyone else. The meter which measures the number of units you use is connected to the main fuses and then to the distribution board which carries the fuses for all the circuits in the house, lighting points, cooker, water heater and socket outlets.

Each major fixed appliance, like cooker, water heater and fixed washboiler usually has its own circuit back to the distribution board but the socket outlets for your portable appliances are nowadays wired up in a ring main circuit which, as its name implies, is a pair of wires which starts and ends at the distribution board. A number of socket outlets are fed by this pair of wires and they are all of the same type and size so that any of your portable appliances can be plugged into any of the sockets. Each plug contains a fuse which should be appropriate to the appliance it is wired to—a 13 amp. fuse for a portable fire, a 3 amp. fuse for a lamp or radio and so on.

All appliances should be 'earthed' for safety. This means that their metal casing is connected to an earthing wire, which ensures that if the insulation should break down for any reason the casing cannot become 'alive' and give a shock to anyone touching it. When your electrician installs a fixed appliance like a cooker or water heater, he will make sure that the earth connection is properly made, but if you connect a plug to a portable appliance yourself be sure to connect the green wire of the flex to the earth pin (marked 'E'), the red wire to the pin (marked 'L') and the black wire to the pin (marked 'N'). Not only will this ensure that the casing of the appliance is properly earthed, but also that the switch on the socket outlet, and any switches in the appliance itself, disconnect the live wire when switched off.

For safety, all portable appliances with exposed metal parts, irons, kettles, fires, toasters, mixers, spin dryers, washing machines and similar equipment, should be used only from a 3-pin socket outlet to ensure that they are earthed. Earthing is not usually possible with wooden table or standard lamps; electric shavers are usually made with an all-insulated construction so they do not need earthing and some vacuum cleaners are made with 'double insulation' so they do not require earthing. If an appliance is supplied with a 3-core flex it means the manufacturer intended it to be used with a 3-pin plug to ensure that the casing is earthed: for safety, always use it this way.

It is wise to look over the flex of your portable appliances regularly and if you see that the outer covering is becoming chafed, or the flex badly kinked or worn, have a new flex fitted. If you do this job yourself, be very sure to buy the right sort of flex for the appliance—the right size to carry the current, the right covering to withstand the temperature or dampness or handling it may get in use (your electrical dealer or Service Centre will advise you) and always connect the green wire to the earth terminal (marked 'E' or coloured green), the red wire to the live terminal (marked 'L' or coloured red), the black wire to the neutral terminal (marked 'N' or coloured black). When you connect the wires to their terminals do not leave stray whiskers of wire sticking out—twist the strands firmly together to avoid this—and do not remove any more of the insulation than is absolutely necessary. Tighten up the terminal screws or nuts really firmly and see that the flex is properly clamped in the cord grip which is provided to prevent strain coming on to the terminals if the flex gets a tug.

Unless you feel quite confident that you can do this sort of repair work properly yourself, take the appliance to your dealer or Service Centre and have it done by a qualified electrician. Never join lengths of flex by twisting the wires together and wrapping with insulating tape—such joints can cause trouble and danger—buy the right length of flex and fit it properly. Never use a greater length of flex on a portable appliance than you need—it only gets in the way and becomes damaged and dangerous. The trouble is that there are usually not enough socket outlets in the house. If you are having a house built it costs very little to provide enough outlets for all your appliances in the places you are likely to need them—however many you put in you will probably wish later that you'd had a few more !

Portable appliances should never be used in a bathroom. If you want a heater to warm the bathroom, there are models specially made for the purpose and they should only be installed by a qualified electrician. They are permanently fixed out of reach and controlled by a switch operated by a cord.

All the circuits in your house are fused and if the socket outlets are connected in a ring main they have a fuse in the plug as well. Fuses are provided to protect the wiring from overloading and if a fuse blows it means that the circuit it is in is overloaded. This may be because you have connected into the circuit an appliance which takes more current than the circuit was intended for, or it may be that an appliance has developed a fault which has blown the fuse. If a fuse blows it means that something is wrong, so before you mend the fuse, try to find the fault first and correct it.

The fuses in plugs as used in ring main circuits are of the cartridge type and are simply replaced by slipping in a new fuse of the correct rating to suit the appliance. Cartridge fuses of a different type are used in some distribution boards, too. If yours is of this type, make sure you have a few spare cartridges of the appropriate ratings handy—there is usually a stowage provided for spare fuses in boards of this type. Most distribution boards use re-wirable fuses, however, and a supply of 5 amp., 15 amp. and 30 amp. fuse wire should be kept in a handy place. Never re-wire a fuse with a heavier wire than it had before—you lose its essential protection if you do.

ELECTRIC APPLIANCES

When you buy a new appliance for your home, you will find in many cases that your choice will be made quite easily according to your requirements as to size and price or your personal taste in colour and styling. But in some instances you may be perplexed by the number of different types you see in catalogues or showrooms and guidance here may be useful.

There is a very wide range of room warmers from which to choose, but they can be reduced to a small number of types intended for particular duties, as follows:

Electric Fires. Some fires have bright polished reflectors and rod-shaped heating elements, some have no reflector but a slab-shaped element in which a coiled wire is supported. Both types do the same job—provide radiant heat almost as soon as they are switched on—but the reflector type throws the heat forward in a more concentrated beam and provides a somewhat higher proportion of radiant heat, that is, more radiant heat and less warm air flow. Fires of these two types are ideal for giving heat quickly, particularly in a room which may not need heat for long periods at a time, because you feel the warmth as soon as you switch on. In bedrooms, dining room or the sitting room on chilly evenings they are ideal.

Some models are portable, some designed to be fixed to the wall. Some are made with lighting or coal or log effects and some are designed to screen the empty fireplace in summer. You choose from these according to your requirements, taste and pocket. A special type of reflector fire is made to fix to the wall out of reach and is suitable for bathrooms or the nursery if you are sure that inquisitive youngsters cannot reach them.

Convectors. These are designed to provide a stream of warm air that will circulate to all parts of the room. They do not provide that instant feeling of warmth which characterises the electric fire, but given a little time they warm the whole room more evenly. If you have a big sitting room and find that the coal fire or electric fire at one end leaves the other end of the room cold and draughty, a convector will probably put this right.

Convectors come in many shapes and sizes, some designed to be fixed to the floor or wall, others light and portable. A portable convector is a very handy general purpose appliance—to air the guest room, to leave on in the hall on a cold night and to top-up the heat in any room which is not as cosy as you would like it.

Heating Panels (or panel heaters or oil-filled radiators). They are generally flat casings with heaters inside. They provide low-temperature radiation and a flow of warm air and are ideal for background heating in a room or hall which you want to keep warm for long periods. They take a little time to warm up and usually store the heat for an appreciable time after switching off. Ideal for controlling with a room thermostat to maintain a constant temperature.

Some models are portable, some made for fixing to floor or wall. Properly installed they are very safe, allowing no access to live parts and being protected by a built-in safety cut-out from overheating. Their surface temperature is usually limited to a value between 170°F. and 210°F. so they cannot cause a serious burn if touched.

One special type is a higher temperature radiator, such as the Creda California, which provides much more radiant heat and less warm air stream. Ideal for the sitting room in between seasons because it does not dry the skin, or cause the eyes to smart as an electric fire may do if you sit in front of it for long periods.

Fan Heaters. These provide a forced draught of warm air at floor level. They are effective in warming a room much more quickly than an ordinary convector because they force the air to circulate at once. They also keep the warmest air where you need it most—near the floor.

Some models have variable speed motors and are mounted in frames so they can be tilted.

Miscellaneous. There are other types of heaters for special duties— greenhouse heaters, tubular heaters which look like water pipes and are mounted on the skirting board and, of course, floor-warming cables for installation in new houses to provide central heating. There are also heated underlays for carpets which provide a pleasant background warmth.

Water Heaters. This, perhaps, is the most confusing group of appliances for the layman to understand—there seem to be so many different types. Always take advice from your electrical contractor or Service Centre before buying a water heater, but these notes may be of some help.

Immersion Heaters. If you already have a hot water system in your house, heated perhaps by a kitchen boiler or fire-back boiler in a sitting room, you can have an immersion heater fitted in the hot water storage tank or cylinder to give hot water at all the hot taps in the house. This is a very simple way to provide constant hot water and does not cost much to install. The immersion heater is controlled by a thermostat and can also be switched on and off by hand, so you can either leave it running to provide hot water always or just switch it on when required to boost the supply from the boiler.

In summer you can let the boiler out and use the immersion heater.

When an immersion heater is installed it is most desirable to have the hot water tank lagged to save electricity. In some big houses the pipe runs may not be suitable for an immersion heater to give a reasonably economic service, so consult your electrical contractor or Service Centre.

Non-Pressure Type Heaters. To provide hot water at one point only, this is the cheapest and most economical heater to install because it needs only one pipe connection. Special small models like the Creda Crusader are designed for the kitchen; compact, smart in appearance and of high loading with 3 gallons storage capacity, they will provide all the hot water you need for the daily household jobs but *not* enough for filling a washing machine or doing a full household wash by hand. The water tank is tinned and the heater is usually plumbed to the main water supply so the water is suitable for filling the kettle and for cooking purposes generally.

Larger models—12 or 20 gallons—are for bathrooms to give one or two baths in succession respectively. Non-pressure type heaters serve only one point but they have a swivelling outlet pipe so they can sometimes be positioned in a bathroom to serve bath and basin.

Pressure Type Heaters. These are multi-point heaters that will feed as many taps as they are piped to. They are fed from the cold water tank in the roof and provide a complete hot water service. Sizes range from 5 gallons to 100 gallons, but for normal households a 20 or 30-gallon size is suitable.

One special type is the Creda Centrepoint which is designed for fitting under the draining board by the kitchen sink. In this position it is most efficient because of the very short pipe run to the hot tap at the sink where draw-offs are most frequent.

Cistern Type Heaters. These are multi-point heaters which provide a complete hot-water service because they include their own cold water cistern and ball-valve. They are usually plumbed to the main water pipe and are ideal for flats where an existing cold water cistern is not installed.

Cistern type heaters are available in a wide range of sizes—twelve gallons is suitable for a one-person flat, but for a family flat a twenty- or thirty-gallon-size is desirable. Cistern type heaters must be installed above the level of the highest tap they serve.

Cookers. The cooker is undoubtedly the most important appliance in the home, and it is a tribute, of which we in the industry are very proud, that so many millions of housewives have chosen electric cookers to provide this most essential service. But to many women, their electric cooker is something more than just a useful and convenient labour-saving appliance— it is their colleague in the kitchen with whose help they conjure up attractive meals which delight the palate and earn the praise of their family. Perhaps it is the knowledge of this almost personal relationship between the owner and her cooker that makes cooker design such an enthralling occupation both for the engineer and his partner, the home economist.

There is more to choosing a cooker than an appraisal of the appearance and price of the models you see displayed. There are four types of cooker.

Table Models, which consist of a small oven with an element at the top for grilling and a boiling surface on the hob. They are suitable for the bachelor flat, bed-sitter or the week-end cottage, and provide reasonable facilities for cooking the light meals appropriate to such surroundings. Usually, they can be operated from an ordinary 13-amp or 15-amp socket outlet and, as their name implies, are designed to stand on any convenient low table although metal stands and cabinets are often available for them.

Standard Models, of which the Creda Stargazer is certainly the most famous. It has two boiling plates and a grill boiler on the hob, a hotcupboard below, a full size oven and a storage drawer in the base. For family use, they provide all the cooker facilities you need with great economy in price and running cost. The Creda Stargazer has a glass panel in the oven door, through which you may see the food cooking without letting in a draught of cold air, and it can be supplied with an oven timer to switch the oven on and off while you are away from the kitchen.

There is an entirely new type of standard cooker which has just been developed—it is called the Creda Mercury. The hob and boiling plates are of unique design, easier to clean and faster to boil than any before. It has a grill much larger than usual, a carefree oven, heated drawer and many other really new features. You should certainly see this cooker in the showrooms.

Luxury Models, of which the Creda Carefree is a notable example, include all the usual features of the standard cookers with many luxury features besides, such as a clock-faced timer with illuminated dial, hob light, very large oven, heated drawer for warming plates and dishes and keeping food hot and, of course, a most attractive appearance. The Creda Carefree oven was specially designed for use with an oven timer and its cooking performance is exceptionally good.

Horizontal Models. Because so many British kitchens are small, space for all the appliances you want is often hard to find and the traditional British cooker is made as narrow as possible to save such valuable space. But for those whose kitchen space is not too cramped there are wider cookers in which such luxury features as a four-plate hob with lots of draw-off space, separate grill, very large oven, heated drawer and generous utensil storage cupboards are incorporated. The Creda Super Comet has all these features and many others, including oven timer, colour-glance controls which indicate with coloured lights the setting of the control knobs and a hob light.

For country-houses and small hotels and boarding houses, there is a two-oven, five plate cooker called the Creda Restaurant Range.

Refrigerators. In the choice of refrigerators, the purchaser is confronted with two basic types—those which are operated by a compressor and those of the absorption type. The latter are usually of smaller size and lower cost than the compressor type, they are quite silent in operation but use somewhat more electricity for their size. Compressor types are available in sizes from 2 cubic feet upwards and are powered by a 'sealed unit' which usually has a five-year guarantee.

Refrigerators are made in various styles, wall mounting, free standing and for building into kitchen cabinets. Some have vitreous enamelled table tops which add usefully to the table area in small kitchens, others have taller cabinets with more shelf space within reach without stooping.

Deep-freeze Cabinets are also available for those who have produce which they can store in times of plenty to use off-season. Fresh vegetables, fruit, poultry, etc., can be stored for long periods by this means.

Laundry Equipment. There have probably been more developments during recent years in the field of home laundry equipment than in any other and the housewife to-day can have a washing machine—heated or not, wash-boiler, iron, rotary ironer, plate ironer, drying cabinet, tumbler dryer and, most necessarily, a good supply of hot water. But the most amazing recent development is the spin dryer, the Creda Debonair, which has transformed washday from an apparently endless drudgery to a precisely-timed operation for many thousands already.

The Spin Dryer extracts water from the washing by spinning it at high speed for a few minutes, the clothes being firmly supported in the drum during this operation so they cannot be damaged or chafed or felted. In four minutes, a 6 lb. load is made ironing dry at negligible cost for electricity, and ironing can proceed without delay whatever the vagaries of the climate.

The Creda Debonair is easily moved because it is mounted on wheels, it has a safety lid lock and brake and can be operated from any three-pin socket outlet.

Washing Machines. Basically there are three types of washing machine, those with revolving drums, which are often fully automatic; those with paddles which oscillate to and fro and those with impellers in the side or base of the washing bowl. All three types wash effectively: the paddle type is usually regarded as the gentler washing action but the impeller type may wash more quickly and is usually lower in cost. The sizes and prices of these machines cover a wide range; some have powered wringers, others have hand wringers. Some are small enough to be stowed under the draining board when not in use, others have useful table tops. The fully automatic machines are a fixed installation because they are plumbed to the water supply and drain. Many washing machines are available with heaters which enable them to be used as boilers as well as washing machines; the heaters are useful, too, if the hot water supply is not adequate for the washing to be done.

Washboilers are the modern equivalent of the old copper. The full-sized models are usually of ten gallons capacity but smaller boilers, light, portable and easily stowed away when not in use, are available for those who wish to boil a smaller quantity of washing. Washboilers are provided with control switches to enable the full loading to be used to bring to the boil and then to reduce to a slow boiling condition. A boiler with a 3 kw. loading will take about $1\frac{1}{2}$ hours to bring 8 gals. of cold water to boiling point: a small boiler with 2 kw. loading will bring 4 gals. to the boil in about an hour and ten minutes.

Ironing Appliances. There are three types of ironing appliances to choose from of which the ordinary hand iron is by far the most widely used. Nearly all are now fitted with thermostats to control the temperature of the sole-plate to suit various fabrics.

The full weight irons are made with cast-iron soleplates and weigh from about 4 lb. to 6 lb.; lightweight irons have soleplates of aluminium alloy and weigh about $2\frac{1}{2}$ lb. Small irons with fold-away handles are made for travellers; they are usually light in weight and some can be adapted to work on a variety of voltages such as may be encountered when travelling the world. Steam irons supply a stream of steam through grooves in the soleplate to the material being ironed and are of two types: the kettle type in which the body of the iron is a boiler in which steam is generated and fed to the soleplate, and the flash type in which steam is generated by dripping cold water from a tank in the body of the iron on to a hot spot where it is converted to steam and led to the grooves in the surface of the soleplate. With the latter type it is possible to turn the flow of steam on and off as required very readily.

When choosing an iron, pay particular attention to the 'feel' of the iron in your hand and select one which is comfortable, because a well-balanced iron with a hand grip which suits your hand can do much to reduce the fatigue of ironing. So will a well-designed, strong and stable ironing board.

Rotary ironers have a padded roll which is turned by an electric motor and a heated metal shoe extending along it which bears against the material being ironed. It takes a little practice to become proficient in using these ironers, but once the technique has been mastered they save much time and fatigue.

Plate ironers have a padded base rather like an ironing board on which the article is laid out and a heated hinged metal top plate is pulled down on to it to achieve the ironing effect. Again, some practice is needed to make full use of a plate ironer, but once you are used to it its value will be appreciated.

Drying Appliances. With the advent of the Creda Debonair, tumbler dryers and drying cabinets are of less interest because the Debonair brings the clothes you iron to ironing dryness in a few minutes and those you don't iron, like woollens and blankets are ready for the slow natural drying process which is essential to preserve their texture. The tumbler dryers have a rotating drum in which the clothes are tumbled while subjected to a stream of hot air. Drying cabinets have rails on which the clothes are hung and a stream of hot air is passed through them either by a fan or by natural convection. The warm, very damp air which issues from both tumbler dryers and drying cabinets will make the room in which they are installed very damp unless it is well ventilated. The water extracted from your washing by the Creda Debonair runs into a bucket—it does not dampen the air in your home. Heated dryers use quite a lot of electricity because they rely on hot air to evaporate the water from the clothes—the Debonair uses only a negligible amount as shown in the example at the beginning of this chapter.

CARE OF APPLIANCES

The factors which may govern your choice of the majority of well-known home appliances have been discussed above and space prohibits a similar consideration of the many other valuable aids to easier and more comfortable living which electricity provides. It might be invidious to select from this wide range particular examples for mention here, but a visit to the showrooms of your local retailer or Service Centre will enable you to appreciate the study which many manufacturers are devoting to household tasks and their efforts to make appliances which will lighten them.

Those who are moving into a new house, and particularly those who are building a new house, have a wonderful opportunity to plan now for the use of modern electric appliances and it is characteristic of the use of electricity in the home that even if money will not stretch to *all* the comforts and labour-saving devices now, plans can be made to acquire them year by year.

No apology need be made for emphasising once again the importance of enough socket outlets in every room and in the hall and landing so that the appliances you have now and those you will undoubtedly acquire as time goes on can be used in the most appropriate places without the nuisance of long flexes trailing across the floor. If you are building a new house or having some part of your present home modernised or redecorated, consider whether you are taking full advantage of the opportunity to install enough socket outlets—it may not be so convenient later.

In the design of electric equipment for the home a great deal of care is taken to make it easy and safe to operate, but the manufacturer must rely on the co-operation of the purchaser. With each Creda product there is an instruction booklet or card which tells how the appliance is intended to be connected and used. Please read the instructions carefully and, if you can, put it by where you can find it again for reference. Remember always the rules for connecting portable appliances to plugs so that metal casings are properly earthed and if an appliance becomes broken or damaged in use have it repaired—don't go on using it in what may be a dangerous condition.

If you decide to repair or clean an appliance yourself, be very sure it is disconnected from the mains before you start. Cookers are controlled by a control unit on the wall beside them: switch this off before you start cleaning if you are going to do more than give the splash plate and hob a wipe over. In the case of portable appliances, pull the plug right out of the socket.

Reflector fires sold nowadays are required by law to be fitted with an effective guard which must comply with certain regulations, but this does not make them safe for children who may be attracted by the bright element and try to prod it with the poker as they have seen you do to the coal fire. If you lift the guard to clean the reflector yourself, pull the plug out of the socket first and be sure you leave the guard securely fixed when you have finished.

No matter how much care is devoted to their design, most kitchen equipment cannot be completely safe for small children. Cookers get hot, boiling saucepans can be pulled from the hob, irons and wringers and kettles and dryers can be dangerous to inquisitive small fingers.

Most appliances like cookers, refrigerators and washing machines have gleaming white or coloured enamel which will keep its lovely gloss if you wipe it over with a cloth wrung out of warm soapy water. None of these finishes will withstand the use of harsh abrasives which will spoil the gloss.

In all its many applications, electricity is the cleanest, the safest and usually the cheapest power and fuel to use in the home. It can relieve you of so much drudgery in cleaning and washing and drying at very small cost. It can supply constant hot water just where you want it and of course it is the perfect way of cooking—automatic, clean, precise. It supplies luxurious warmth in your home in any degree you choose, from whole-house heating to the quick warm-up of the bedroom on a chilly night. It guards your health by keeping food fresh and saves eye strain with bright light just where you need it.

Creda products make the most of electricity in the home; they are produced in a superbly equipped modern factory at Blythe Bridge in Staffordshire. You will see Creda appliances in every Electricity Service Centre and nearly all electrical showrooms. Year by year you will see new Creda products which have been designed to give you the best service electrically.

General Information About Cooking

BY JOAN WHITGIFT

THE CHEAPEST and most important ingredient of any dish is imagination! Good food is not necessarily expensive food; it can be the cheapest cut of meat, well cooked, seasoned with discretion, garnished with tact and served with an eye to what appeals to the appetite.

We all get into a rut sometimes, even the housewife. It is so easy to buy the traditional roast and to cook it with the usual trimmings, week after week, that we don't bother to think about it any more. The family likes roast beef—why experiment?

Well, to start with, they are your family. They won't want to hurt your feelings. After all, they feel, if it is roast beef *again*, it's still a jolly good meal. Maybe, however, you have sometimes caught that faint sigh as you serve the cold joint for the third time. Or have you fancied they suppressed a groan when you told them you had hashed it?

I don't care how healthy their appetites are, they still would enjoy stimulating, interesting food. They will soon let you know if there are some things they enjoyed more than others, and will take a real interest in your experiments.

So there, I believe, you have on the one hand families that would thoroughly enjoy more original and imaginative food, and on the other hand—the housewife.

Most housewives would like to experiment but are a little nervous of reactions. There is great pleasure in watching the family tuck in to a meal, a real joy in seeing plates wiped clean, but many a woman reads a recipe, gloating over it a little because it sounds attractive, and fears to make it in case it should not have a good reception from the family.

I think every woman should bear in mind the list of the few flavours that she knows are not enjoyed in her household. A lot of people don't like garlic, for example. If your family is of them I would not try to convert them, because if you do you will be almost certain to spoil appetites and give cause for criticism.

Suppose, then, you encounter a dish that has garlic in the recipe. Suppose it is a dish that you would like to make, that you think would be economical, easy and nourishing. It is pretty obvious that you simply leave out the garlic— so obvious that you must wonder at my mentioning it.

I do mention it because I think that it is very difficult and sometimes impossible to persuade people to overcome their prejudice for a flavour.

It is, on the other hand, easy to persuade people to decide to like a *food*. 'My family doesn't like fish!' How often have I heard women make a remark like that, and what nonsense it is! What they mean is that their families don't like fish (or whatever it may be) *the way they cook it*.

And once a woman recognises that fact, she says to herself, 'What's the matter with me that I can't cook fish so that my family eat it and enjoy it?' That's when a housewife turns to a cookery book—one (like this, I hope) that she can browse through to get an idea or two.

Away with the easy, rather lazy, method of catering! Let us be original. Let us have the families wondering what it is, tasting, considering—and asking for more.

PLANNING A MEAL

A good housekeeper never completely plans her shopping for a meal. She has a rough menu in mind and changes it according to what looks best in the shops. She thinks something this way: 'It's a cold day. It would be nice to start with some soup, and I've plenty of stock. I wonder what vegetables are good? Then they would enjoy a pie—veal and ham?— steak?— rabbit? I must see what the butcher's got. And something fruity to follow, something not too stodgy. A flan? No, certainly not; they can't have pastry twice in one meal. Tinned peaches? Oh dear, how *dull*! A lemon soufflé—just the thing. What's the price of eggs?' and so on. That way good and inexpensive meals are concocted.

I once gave myself an exercise in shopping. I bought the cheapest meat and the cheapest fish I could find and brought them home to see what I could do with them. The resultant dishes were good, but when I added it all up, I found that this was not the least expensive catering. The cheapest food may be extravagant, it may cut to waste, need extra long cooking and so much disguise in the way of additions that it is no longer cheap. There is an art in buying, and it comes of long practice.

However, there are a few rules, and I'll list them for your benefit.
1. Don't ever buy more than you need. If you want two tomatoes, buy two tomatoes and not a pound. Some foods which will keep, on the other hand, may be cheaper to buy in quantity.
2. Study a piece of meat before you buy it. Has it a large bone, a lot of fat, will those chops be good value by the time they are trimmed?
3. If you are not sure how to cook something you are buying, ask the salesman. If he is a good one he will know how and tell you.
4. When you are buying it ask yourself not only how you are going to cook it, but whether you can reheat it to make a palatable meal for the following day.
5. Look at each prospective purchase and ask yourself if it is fitting in with the menu you had half-planned before you came out.
6. And finally, and most important, is your menu shaping itself into a balanced meal?

Experienced housewives have a rough idea of how to balance a meal even if they don't know the expression. (It's a bad one anyway, and nutritionists frown upon it as being a loose term that could mean anything or nothing.)

A housewife, when she is planning the family meal, visualises it in her mind and can tell if it is not properly proportioned. She won't say that; she'll probably decide it is "too starchy," or "too stodgy," or "not enough to fill them," or, maybe, "too colourless"; and any of these things will mean that it is not balanced.

It is not the place of this book to go into a long treatise on diet, and in any case most housewives have neither time nor inclination to study the subject. A housewife's object is to keep her family feeling that they've had a jolly good meal when they get up from her table.

Nevertheless, our bodies are tricky bits of machinery and must have all the correct stuff to make the wheels go round. There are dozens of different things that we must have to be healthy, but fortunately several are in each food so that our catering is not as difficult as it might be. They are divided into six categories listed here, though if I were you I shouldn't worry too much about them. They are:

Carbohydrates; Proteins; Fats; Vitamins; Minerals; Water.

People who do not have proper feeding are unhealthy, suffer from fatigue, headaches, eyestrain, bad complexions, over- or under-weight, and in extreme cases of bad diet some very nasty diseases can result. Set your minds at rest! Many of the things we need appear automatically in our food. As a caterer, all you have to do is to ensure that you give *all* of them in sufficient quantities.

Serve at least once a day and, if possible, at every meal, a helping from each of the following squares. Provided your family has had plenty to eat and feels well-fed, and provided you have given them something from each of these vitamin squares, they are certain to get enough proteins, carbohydrates, fats and mineral salts.

1	2
meat, both red and white, poultry, fish, cheese, offal, bacon, nuts, eggs, haricot beans, soya, lentils	butter, margarine, lard, milk, dripping

3	4
soup, tea, coffee, water, fruit juices	Carrots, tomatoes, liver, cod's roe, wholemeal bread, Marmite

5

oranges, tomatoes, lemons, watercress, grapefruit, green vegetables

That leaves out foods like bread, cakes, sugars, jam, porridge, salt and potatoes. They are necessary to us, but as one could hardly cater without them, you need not pay any special attention to them.

When you are planning a meal, glance over those five squares and make sure that you have provided something from each. Then you can't go wrong. The greatest temptation is to exclude square 5. When you are planning roast beef and Yorkshire pudding there seems no place for fresh fruit or vegetables but you must make one. Serve plenty of green vegetables, some watercress, some lemon, orange or lime juice to drink, or if all else fails, a pudding with a lemon juice sauce—anything to get that Vitamin C.

I think it is when you are catering only for yourself that your diet gets most neglected. How many mothers just have bread and cheese and a cup of tea for lunch? It may be enough, but it does not completely nourish. Substitute a glass of milk for the tea and have some fresh watercress and tomatoes with your cheese and you'll be getting somewhere!

Many a dish, delicious and imaginative, I have seen completely spoiled by its appearance, and I consider that appearance is almost as important as flavour. It is no use presenting good food that does not look appetising. Your family will refuse it before they've tasted it.

Some people seem to find this so difficult that a few words of help may not be amiss, and I do assure you that the following ideas have made all the difference to my own cooking.

Whatever you are dishing up, pretend you are preparing it for being photographed in colour. You will immediately become more alive to the appearance of the food. Probably you will want to add colour to the dish— a few slices of tomato and a sprig of watercress. Then you will find yourself criticising the shape and colour of the dish on which you intended to serve the food. Would a smaller one, or a different shape, be more decorative? Does it clash with the food? And as you garnish it with, maybe, a forcing of potatoes or piping of cream, something will stay your hand from dividing a round dish with two diagonal lines so that your photograph looks like noughts and crosses. Try to make it look a bit different, so that even the appearance of the dish is original. Then, if it has an original flavour it will be accepted.

EASY MEASUREMENTS

In most books when a recipe speaks of a "spoonful," it means a *rounded* spoonful—as much above as below the spoon. Unless otherwise stated this interpretation is followed throughout the recipes here. Nevertheless, and because one might forget, most receipes tell you to use flat spoonsful.

A flat spoonful is obtained by running the blade of a knife across the top of a filled spoon, knocking off any food that comes above the rim. Two flat spoonsful therefore equal one rounded spoonful.

A heaped spoonful has twice as much above the spoon as below. Three flat spoonsful therefore equal one heaped spoonful

2 flat or 1 rounded tablespoonful	sugar	=	1 ounce
2 ,, ,, 1 ,, ,,	rice	=	1 ,,
2 ,, ,, 1 ,, ,,	currants or sultanas	=	1 ,,
3 ,, ,, 1 heaped ,,	flour	=	1 ,,
3 ,, ,, 1 ,, ,,	custard powder	=	1 ,,

Butter and margarine are sold in half pound packets, and the simplest method of arriving at correct quantities is to mark the fat in one-ounce sections.

For measuring liquids a half pint tumbler is the most accurate, although a breakfast cup holds half a pint. A gill is a quarter of a pint.

Another method is to buy yourself a set of British Standard spoons and cups which of course make for greater accuracy. Don't, by the way, be led astray by American recipes which often give the ingredients in spoons and cupsful. The U.S. standard measures are different from the British, and an American recipe has to be "translated" before we can use it.

On the whole, I think the actual weights are the safest, and in all the recipes in this book the quantities are given in pounds and ounces.

POSITIONING FOOD IN THE OVEN

The heat is so evenly distributed through the Creda oven that it does not much matter where the food is placed in it.

The meat roasting pan, which is of necessity large, would however interrupt the circulation if it were put in the centre of the oven. The proper place for it is towards the bottom of the oven. In the Carefree, Stargazer and Mercury cookers it should stand directly on the floor of the oven. In the Super Comet it should slide on the bottom runners.

It is most convenient to put quick cooking, such as Yorkshire puddings and small cakes or pastry, to the top, leaving the rest of the oven free for other cooking. Nevertheless, if cooking a whole batch of two or three trays of cakes, scones or biscuits, you can quite easily put them in the oven together on three runners with perfect results; two sponge sandwiches will cook together, one two runners from the top and the other on the bottom runner, and four Christmas cakes, two on the third runner from the top, two on the bottom runner, will cook evenly and in the same time.

Slow cooking, which very frequently has to be done at the same time as a roast, is best placed in the centre where it is most easily attended to.

Provided that the oven is at the correct temperature, the food will be well-cooked wherever it is placed. Owing, however, to the necessity for planning the food so that several dishes are cooked together, you may find it more simple to put quick cooking to the top and bottom and slower cooking in the centre.

COOKING BY TIMER

Most food can be put in a cold oven and will start to cook while the oven heats up. Very little experiment will prove that this statement is correct and I suggest that, to convince yourself, you put a Yorkshire pudding or a toad-in-the-hole towards the top of a cold oven, and dial 425°F. By the time the oven is hot the batter will be well on the way towards being cooked and in another 15 to 30 minutes, according to the size, it will be as perfect as if it had gone, orthodox fashion, into a hot oven.

If you are to gain the maximum benefit from the timer, it is very necessary that you should be quite confident that food will not spoil if cooked by this method. Once having assured yourself that this applies to nearly everything you bake you will also find that most food can safely stand in the cold oven for several hours before starting to cook.

There are two things that you are likely to ask of your timer. You may want to put a complete meal in the cold oven at nine o'clock in the morning and expect to come back at seven o'clock in the evening to find it hot, cooked and ready to dish up. Or you may want to put a cake in a hot oven and go away and leave it, secure in the knowledge that the timer will switch off the heat and that when you return the cake will be cooked, cold and ready to put on the tea table.

Timers differ and there are several on the market, so for instructions on its use you are advised to refer to the book that will have been delivered with your cooker.

Every recipe in this book tells you where in the oven to place it, what temperature it takes, how long to cook it and how many servings it will give. These instructions are for food as I like it. You may prefer yours to look slightly different—paler, or crisper or darker—and because it is impossible to suit everybody I shall have to ask you to vary the times and temperatures to suit your personal taste. In the same way you may criticise my servings as being inadequate for your hungry family. Make a note of any alterations you want in the margin against my recommendations so that you will get things just right the next time!

At the foot of each recipe is a temperature guide and there is also a chart on page 26.

PRESSURE COOKING

Pressure cooking is an art in itself, and pressure cookers are useful and easy to use. Instructions and recipes are always supplied with the pressure cooker and as all makes differ slightly in operation it is unnecessary for this book to give them. One or two points deserve attention, however, not least being the fact that it is unwise to put a pressure cooker in any sort of oven. Always pressure-cook on the hob.

Put the pressure cooker on a boiling plate that it fits and turn to high. When pressure is reached reduce the heat. In addition to the steaming of puddings, a pressure cooker is excellent for soups and vegetables in which flavour is increased and nutritional values conserved. The pressure is also helpful in making meat tender and it is a good idea to pressure-cook a "doubtful" joint before roasting.

DEFINITION OF COOKING TERMS

Au Gratin: Food that has been coated with sauce and sprinkled with breadcrumbs before browning in the oven or under the grill. Cheese is frequently substituted for the breadcrumbs. This dish is served in the vessel in which it has been cooked.

To Baste: To moisten with hot gravy or fat. Fruit, such as baked apple, is basted with hot syrup.

To Bind a Mixture: To add sufficient liquid, either water, egg, sauce, milk or fat, to hold together the dry ingredients of a recipe.

To Blanch: To cleanse, whiten, soften, remove strong odours and flavours or to clear vegetables and nuts of skin, by steeping in cold water or plunging in boiling water.

To Blend: To mix flour or other dry farinaceous food with a small proportion of cold liquid, adding it very gradually, stirring all the time to keep it smooth and creamy.

To Cream: To beat a mixture with a wooden spoon (usually fat, sometimes with sugar) until it is soft, white and fluffy.

To Dice: To cut food into small cubes.

To Fold: To add a light mixture to a heavy one.

A good example is the folding of stiff-whipped white of egg into a cake mixture. The heavier mixture is cut with a metal spoon, each movement putting some of the lighter mixture into it.

To Marinade: To stand the food in a flavouring "pickle" before cooking. This is usually made of herbs, oil and vinegar.

To Mask: To cover food with a coating of sauce.

To Poach: To simmer in a small quantity of water, milk, syrup or other liquid until cooked.

Raspings: Grated, toasted breadcrumbs.

Temperature

The following temperatures must be regarded as a rough guide. Personal taste, experience and nature of the food (the thickness, for example, of a joint of meat)

Food	Temperature and Time		Position in Oven
MEAT			
Beef	400°	20 mins. to lb.	In meatpan on floor of oven
Mutton	400°	30 mins. to lb.	In meatpan on floor of oven
Lamb	400°	25 mins. to lb.	In meatpan on floor of oven
Stuffed meats	350°	30 mins. to lb.	In meatpan on floor of oven
Pork	400°	35 mins. to lb.	In meatpan on floor of oven
Veal	375°	30 mins. to lb.	In meatpan on floor of oven
Venison	375°	30 mins. to lb.	In meatpan on floor of oven
FISH			
Cutlets	350°	20 to 30 mins. according to thickness	In meatpan on floor of oven
Whole fish, stuffed	325°	10 to 15 mins. to the lb.	In meatpan on floor of oven
BAKING			
Bread, full oven	475°	50 to 60 mins., reducing to 425° after first 8 mins.	Centre and floor of oven
Bread, single loaf	475°	45 to 50 mins., reducing to 425° after 8 mins.	Centre oven
Scones	475°	9 to 12 mins.	Second runner from top and bottom runner
Small cakes	425/450°	15 to 20 mins.	Second runner from top and bottom runner
Rich fruit cakes	275/300°	According to size	Bottom runner
Plain cakes	350/375°	1½ to 2 hrs. according to size	Bottom runner

26

To Reduce: To boil quickly and drive off some of the water, thus giving a denser consistency or more concentrated flavour.

Roux: The basis of good sauces and soup. Flour and fat are cooked together and then liquid added, till the mixture is of the desired thickness.

To Sauté: To toss food in a little hot fat till the fat is absorbed. To cook by this method at low temperature and without colouring the food.

To Score: To make light cuts in the surface of the food.

To Sear: To brown rapidly at a high temperature.

To Shred: To cut up finely with a sharp knife.

To Simmer: To heat a liquid so that it maintains a temperature of 180° F. to 185° F. At this point water will be just moving.

Chart

must also be taken into account. Every recipe that is suitable for cooking by baking or roasting in the following chapters gives advice as to temperature and timing.

Food	Temperature and Time		Position in Oven
BAKING (*cont.*)			
Short pastry	400°	15 to 30 mins.	Second runner from top
Puff pastry	425/450°	Till brown	Second runner from top
Plate pies	425°	40 to 50 mins.	Second runner from top and Second runner from bottom; reverse positions after half the cooking time
Sponges with fat	375°	20 to 30 mins.	Third from top
Sponges without fat	375°	25 to 30 mins.	Third from top
Casserole cooking	300/350°	According to quantity	Centre or floor of oven
Bottling	200/250°	50 to 70 mins.	Floor of oven
Yorkshire Pudding	400/425°	20 to 30 mins.	Top of oven
Milk Puddings	275/300°	1½ to 2 hours	Centre oven
Egg custards	250°	45 to 60 mins.	Centre oven
Meringues	175°	Till dry	Any
POULTRY			
Chicken	375°	1 to 1½ hours	In meatpan on floor of oven
Duck	375°	15 mins. to lb.	In meatpan on floor of oven
Duckling	350°	35 to 45 mins.	In meatpan on floor of oven
Goose (10 to 12 lb.)	325°	2 to 2½ hours	In meatpan on floor of oven
Grouse	375°	35 mins.	In meatpan on floor of oven
Guinea fowl	350°	25 to 35 mins.	In meatpan on floor of oven
Partridge	375°	25 to 35 mins.	In meatpan on floor of oven
Pheasant	375°	45 to 50 mins.	In meatpan on floor of oven
Quail	350°	25 mins.	In meatpan on floor of oven
Rabbit	350°	60 to 80 mins.	In meatpan on floor of oven
Turkey (10 to 12 lb.)	300°	2 to 2½ hours	In meatpan on floor of oven

Flavourings and Stuffings

Herbs, Flavourings and Seasonings

FRESH HERBS are best, of course, and if you have a garden or even only a window box it is good to grow them for yourself, cutting them as you want them.

The most frequently used flavourings are listed below against the foods into which they are usually introduced.

Almond: For marzipan, sauces, moulds, cakes.

Angelica: Decorations on cakes and puddings.

Bay leaf: For sauces, fish, meat.

Borage: For cold beverages and salads.

Bouquet garni: A sprig of thyme, a bay leaf and two sprigs of parsley, tied with cotton and used to flavour stews and sauces. It is removed before serving. The equivalent dried herbs can be tied in a muslin bag if fresh herbs are not available.

Carraway seeds: Occasionally used in stews, but most common in cakes.

Chervil: An aromatic herb. Used in salads.

Chives: As a substitute for onion. Used in salads, soups, sandwich spreads.

Cloves: Most frequently used with apple, but also as a flavouring for some meat dishes.

Cayenne: Very hot red pepper for cheese dishes and sauces.

Fennel: For fish dishes.

Garlic: For meat dishes, salads and sauces.

Ginger: In cakes and puddings, usually powdered, but also the chopped root is used.

Maraschino: Liqueur used in desserts.

Marjoram: For forcemeat.

Mint: For sauces; occasionally used as a garnish and in salads; also good with summer cups and cold fruit drinks.

Mixed dried herbs: For forcemeat.

Nutmeg: Used in puddings.

Parsley: For sauces, garnishes.

Paprika: Red pepper for sauces.

Peppercorns: For soused dishes and pickles.

Ratafia: Used in some sweet dishes as an alternative to almond.

Sage: For stuffing.

Sorrel: Used in sauces with fish, and in cooking fish.

Spice, Allspice: A mixture of spices; nutmeg, cinnamon, mace are the most common.

Spice-pickle: A mixture of spices, vinegar, ginger, onion and water, used for pickling fruits, vegetables and some fish.

Vanilla: For chocolate or coffee dishes, some cakes and puddings.

Stuffings

FORCEMEAT

2 ozs. breadcrumbs	1 tablespoonful chopped parsley
1 oz. chopped or shredded suet	a pinch of mixed herbs if liked
grated rind and juice of ½ a lemon	pepper and salt
1 egg	

Mix all the ingredients together, adding a little water to bind if necessary. Use as a stuffing, or with well floured hands, roll into small balls and cook in a stew or roast round a joint, adding after cooking has started so that they cook for a maximum of 30 min.

SAGE AND ONION

½ lb. onions	1 level teaspoonful powdered sage
2 ozs. breadcrumbs	pepper and salt

Peel the onions and boil till tender. Drain and chop finely. Mix with other ingredients and use as stuffing.

SAUSAGE

1 lb. sausage meat	1 teaspoonful chopped parsley
pinch of mixed herbs	1 teaspoonful chopped onion

Mix the ingredients thoroughly and use as stuffing.

CHESTNUT (A)

½ lb. chestnuts	1 tablespoonful lemon juice
2 ozs. breadcrumbs	1 tablespoonful chopped parsley
1 oz. grated suet	salt 1 egg

Slit the skins of the chestnuts and boil for 30 mins. or till tender. Shell them while still hot. Press through a sieve.

Mix with the other ingredients, binding with the egg. Use as a stuffing for turkey.

CHESTNUT (B)

1 lb. cooked, sieved chestnuts	4 sticks chopped celery
4 ozs. soaked and chopped dried	2 ozs. breadcrumbs
apricots	1 egg salt

Mix the ingredients thoroughly and use as a stuffing for turkey.

Garnishes

FRIED PARSLEY

Wash the parsley, break off the stalks. Dry the leaves thoroughly and put them in a frying basket. Get fat smoking hot and draw away from boiling plate. Lower the parsley carefully into the hot fat. When spluttering ceases, withdraw the basket for a few seconds and then lower again into the fat. Lift out the basket, drain the parsley of all fat.

It should be crisp and green.

MAÎTRE D'HÔTEL BUTTER

½ oz. butter
2 or 3 drops lemon juice

1 dessertspoonful finely chopped parsley
pepper

Cream all the ingredients together. Shape into squares and cool in the refrigerator. Serve on grilled meat or fish just before sending to the table.

CROÛTONS

Small pieces of bread cut into fancy shapes and fried till crisp and pale brown.

AWAY FROM THE ORDINARY

Roast pork usually is accompanied with apple sauce. Try these instead:
(1) Very young beetroots, boiled, skinned and served as you would a vegetable for garnishing the joint.
(2) Stewed prunes, unsweetened, passed through a sieve and made into a thick sauce with lemon juice.
(3) Sweet oranges, sliced and heated very gently in their own juice.
(4) Red currant and horseradish sauce (see page 38).

Lamb has red currant jelly and mint sauce, but it is interesting with:
(1) Three tablespoonsful of cherry jam, heated to melt in the juice of a lemon, with 1 tablespoonful of chopped mint. Serve cold.
(2) Peel a lemon, removing the pith and cut into thin rings. Drop them in ½ pint of curry sauce. Serve hot.
(3) Beat some milk or cream into 2 ozs. cream cheese till it is as thick as whipped cream. Add 1 teaspoonful of chopped chives, a teaspoonful of chopped mint, 2 tablespoonsful of finely chopped parsley, pepper and salt to taste.

Beef has horseradish sauce, but it is a change with one of the following:
(1) Caper sauce, well-flavoured with paprika.
(2) Add 1 oz. of coarsely chopped walnuts to ½ pint of mustard sauce. Serve hot.

Try garnishing *fish* with wedges of orange or thin slices of pineapple instead of lemon. Try stuffing it with a forcemeat stuffing to which you have added some blanched almonds.

Vegetables stuffed with plain boiled rice mixed with chopped almonds and enough thick cheese sauce to bind are delicious. Use this stuffing for peppers and large Spanish onions.

Sauces

SAUCE makes the dish! It gives that touch of something different—that glamour to quite a modest little meal. A point you have to consider very carefully is what you want the sauce to do, in addition to improving appearance and providing decoration. Is it to bring out the flavour of the food? If so, it should be made from some of the liquid in which the food was cooked. Is it to provide a contrast, as you might want to with a rather flavourless fish or vegetable, or to counteract the richness of a food as you do when you serve something acid, like apples, with rich meat?

Choosing a sauce is an art—if you haven't the flair for it stick to the traditional combination, but there is really no limit to the variations and originality that you can use.

There are a few terms in the making of a sauce that may need explanation:

A roux. This is the term for cooking flour and fat together prior to the addition of liquid in the correct proportions.

A panada. This is a thick binding sauce and is used in the foundation for croquettes, soufflés and réchauffes.

A purée. This is the result of pressing food through a sieve to break it into a fine mash.

Tammying. This is straining through a finely woven cloth.

A chaudfroid. This is a sauce which has aspic added to it to make it set. It is used as a glaze for certain foods and gives a high gloss to the dish.

REASONS FOR FAILURE

If a sauce is a failure it is for one of the following reasons:

(1) It may be lumpy. This is usually through insufficient mixing before cooking or through mixing over the heat. The sauce should be smooth before it is put on the boiling plate to cook. To correct it, tammy or strain through a fine sieve.

(2) It may be too thick. This is due to careless apportioning of the ingredients. Add more liquid and correct the seasoning. It may be too thin for the same reason. Never add more flour as there is a tendency for the sauce to become lumpy at this stage, but boil gently to reduce it until it is of the right consistency.

(3) Through over-long standing before cooking it may get thin. Do not leave the sauce standing on the hob. Serve it at once if you can, and if not, stand the saucepan in a bowl of hot water or a bain marie when it will not lose its texture.

(4) It may form an unsightly skin on the top. To prevent this lay a piece of greaseproof paper across the top of the sauce and cover with the lid of pan.

(5) It may " catch " through careless cooking and taste burnt. There is nothing you can do about this—throw it away and start again.

For easy classification sauces are usually divided into four types:
(1) Roux and blended sauces.
(2) Sauces thickened with egg.
(3) Unclassified sauces.
(4) Cold sauces and dressings.

Roux and Blended Sauces

Pouring	*Coating*	*Panada*
¾ oz. butter or margarine	1 oz. butter or margarine	2 ozs. butter or margarine
¾ oz. flour (plain)	1 oz. flour (plain)	2 ozs. flour (plain)
½ pint liquid	½ pint liquid	½ pint liquid

ROUX METHOD

The method for making the above three basic sauces is the same in each case. Follow these instructions exactly and the sauce will not be lumpy:

Put the fat and the flour in a pan over a very low heat and stir them together until the mixture looks like fine wet sand. Remove the pan from the heat and add half the liquid very slowly, stirring all the time until it is smooth. Cook slowly for 2 mins., stirring all the while. Remove from the boiling plate again and add half of the remainder of the liquid. Stir till smooth and cook for another 2 mins. Remove from the heat a third time, add the last of the liquid, stir till smooth and cook, stirring all the time, for 7 mins.

BLENDED METHOD

Blend the flour in the cold liquid and stir till smooth. Strain into a saucepan and bring slowly to the boil, stirring all the time, and cook for 7 mins. Now break the fat into small lumps, drop them into the sauce and beat thoroughly.

METHOD FOR BROWN SAUCE

Thinly slice a small onion and dice a small carrot. Fry them in ½ oz. dripping until of a rich brown colour. Remove the vegetables and add ½ oz. of flour to the dripping and cook, stirring all the time. Remove from the heat and add ½ pint of household stock, following the instructions for white sauce. Simmer for half an hour, remove all fat and scum, and strain.

VARIATIONS

With the base, made preferably by the roux method which is smoother, and with suitable seasoning (you should always *taste* a sauce before you serve it, to make sure it is to your liking) you can make the following:

ALLEMANDE SAUCE

To ¾ pint of white pouring sauce made with white stock add one well-beaten egg, seasoning and a dash of nutmeg. Cook without boiling for a few minutes and then beat in ½ oz. of butter. Strain and re-heat before serving.

ANCHOVY SAUCE

Add 2 teaspoonsful of anchovy essence to ½ pint of pouring fish sauce. Beat in a few drops of lemon juice just before serving. Season to taste.

Stuffed sole, roast loin of lamb, onion sauce and steamed jam pudding

French liver and bacon

BECHAMEL SAUCE

To ½ pint of cold milk add 1 shallot, 1 small piece of carrot, 1 piece of celery, a bay leaf and 6 peppercorns. Bring to the boil, leave to infuse for half an hour and strain. Cool. Make a white coating sauce with the milk, cook for 7 to 10 mins. and then stir in a tablespoonful of cream just before serving. Season to taste.

BRANDY SAUCE

To ½ pint of white pouring sauce add 1 tablespoonful of brandy and a teaspoonful of sugar.

CAPER SAUCE

To ½ pint of white pouring sauce, made half-milk, half white stock, add 1 heaped dessertspoonful of chopped capers and 2 teaspoonsful of caper vinegar. Season to taste.

CHEESE SAUCE

To ½ pint of white coating sauce made with milk and slightly cooled, season and add 1 oz. finely grated cheese. If sauce is for an au gratin, it is a good idea to sprinkle a little more cheese over the top of the dish to improve the appearance and assist browning during cooking.

EGG SAUCE

To ½ pint of white pouring sauce made with milk, or half milk, half white stock, add a chopped hard boiled egg just before serving.

ESPAGNOLE SAUCE

Make a brown coating sauce, adding a few diced mushrooms and 1 oz. of chopped ham or bacon when you fry the vegetables. Add a teaspoonful of sherry and 2 tablespoonsful of tomato pulp to the sauce after it has simmered for an hour. Then tammy or strain, re-heat, taste and season.

FENNEL SAUCE

1 oz. butter or margarine	pepper and salt
¾ oz. flour	2 tablespoonsful chopped cooked
½ pint hot (not boiling) water	fennel

Melt the fat, add the flour and cook for 3 mins. without browning. Remove from the heat and, very slowly and beating all the time, add the hot water. When quite smooth, bring to the boil and simmer 10 mins., stirring continuously. Season to taste.

Wash and pick from the stalks a good bunch of fennel and boil till tender. Drain, chop and stir it into the boiling sauce. Serve with fish.

FISH SAUCE

A plain fish sauce is made exactly as an ordinary white sauce, except that you use half milk, half fish stock.

THIN GRAVY

Remove the meat from pan after cooking and pour off the fat. Add quarter to half a pint of stock or water to pan with pepper and salt to taste and stir with a fork.

Pour this into a saucepan and bring to the boil.

THICK GRAVY

Remove meat from pan after cooking and pour off all except a teaspoonful of fat. Add one flat dessertspoonful of plain flour and stir well with a fork. Scrape into a saucepan and cook slowly, stirring all the time for 4 mins. Add half pint of water, pepper and salt and stir with a spoon before bringing to the boil.

MUSTARD SAUCE

To ½ pint of white pouring sauce add a pinch of castor sugar and 1 rounded teaspoonful of mustard mixed in 1 tablespoonful vinegar. Beat thoroughly and re-heat.

ONION SAUCE

To ½ pint of white pouring sauce made with milk or stock, add 1 large or two small boiled and finely chopped onions. Season to taste.

OYSTER SAUCE

Scald 6 oysters, using their own liquor. Strain, beard and cut them into large pieces. Make ½ pint of white pouring sauce using milk and the liquor. Add the oysters, re-heat and beat in a little lemon juice just before serving.

PARSLEY BUTTER SAUCE

To ½ pint of white pouring sauce made with milk, add 1 heaped teaspoonful of finely chopped parsley. Reheat for not more than 2 mins. Then beat in ½ oz. butter dropped in small pieces into the sauce.

PIQUANT SAUCE

1 small grated onion	2 dozen chopped capers
2 tablespoonsful vinegar	½ oz. of chopped gherkin
½ pint brown sauce	pepper and salt

Boil the onion in the vinegar until reduced to half. Then add the other ingredients and simmer for 5 mins.

SHRIMP SAUCE

Add ½ gill of picked shrimps to ½ pint of pouring fish sauce. A teaspoonful of anchovy essence adds to the flavour.

SHERRY SAUCE

½ pint béchamel sauce	½ wineglassful sherry

Cook the sauce for 7 to 10 mins., then stir in the sherry and beat well. Season to taste.

34

Sauces Thickened with Egg

In these sauces egg is used instead of flour to thicken the liquid. Great care must be taken in cooking or the egg may curdle.

CUSTARD SAUCE

1 egg	½ pint milk
castor sugar to taste	1 vanilla pod

Beat the egg in a basin with the sugar while the milk with the vanilla pod is coming slowly to the boil. Remove vanilla, pour milk on to the egg stirring all the time. Return to pan, cook very slowly and stirring all the time. Do not allow to boil. When thick serve immediately.

Alternatively, you can turn the milk and egg into a pie dish and bake at 275° for an hour.

GERMAN EGG SAUCE

2 egg yolks   1 gill sherry   ½ oz. castor sugar

Whisk in a basin over hot water till thick and frothy.

HOLLANDAISE SAUCE

1 tablespoonful lemon juice	2 egg yolks
1 tablespoonful water	2 ozs. butter

Put the lemon juice and water in a double cooker or a basin that will fit over a saucepan. Add the egg yolks slowly and beating all the time. Cook very slowly over hot water until the mixture thickens. Then add the butter, dropping it into the sauce in small lumps and beating thoroughly. Taste, season and re-heat but be careful not to let it boil.

Cold Sauces

These include mayonnaise sauces and salad dressings to serve with cold dishes.

Everyone has her own pet mayonnaise, and you can take a number of flavourings to suit your particular fancy or the food you are serving with it. Chopped parsley or mint, a smear of garlic, snips of chives, caper vinegar, a suspicion of grated cheese, lemon juice, anchovy essence—any of these will make a mayonnaise that little bit different.

CUMBERLAND SAUCE

2 tablespoonsful red currant jelly	about ¼ gill sherry
1 tablespoonful French mustard	

Mix the red currant jelly and mustard in a basin and then beat in enough sherry to make the consistency of thick cream. Serve with cold meats and cold game.

FRENCH DRESSING

3 tablespoonsful salad oil
1 tablespoonful vinegar

pepper and salt
1 teaspoonful mustard

Place the oil in a basin with the seasonings. Add the vinegar a drop at a time, beating all the while.

MAYONNAISE

1 egg yolk
½ teaspoonful dry mustard
salt

pepper
½ gill salad oil
2 tablespoonsful wine vinegar

Place the egg yolk in a basin with the seasonings and add the oil a drop at a time, beating all the while. It will turn thick during the beating. Now beat in the vinegar, adding it very gradually. It should be the consistency of thick cream.

SALAD CREAM

1 hardboiled egg yolk
pepper and salt
1 dessertspoonful lemon juice

½ gill wine vinegar
2 tablespoonsful cream

Pass the egg yolk through a sieve, add seasonings and lemon juice, beating all the time and then gradually beat in the vinegar. Stir in the cream just before serving.

BOILED SALAD DRESSING

1 dessertspoonful cornflour
1 teaspoonful dry mustard
½ teaspoonful salt
1 teaspoonful sugar

1 egg
1 gill milk
1 gill wine vinegar
2 tablespoonsful salad oil

Mix the dry ingredients with the egg in a basin. Bring the milk and vinegar to the boil and add to the mixture. Cook it in a double cooker until thick and creamy. Cool and gradually whisk in the salad oil.

TARTARE SAUCE

½ pint mayonnaise
2 flat dessertspoonsful chopped
   parsley
¼ teaspoonful finely chopped shallot

1 flat teaspoonful chopped capers
1 flat teaspoonful finely grated
   raw carrot

Stir all the ingredients into the mayonnaise and serve cold.

Miscellaneous Unclassified Sauces

This section includes all those sauces, both sweet and savoury, which are not thickened by a roux or egg.

APPLE SAUCE

1 lb. of good cooking apples peeled,
   cored and cut into chunks

½ oz. butter or margarine
½ oz. sugar   ½ gill water

Cook the apples in just enough water to prevent them from 'catching.'
Beat them to a pulp and add the butter, sugar and either a piece of lemon
rind or one or two cloves. Re-heat, beat smooth with a wooden spoon, remove
flavouring and serve.

BLACK BUTTER

1½ ozs. butter
1 teaspoonful finely chopped parsley

½ teaspoonful vinegar
2 drops of lemon

Cook the butter in a saucepan until it turns brown. Remove from the
boiling plate and add the other ingredients. Stir, and cook for another
minute.
Serve with fish.

BREAD SAUCE

1 medium onion
3 cloves
6 peppercorns

½ pint milk
1 gill white breadcrumbs
½ oz. margarine

Infuse the onion, cloves and peppercorns in the heated milk for half an
hour. Strain, return to the pan and add the butter and the breadcrumbs,
beating well. Stir until the sauce comes to the boil.

CARAMEL SAUCE

4 ozs. of loaf sugar
1 gill water

Place the sugar and water in a small pan and dissolve. Boil, without stirring
or shaking, till rich brown.

CHAUDFROID SAUCE

¼ oz. gelatine
¼ pint aspic jelly

½ pint béchamel sauce
½ gill milk
juice of half a lemon

Dissolve the gelatine in a very little hot water and add to the aspic jelly.
Add to the sauce with the remaining ingredients and simmer for 2 to 3 mins.
Strain or tammy and use as a coating when it is cold and nearly set.

CORNFLOUR SAUCE

¼ oz. cornflour
1 teaspoonful sugar

½ pint milk
lemon rind

Blend cornflour in a little milk. Bring the remainder of the milk with the
lemon rind to the boil. Remove flavouring and add the blended cornflour.
Boil for 5 mins., add the sugar and serve.

CRANBERRY SAUCE

Stew 1 lb. of cranberries in half a gill of water till tender. Press them
through a sieve and return to the pan with 4 ozs. of sugar. Re-heat and add
½ gill of port wine just before serving.

CURRY SAUCE

½ oz. curry powder
½ oz. butter
½ pint white stock or water
1 tablespoonful coconut
(can be omitted)
1 small chopped onion

1 small chopped apple
1 tablespoonful sultanas
1 lemon (juice only)
1 teaspoonful apricot jam
salt
1 teaspoonful chutney

In an enamel pan, fry the onion in the butter. Stir in the curry powder and fry for a few minutes. Add all the other ingredients except the chutney. Simmer for half an hour. Add the chutney, re-heat and serve.

HARD OR BRANDY BUTTER SAUCE

4½ ozs. icing sugar   3 ozs. butter   brandy

Sieve the sugar into the butter and cream together. Gradually work in enough brandy to flavour it well. Chill and serve with Christmas Pudding.

HORSERADISH SAUCE

Wash, scrape, dry and then grate 2 oz. horseradish: place it in a sauceboat with a pinch of dry mustard, pepper and salt. Then add a gill of whipped cream, stirring thoroughly, a tablespoonful of wine vinegar and the juice of a lemon.

JAM, MARMALADE OR SYRUP SAUCE

1 oz. sugar
1 gill water or fruit juice
1 teaspoonful cornflour or arrowroot

2 tablespoonsful jam, marmalade
or syrup
rind and juice 1 lemon

Dissolve the sugar in the liquid and add the jam, lemon juice and rind. Simmer for ten minutes and then strain. Return to the pan and add the cornflour blended in a small quantity of water. Cook for five minutes, stirring all the time.

MINT SAUCE

1 tablespoonful castor sugar
2 heaped tablespoonsful of finely
chopped mint

2 tablespoonsful hot water
½ gill vinegar

Place sugar, mint and hot water in a sauceboat and stir until the sugar is melted. Add the vinegar and serve cold.

RED CURRANT AND HORSERADISH SAUCE

4 tablespoonsful red currant jelly   1 tablespoonful horseradish sauce

Mix well together and serve with pork chops or roast pheasant.

TOMATO SAUCE

Sauté 1 sliced onion, 1 chopped carrot and ¾ lb. sliced tomatoes in ½ oz. butter. Blend ½ oz. of flour in ½ pint of stock or water and add to the vegetables. Simmer for ¾ hour. Pass through a sieve and re-heat. Season, adding sugar if liked.

Soups

ONCE you've got a good stock you can almost say you have a good soup. Nevertheless, you should not feel, because the stockpot is empty, that you cannot serve soup. Water or milk or a mixture of both can act as a substitute for stock if need be, and many a tasty soup came straight out of a tin. Canned soups are, indeed, the easiest of all, since all you need is a tin opener and seasoning!

You can give greater variety if you make them yourself, however, and of course they are cheaper, as the stock is made from bones and scraps. If you open a book of high-class recipes you will find you're told how to make first and second stock, and the method is given below though you will probably choose to make a household stock. This last one has the advantage that it does not call for expensive meat; it is made from the end of the joint and from bones.

All soups and stocks need long simmering and provided they are put in a fireproof dish and carefully sealed with plenty of greaseproof paper or, preferably, aluminium foil, this long cooking can be done in the oven. (This is particularly useful when cooking a complete meal by timer control.)

When serving soup allow approximately one third of a pint for each person, unless it is only a very light following menu when you may wish to increase the quantity to half-pint per person. Always sample a soup before serving and add salt to suit your personal taste.

Stocks

FIRST STOCK

For brown stock use shin of beef and for white, knuckle of veal. Wash the meat and cut it into small cubes. Cover it in a saucepan with cold water, allowing a quart to every pound of meat, and bring it very slowly to the simmer. After half an hour, add 1 teaspoonful of salt, a small whole onion and 6 peppercorns, and continue to simmer for another $2\frac{1}{2}$ hours. Strain it, and cool, removing any fat from the top.

SECOND STOCK

Take the meat drained from the first stock and add $1\frac{1}{2}$ pints of water to every pound. Bring very slowly to the simmer, add an onion, a carrot and, if liked, a stick of celery and simmer for at least three hours.

VEGETABLE STOCK

Peel and cut into large chunks 1 lb. of mixed vegetables. Drain them and sauté in $\frac{1}{2}$ oz. of dripping. Then add 1 quart of water, salt and 6 peppercorns. Simmer for an hour.

Strain and cool.

FISH STOCK

1 cod's head, or trimmings of	1 stick of celery	2 cloves
white fish weighing 1 lb.	6 peppercorns	salt
1 onion	bunch of herbs	1 quart of water

Clean the fish and bring it very slowly to the boil. Add the other ingredients and simmer for 30 mins.

Strain and cool.

HOUSEHOLD OR FAMILY STOCK

For this you need cooked or uncooked bones (the carcase of a chicken is excellent), giblets or the end of the joint. Cut away all the fat and break the bones. Add salt, 6 peppercorns, an onion, a turnip; cover with water and simmer for several hours. Strain, cool and skim off fat.

If you keep a stockpot going, never leave any vegetables or bread in it, as these will go sour. Boil at least once a day. Recipes for stock are always in the chapter on soups, but remember that your stockpot is also useful for sauces, gravies and réchauffées.

TERMS IN COOKING SOUPS

There are a few instructions in the making of soups that might not be clear to the beginner, and one or two definitions may be helpful.

CLEARING A SOUP is making it free of all blemishes. Straining is not enough, as tiny particles of meat or vegetables pass through the sieve with the liquid. White of egg, whisked into the soup as it cooks, coagulates and collects any of these stray particles. They all float with the egg to the top of the liquid and can be skimmed off. Very often the smashed shell of the egg is also added with the white, and the two together collect all the pieces and leave the soup perfectly clear.

SIEVING A SOUP is a different matter, and is more than just straining. When you are making thick cream or purée soups, you want to get the vegetables or pulse into such tiny pieces that they form part of the cream. You cook it altogether, and when the food is soft stand a large sieve over a basin. Pour the soup into the sieve. Take a wooden spoon and press the food through the sieve, scraping the underside so that it all falls into the liquid.

If you don't add something to the soup to keep these tiny pieces of mashed food suspended in the liquid you will find that the heavy part of the mixture will fall to the bottom of the tureen, so that you will get thick soup at the bottom and nearly clear soup at the top. So you add cooked flour which gives the liquid sufficient " body ", the technical term for which is a *liaison* to hold the heavy food. Liaisons can be given by adding cornflour or plain flour blended in milk or water, a roux (see page 32) or egg yolk.

The soup must be re-heated after the addition of a liaison, but should not be cooked for more than 10 mins. When egg yolk is used the soup must never be allowed to boil.

GARNISH. In many instances the garnish is given in the recipe. Clear soup is often served with cooked noodles or tiny cubes of diced and cooked root vegetables lying in the bottom of the tureen. Croûtons, which are small dice or fancy shapes of fried or toasted bread are sometimes floated on the top. Don't use too many, they are supposed to be a decoration, *not* part of the dish.

There are several basic recipes for soups, and once you know them you have any soup you fancy at your finger-ends.

REASONS FOR FAILURE

If you spoil a soup you have probably done one or other of the following:

(1) If a cream soup is lumpy you either did not sieve it carefully, or the roux sauce was lumpy when you added it to the soup, or you added the roux sauce to too hot a soup. The best method of clearing lumps is to strain the soup through a sieve.

(2) If the soup is too thick, add a little milk or water or stock. Taste and re-season to correct the flavouring before you serve it.

(3) If the soup is too salt, or should you want to use for stock the liquid in which salted meat has been cooked, boil some potatoes in it.

(4) If the soup looks or feels greasy on the palate, let it get quite cold. Sometimes a biscuit of hard fat will form on the top and this can be removed by lifting it off, but in any case the fat will rise to the top of the liquid and if you lay a piece of clean blotting paper on the surface the fat will be absorbed.

Thin Soups

Strain and remove all trace of fat from a good household stock. Season it well and serve hot. Some people like to put a very little pearl barley, macaroni or lentils, or even one or two dumplings in this type of soup.

CONSOMME

This needs a special brown stock made from lean beef. Allow 1 lb. of beef to the quart of water. Cut it in thin slices and scrape the pieces with a knife so that as much as possible of the juice is extracted. Then put meat and juice into a pan, cover with the water and simmer very slowly for 2 hours. Strain the soup, separate the white of an egg, crush the shell and whisk both into the slightly cooled soup. Bring slowly to the boil again and skim. Season and re-heat.

COLD CONSOMME (*facing page* 81)

| 1 lb. lean veal | 1 onion | 1 flat teaspoonful salt |
| 1 quart water | 6 peppercorns | 1 piece celery, if liked |

Cut the veal into small pieces, having removed all fat. Put all the ingredients in a saucepan and simmer for at least two hours. Strain. Then allow to cool and remove all fat from the top. Re-heat and whisk in the white of an egg and the shell to clear. Strain a second time.

Leave till quite cold when it will be a thick jelly.

Broths

These can be served with meat in them, almost like a thin stew, or with the meat strained from it. In each case they are thickened with some farinaceous food, such as barley, rice or macaroni.

SCOTCH BROTH

2 lbs. scrag end mutton	1 onion
2 ozs. barley	1 leek
2 quarts of water	1 piece celery, if liked
1 small carrot	pepper and salt
1 small turnip	

Remove fat, wipe the meat and cut it into small, neat pieces. Put it in a saucepan with the barley and the water. Bring fairly rapidly to the boil and then simmer gently for an hour, skimming it when necessary. Leave it to get cold and then remove any fat that has collected on the top. Remove the bones. Clean and peel the vegetables, cut them into dice, add to the soup, season and cook for another hour. Serve very hot with a sprinkling of chopped parsley.

FAMILY BROTH

To the liquid in which a leg of mutton has been boiled, add:

1 onion	1 carrot	} *Cleaned, peeled and diced*	3 ozs. pearl barley
1 leek	1 turnip		pepper and salt

Bring to the boil and simmer for 2 hours.

Thickened Soups

These are usually made from a purée of vegetables, and are thickened with flour or cornflour, or they are made from lentils or split peas.

CREAMED VEGETABLE SOUP—BASIC RECIPE

1½ lbs. potatoes	a pinch pepper
¼ oz. of bacon, dripping or other fat	1 teaspoonful salt
1½ pints white stock or water	

1 oz. fat	
1 oz. flour	} made into a sauce (see page 32)
1 gill milk	

Clean and peel the potatoes and chop them into pieces about the size of a walnut. Drain them and sauté them in the dripping, being careful not to cook them long enough to change their colour. Add the remainder of the ingredients, including the stock, and bring to the boil. Simmer for 1½ hours. Pass soup through a sieve, pressing the vegetables through with a wooden spoon.

Add the sauce to the slightly cooled soup and whisk well. When thoroughly mixed, bring to the boil again, stirring all the time and cook for 10 mins. Serve very hot, with a sprinkling of chopped parsley.

To the quantities in the above recipe, substitute for the potatoes any of the following vegetables: Jerusalem artichokes, celery, mushrooms, onions, or equal quantities of leeks and potatoes.

There are a few vegetables which make excellent soups and which, owing to their texture, cannot be sautéed in fat. An example of this is cabbage soup.

CABBAGE SOUP

1 lb. cabbage	1 gill milk	1 oz. margarine
1 pint white stock	½ oz. flour	pepper and salt

Wash and shred the cabbage and drop it into boiling stock. Boil gently for about 25 mins., or until the cabbage is tender. Press it through a sieve. Blend the flour in the milk and add it to the soup. Bring to the boil and cook for 10 mins., stirring all the time. Cut the margarine into small pieces and beat it into the hot soup. Taste and season the soup. Add a few drops of green colouring to green vegetable soups to improve the appearance. Don't use too much—soups should have a whitish colour to indicate they are a cream.

VARIATIONS OF THE ABOVE RECIPE

To the quantities in the above recipe, substitute for the cabbage any of the following: Brussels sprouts, spinach, turnip tops, green peas or vegetable marrow.

Carrot soup is made in the same way but you will require an additional ½ pint of water or white stock.

FAMILY SOUP

Shred on a suet scraper 1 lb. of mixed vegetables (anything you fancy, but root vegetables are easier) and sauté in ½ oz. of margarine or dripping. Add ¾ pint of stock or water and ¼ pint of milk. Cook for 15 mins. Blend ½ oz. of flour in ½ gill of milk or water and add to the soup and boil, stirring all the time. Cook for 10 mins., season and serve very hot.

CHESTNUT SOUP

1 lb. chestnuts	dash of grated nutmeg
1½ pints vegetable stock	1 oz. flour
1 onion	½ pint milk
½ stick celery	pepper and salt

Cut the ends of the chestnuts, boil for 20 to 30 mins. and drain. Remove the outer and inner skins. Put them in a saucepan with the stock, onion, celery and simmer till tender. Pass through a sieve, thicken with the flour blended in the milk and cook another 10 mins. Season and serve very hot.

PULSE SOUPS—BASIC RECIPE

6 ozs. lentils	1 quart water or white stock
1 onion	1 oz. flour
1 turnip	1 oz. dripping ⎱ made into a sauce (see page 32)
1 piece celery	1 gill milk
bunch herbs	pepper and salt

Wash and leave the lentils soaking in plenty of water overnight. Drain. Wash, peel and dice the vegetables. Put them together in a pan with the water or stock and the herbs. Bring to the boil and simmer for 2 hours with a tightly fitting lid on the pan. Pass the soup through a sieve, pressing the lentils and the vegetables with a wooden spoon. Remove the herbs.

Make a sauce with the dripping, flour and milk. Add it to the soup, stirring very thoroughly and watching that there are no lumps. Season with pepper and salt, and when it tastes as you like it, re-heat and serve very hot.

VARIATION OF THE ABOVE RECIPE

The basic recipe can be varied by the substitution for the lentils of split peas, dried haricot beans or butter beans, or barley.

All these cream soups can be made more interesting with a change of flavouring and the addition of colour. For example, a potato soup is improved if you chop a few leaves of mint very finely and stir them in just before serving. A more common garnish is a sprinkling of parsley. An occasional touch of garlic, or a sprinkling of grated cheese is pleasant. Chives, cut in $\frac{1}{4}$ inch pieces and floated on the top, look pretty and give a slight flavour, and some people like a suspicion of cinnamon or caraway.

TOMATO SOUP

Tomato soup can be made in the same way as you make potato soup, but it is better with more milk and fat to make it creamy:

1 lb. ripe tomatoes	1½ ozs. flour
1 onion, peeled and sliced	¾ pint milk
2 ozs. fat bacon	1 teaspoonful sugar
1 pint white stock	pepper and salt
2 ozs. margarine	

Cut the tomatoes in four, put in a pan with the thinly sliced onion and the bacon cut in small pieces. Add the stock, bring to the boil and simmer for 1½ hours. Strain the soup through a sieve, helping it with a wooden spoon but without pressing it more than enough to extract the liquid.

Blend the flour with about a gill of milk and add it to the soup, stirring it carefully. Then add the remainder of the milk, a little sugar, season with pepper and salt and bring it to the boil, stirring all the time. Cook for 10 mins. when it should be thick and creamy and then beat in the margarine.

Miscellaneous

KIDNEY SOUP

½ lb. ox kidney	1 turnip
1 onion	a piece of celery
1 oz. dripping	1 carrot
1 oz. flour	bunch of herbs
2 pints stock or water	pepper and salt

Wash, skin and dry the kidney, cut in small pieces removing the core. Clean and skin the onion and cut it into thin rings. Get the dripping smoking hot in a pan and fry the kidney till it is brown. Lift it out and fry the onion. Add the flour and fry till brown, and then return the kidney to the pan. Add the stock, bring it slowly to the boil, skimming occasionally. Cut the vegetables into neat pieces and add them to the soup with the bunch of herbs and simmer for at least 3 hours. Strain it through a sieve, leave it to get cold and remove any fat. Chop the pieces of kidney very finely and add them to the soup. Bring it to the boil, season and serve very hot.

OXTAIL SOUP

Substitute the oxtail and proceed as for kidney soup, decorating the soup in the tureen with thin rings of cooked carrot and meat chopped from the oxtail.

MULLIGATAWNY SOUP

1 lb. knuckle of veal, lean mutton or rabbit	1 quart water or stock
1 apple	1 tablespoonful grated coconut
3 carrots 2 onions	1 dessertspoonful chutney
¾ oz. dripping	1½ ozs. flour
1 teaspoonful curry powder	1 teaspoonful mulligatawny paste
½ rasher bacon	a squeeze of lemon
	pepper and salt

Cut the meat into small pieces. Wash, prepare and dice the apple and vegetables. Melt the fat in the pan and fry the meat and vegetables with the curry powder. Add the bacon and the stock, cover the pan and simmer till the meat is tender. Stir in the coconut and add the chutney. Mix the flour and mulligatawny paste with a ¼ gill of stock and add to the soup. Strain through a very fine sieve or a kitchen cloth. Add the lemon juice, season, and garnish with neat pieces of the meat. Serve with plain boiled rice.

BISQUES

These are soups made from fish. Any white fish can be substituted in the recipe given below, and the soup can be garnished with shrimps, anchovies or a grating of cheese.

2 ozs. flour	bunch of herbs or a bay leaf
1 pint milk	8 ozs. flaked cod, cooked
1 pint fish stock, white stock or water	pepper and salt
1 onion	

Blend the flour with a gill of the milk. Bring the remainder of the liquid to the boil and add the onion and the herbs and seasoning. Remove from the heat and add the blended flour. Boil for 10 mins., stirring all the time. Rub the fish through a sieve and add it to the soup. Remove the herbs or bay leaf. Taste, correct seasoning if required and serve very hot.

Fish

FISH can be cooked in various ways. It can be boiled, baked, fried, grilled or steamed.

There are one or two points to remember:

1. Fish is divided into two kinds—oily fish like salmon, herring, eels, tunny and mackerel, and white fish like cod, hake, turbot, plaice, and sole.

Oily fish can often be dry-fried and served with a piquante sauce to counteract the oily taste. White fish contains little fat and is therefore more suitable for frying in deep fat or oil. Fish flakes as it cooks and is usually given a protective coating of batter, or seasoned flour, or egg and breadcrumbs to hold it together.

2. White fish, if not carefully cooked, can be tasteless. It has a very delicate flavour and sauces are required either to bring out the flavour or to give it one.

3. White fish looks most appetising if it is served with a bright garnish to give colour. After cleansing, sprinkle the fish with lemon to whiten it. Boiled cod can be delicious, but served unadorned on a white platter with mashed potatoes, it looks pallid and unappetising!

Fish is nearly always bought prepared by the fishmonger, filleted and skinned as you want it. An exception is herrings, and here is a simple way to clean them: lay them on a sheet of newspaper. Take the fish in the left hand, underside down, and cut with a sharp knife through the backbone near the head. When the head is half-severed, take it in the right hand and pull it off. The head with the intestines will come away altogether. Scrape the fish with a knife to remove the scales and cut off the fins and tail. Now wash it and it is ready for cooking.

All fish must be washed and often you will want to trim off the fins which have slipped past the fishmonger's knife. Use cooking scissors for this job— they are easier than a knife.

Methods of Cooking

A list is given below of the usual methods of cooking each particular type of fish. *ALL* white and some oily fish can be steamed.

BOILING	GRILLING	BAKING	FRYING
Hake	*Herring*	*Cod*	*Cod Steaks*
Cod	*Kipper, Bloater*	*Halibut*	*Plaice, Sole*
Halibut	*Plaice, Sole*	*Fresh Haddock*	*Whitebait*
Salmon	*Trout*	*Hake*	*Whiting*
Skate	*Cod Steaks*	*Mackerel*	*Hake*
Turbot	*Halibut Steaks*	*Whiting*	*Fresh Haddock*
Fresh Haddock	*Mackerel, Hake*	*Turbot*	*Scallops*
Smoked Haddock	*Whiting, Skate*	*Plaice, Sole*	*Skate*

Space only permits giving one or two examples of each method, but the recipes can be adapted for any of the fish in the appropriate column of the above table. Differences in flavour and presentation are provided by varying the accompanying sauces.

BOILING

Fish should be poached rather than boiled; that is to say it should be plunged into boiling salted water and immediately turned to a simmer. Use enough water just to cover the fish and allow 5 to 10 mins. to the pound, according to its thickness. Allow 1 teaspoonful salt to the pint of water.

BOILED SMOKED HADDOCK

Smoked fish is already salt enough, so do not add any to the water in this case. Trim the haddock into neat pieces. Wash and drain them, and drop them into a saucepan of boiling water. Reduce to a simmer and cook for 10 mins. or until tender. Drain and serve with melted butter, or with a poached egg on the top of each piece.

BOILED SALMON

Salmon is really rather difficult to cook. If it is overdone it is dry and flavourless and unless carefully treated it loses its colour.

For salmon steaks here are two methods which do not fail:

1. Brush a sheet of greaseproof paper with melted butter and wrap it loosely round the salmon steak. Put it in a steamer over briskly boiling water and cover with a closely fitting lid. Cook in the steam. Allow 15 mins. for a ½ lb. steak and 15 mins. for each additional ½ lb.

2. Brush the cut ends of the salmon steaks with olive oil or melted butter. Have ready in a saucepan enough briskly boiling water just to cover them and add salt at the rate of 1 teaspoonful to the pint. Plunge the steaks into the water and turn *off* the switch. Leave for 10 to 15 mins., remove with a slice, and drain.

3. If you are cooking a whole salmon use method 2. You will require either a large pan or a fish kettle. Place the fish carefully in the boiling water and remove very gently so that it does not break. If the salmon is very large, reduce the heat until the water is just simmering and continue simmering for 5 to 10 mins. before leaving for the 15 mins. with the switch off.

KIPPERS

Wash and trim the kippers and stand them head downwards in a strong china jug. Now fill the jug with boiling water, cover with a saucepan lid and wrap a folded teacloth over the top to keep hot.

Leave for 10 mins., then remove the fish and dry under a hot grill for 2 mins.

With this method you will find that the smell of cooking is not so strong nor does it linger as long.

BOILED TURBOT

Wash and trim the turbot. Bring to the boil enough water just to cover the fish. Add salt and vinegar at the rate of 1 teaspoonful of each to the pint.

Plunge the fish into the boiling water, reduce to a simmer and cook for 5 to 10 mins. to the pound, according to the thickness of the fish.

Any white fish can be cooked by this method. Fillets and small pieces are, however, not so easy as they are apt to "flake" and fall to pieces if slightly overcooked. In fact, you will find that this method is most suitable for whole or half pieces of larger fish; the skin of the fish itself then holds it together.

STEAMING

Fillets and small pieces are much better steamed and two methods are given below:

1. For small fillets. Grease a plate. Lay the fillets on it either flat or packed into neat rolls. Sprinkle with salt and lemon juice and cover with a piece of greased greaseproof paper. Then put a lid of a saucepan or another plate over the top. Stand it on a pan of boiling water and boil rather fast so that there is plenty of steam.

Cooking time is 15 to 20 mins. to the lb.

2. Wrap the fish in a sheet of greased greaseproof paper and stand in a steamer over boiling water. Cover and steam for the same times as above.

GRILLING

Grilling is the easiest and quickest method of cooking fish. White fish needs either a low heat when it has something the appearance of baked fish, or a protective covering, as with fried fish, against the fiercer radiant heat.

1. Brush the bottom of the grill pan with melted butter or olive oil and place the fish in the pan. If they are small fillets, roll them tail first into neat tight rolls. Brush the fish with melted butter. Cook slowly with the grill pan in the runners, leaving till the fish is cooked through. If liked, cook quickly for a final minute to brown the top. For a change, and with small fish like dabs or very small plaice, sprinkle with grated cheese before cooking quickly.

2. Dip the fish first in beaten egg and then in breadcrumbs or fine oatmeal, shaking off any excess crumbs. Thoroughly grease the grid in the grill pan and stand the fish on it. Put a few small dabs of margarine on the top. If the fish is ¾-inch thick or less, cook quickly, if more, cook at a lower heat. Grill for 6 to 7 mins., then turn it over, dab the other side with margarine and cook for another 7 to 10 mins., according to thickness.

GRILLED HERRINGS

Clean, trim and wash the herrings. Score them with three cuts each side. Place them on the grid in the lowest position, put in the grill pan and cook each side for 5 to 7 mins. or until cooked. Serve with mustard sauce (see page 34).

BAKING

Fish can be baked in the oven and served either as a main dish or as an additional course. It can readily be cooked from cold.

48

Curried lamb with plain boiled rice, papadums and chutney

Shrimp pasta

BAKED COD STEAKS

3 cod steaks
lemon juice
pepper and salt
breadcrumbs
3 tomatoes

a few button mushrooms
teaspoonful grated onion
dash nutmeg
½ oz. margarine

Trim, wash and bone the cod steaks; roll them tightly and secure with a small skewer or cocktail stick. Sprinkle them with lemon juice and pepper and salt. Coat them with breadcrumbs. Grease a fireproof dish and arrange the cod steaks in it with halved tomatoes and button mushrooms. Sprinkle the finely grated onion over the dish and, finally, a very little grated nutmeg over the lot. Cut the margarine into small pieces and dot over the whole.

Cook at 350°F. for 30 to 40 mins. any position in oven.

Serves three.

BAKED STUFFED HADDOCK

Have the fish cleaned without cutting off the head but remove tail, fins and eyes. Stuff it with veal forcemeat and sew it up with a needle and thread, making big stitches that are easily cut out after cooking. Take a long skewer and starting at the tail end, push it twice through the fish from one side and back again—like taking two big stitches—finishing at the head so that the fish is threaded on the skewer in the shape of a letter "S." Coat the fish with beaten egg and then with breadcrumbs. Place it in a fireproof dish with a coating of margarine or dripping and pour round the fish a gill of anchovy or brown sauce. Cover the dish with greaseproof paper.

Cook at 350°F. for 30 to 40 mins. floor of oven.

Serves four.

STUFFED SOLES

4 ozs. white breadcrumbs
8 or 10 skinned tomatoes
1 finely-chopped stick of celery
1 egg

1 flat teaspoonful salt
dash of pepper
4 small soles, boned from the
centre

Mix together the breadcrumbs, tomatoes, celery and egg, and season with salt and pepper. Fill the cavities in the centre of the soles with this stuffing, pulling the fish together over the top of it. Place head to tail in a well buttered fireproof dish about 1½ inches deep. Dot with butter and cover the dish with aluminium foil.

Cook at 375°F. for 45 mins. any position in oven.

Serves four.

FRYING

REASONS FOR FAILURE

1. If the fat is not boiling the fish will be "soggy" and greasy.
2. If the fat is overheated the fish will be flecked with little black marks. There is no cure for either of these faults.

The temperature of boiling fat is high enough to spoil fish but a coating will protect it and prevent this occurring. The most common coatings with the methods of using them are given on pages 63 and 64.

Some people use medium-grain oatmeal instead of breadcrumbs after coating the fish with beaten egg.

Fish that can be "dry-fried" like herrings can be washed, dried and rolled in oatmeal. It gives a crisp, nutty flavour to the fish.

The three methods of frying fish are by deep fat, shallow fat or dry-frying —the same methods as with other foods.

DEEP FAT FRYING

Oil is the best fat to use, but clarified beef or mutton fat is also suitable. The fat should be brought to the boil in a fish kettle or a strong saucepan and should fill about two-thirds of the pan. A frying basket to fit the pan is useful, especially for potatoes, but remember that it is a mistake to use it for coated foods.

The fat is not boiling when it bubbles! The bubbles are caused by water in the fat which must be driven off. When ready, the fat is very still and has a faint blue haze about it. The safest test is to take the temperature of the fat with a fryometer but there are some home tests on page 64 which, though approximate, are safe enough. For fish, cut an inch cube of bread and drop it into the fat. If it is crisp and golden in 60 seconds, the fat is at the right temperature.

Immerse the fish gently to prevent splashing and don't put in too many pieces at once or you will take the fat off the boil. Make sure the fat is boiling before you start another lot of fish. Never use a frying basket for coated fish— particularly when it is coated in batter—as this sticks to the basket.

It is an accident unlikely to occur with an electric cooker but every cook should know what to do if she catches a pan of boiling fat on fire! When you are frying in deep fat always have close at hand a lid that fits the pan. Nothing will burn without air. If the fat does catch alight, cover it with the saucepan lid, switch off, and leave it alone till it has gone out. Then take it out of doors before you remove the lid or you will fill the house with the smell of burnt fat!

FRIED WHITEBAIT

These fish are not drawn and it is therefore very important that they should be absolutely fresh. Wash and dry the fish. Drop them into a cloth and sprinkle flour over them. Then shake them in the cloth till they are lightly coated with flour. Turn them into a frying basket and shake out excess flour before plunging them into boiling fat. Toss them in the fat for 2 mins., hold them out of the fat for about half a minute and then re-immerse them, frying for about 2 mins. till they are crisp and slightly coloured. Drain them on kitchen paper and serve them very hot with quarters of lemon and thin slices of brown bread and butter.

FRIED SCAMPI

These are best if they are first dipped in milk and then in seasoned flour, and fried in the same way as Whitebait.

50

This is done in a strong pan. Enough fat is used to coat the pan and prevent the food sticking; the food should be turned so that it cooks evenly on both sides. Shallow frying is more commonly used for fillets and cutlets of fish, and batter as a coating is not suitable.

DRY FRYING

Herrings contain fat, and if you put them in a dry pan in the same way as you would a rasher of bacon, the heat will extract enough fat to cook them.

Unclassified Recipes

DRESSED CRAB

1 medium sized crab, cooked and cold   chopped parsley
the heart leaves of a lettuce   butter
1 tablespoonful of mayonnaise (see page 36)
coralline pepper

Remove the claws, crack them and take out the flesh. Pull off the body from the shell and remove flesh, keeping the two separate. Discard the gills, the stomach and intestines, all recognizable because of their greenish colour.

Wash and dry the shell, and half fill it with coarsely chopped lettuce leaves. Mix the yellow flesh from the shell with the mayonnaise and pile in the centre. Sprinkle with coralline pepper and a very little chopped parsley. Arrange the white claw flesh round the pile of yellow flesh.

Mix a little butter with enough colouring to make it pale green, and pipe it in small dots round the shell.

Serves two.

DEVILLED CRAB

1 medium crab   1 teaspoonful mayonnaise or
1 teaspoonful chopped chutney   piquant sauce
1 teaspoonful breadcrumbs   ½ teaspoonful vinegar

Heat all the ingredients in a saucepan, adding the flaked crab when the rest is hot. Do not boil. Mix thoroughly and fill the washed shell with the mixture. Brown under the grill and serve garnished with chopped parsley.

Serves two.

SCALLOPS

4 scallops   4 pieces of fat bacon   4 croûtons of fried bread

Wash the scallops, loosening them from the shells with a sharp knife, and removing the beard and any dark matter. Only the white and orange of the fish should be left.

Wrap each scallop in a piece of fat bacon and bake at 350° for 25 mins.

Serve on croûtons of fried bread or on the scrubbed and dried shells of the fish.

Serves two.

51

SHRIMP PASTA (*facing page* 49)

½ lb. cooked macaroni
½ pint sherry sauce (see page 34)
4 ozs. shrimps

12 grapes (stoned)
hard boiled egg for garnish
a little cochineal

When the macaroni has been drained turn it into a border mould and press down. Turn out on to a serving dish. Make the sherry sauce and heat the shrimps and grapes in it; adding a little cochineal to turn it a pretty pink. Pour the shrimp mixture into the centre of the macaroni border and decorate with segments of hard boiled egg.

Serves three.

SOLE AU GRATIN

It is a common belief that an *au gratin* dish means that it is sprinkled with grated cheese. This is incorrect. An *au gratin* dish is one sprinkled with breadcrumbs.

1 Dover sole—or any other white fish
pepper, salt and lemon juice
1 teaspoonful grated or finely
   chopped onion
a sprinkle of chopped parsley

4 small chopped mushrooms
1 tablespoonful breadcrumbs
1 tablespoonful melted
   margarine or butter
½ pint piquant sauce (see page 34)

Wash, clean and skin the fish, removing the fins and tail. Score each side with a sharp knife. Season and sprinkle with lemon juice.

Mix the chopped onion, parsley and mushrooms together and put half into a greased *gratin* or fireproof dish. Place the fish on the top, and spread the remainder of the mixture on it. Sprinkle with breadcrumbs and finally with the melted butter or margarine.

Cook at 350° for 25 to 30 mins., centre of oven.

Serves two.

Pour piquant sauce round (not over) the fish and serve from the dish in which it is cooked.

TROUT À LA MEUNIÈRE

6 small trout
1 dessertspoonful seasoned flour
2 ozs. margarine
lemon juice

1 oz. butter
thin slices of lemon
chopped parsley

Clean and dry the fish and toss in seasoned flour, shaking off any excess. Heat the margarine in a pan and fry the fish slowly till golden brown.

Cream the butter in a warm place and beat in a few drops of lemon juice. Shape into squares and chill.

Serve the fish on a very hot dish, place the butter on the top, allowing it to melt with the heat of the fish. Garnish with thin slices of lemon and a sprinkling of chopped parsley.

Sole and halibut steaks are excellent cooked by this method, and all small fresh-water fish. Coarse fresh-water fish should be cleaned and then soaked overnight in water containing salt in the proportion of a tablespoonful to the pint to remove the muddy flavour.

Serves four to six.

CODS' ROES

Tie the cods' roes in a piece of muslin and lower them gently into briskly boiling salted water. Reduce to a simmer, and cook for 15 to 30 mins. If they are small, 15 mins. will be sufficient but the large ones require longer time.

Remove from the muslin bag, and allow the roes to cool. At this stage you can store them. A pound of cod's roe goes a long way and you can use half at once and keep the remainder for a day or so in a cool place.

Cut the roes lengthwise in slices about half to three-quarters of an inch thick, and fry them rather slowly in butter or margarine, until they are lightly browned and thoroughly heated through.

Serve on croûtons of bread and garnish with small sprigs of parsley.

SOFT HERRINGS' ROES

Wash the roes and drain. Plunge into boiling salted water and cook for 5 to 7 mins. Serve hot, on buttered toast, or place them in a fireproof dish, cover with a cheese sauce, sprinkle with grated cheese and brown under the grill.

FISH CUSTARD

fillets of 1 Dover sole or ½ lb. of any white filleted fish
pepper and salt   1 egg   ½ pint milk   butter

Wash and dry the fillets, sprinkle with pepper and salt, and roll them up from the thin end.

Lay the fish in a fireproof dish. Thoroughly beat the egg. Heat the milk until it is just under boiling point and pour it over the egg, stirring all the time. Then pour the custard over the fish, put some small knobs of butter on the top and bake at 275° for about three-quarters of an hour or until set. *Serves two.*

FISH SOUFFLÉ

Panada   2 or 3 eggs
1 oz. flour   pepper and salt
1 oz. margarine   lemon juice
1 gill milk or fish stock   cream
6 ozs. of raw white fish, skinned
  and filleted

Grease a soufflé dish with butter and cut a round of greased paper to fit in the bottom.

Shred the fish as finely as you can.

Make a panada with the flour, margarine and milk or fish stock according to the instructions on page 32. Cool it, and add it to the fish with the yolks of egg. Mash all together with a fork, or better still, pound it in a mortar.

Now press the mixture through a sieve, add pepper and salt and a few drops of lemon juice and a tablespoonful of cream if you have it.

Beat the whites of egg until very stiff and fold them into the mixture. Then put it all into the prepared tin and bake at 375° for half an hour or steam for 45 mins.

Serve from the dish or turn out (both methods are correct).
Garnish with very thin slices of lemon.
Shrimps, crab meat, or tinned fish make excellent soufflés.
Serves two or three.

SOUSED MACKEREL OR HERRINGS

3 herrings or mackerel	6 rings, very thinly cut, from a
1 clove 2 bay leaves	medium sized onion
pepper and salt	wine vinegar water

Clean, wash and trim the fish and place them in a fireproof dish. Add the clove, bay leaves and seasoning and lay the onion rings along the top of the fish. Add sufficient vinegar and water in equal quantities to cover the fish. Cover the dish with greaseproof paper.

Cook at 300°F. for 45 to 60 mins. according to size, any position in the oven. When cold, drain and serve.

Serves three.

STEWED FISH

Coating sauce	$\frac{3}{4}$ to 1 lb. of white fish
1½ gills milk or fish stock	1 hard-boiled egg
$\frac{3}{4}$ oz. flour	½ teaspoonful anchovy essence
$\frac{3}{4}$ oz. fat	a few drops lemon juice

Clean, wash, fillet and skin the fish, and roll the fillets. Make the sauce and add the fillets to it, simmering very gently for about 20 mins.

Remove the fillets from the sauce and place on a hot dish. Keep it hot in the warming drawer.

Add the anchovy essence, lemon juice, pepper and salt to the sauce. Reheat and pour it over the fish. Garnish with slices of egg.

Serves two or three.

FISH SALADS

White fish, shell fish and salmon are those most commonly used for salads.

Cook the fish by boiling or steaming, drain and leave to cool; dress crab or lobster according to recipe.

Arrange in a winter or summer salad of lettuce, sliced beetroot, blanched and peeled tomatoes, etc. For a change, try mixing some grated apple and nuts with white fish. Coat with mayonnaise and garnish with slices of hard-boiled egg.

Meat, Game and Poultry

MEAT is cooked in a variety of ways. It can be roasted, boiled, steamed, stewed, grilled or fried, and the method you choose depends to a great extent on the cut of the meat. Methods are divided into three classes:

(1) Boiling, stewing, steaming or deep frying.
(2) Roasting, baking, 'dry frying', grilling or broiling.
(3) Braising, pot-roasting and sautéing.

A lot of meat is chilled or frozen, but thawed before we see it. There is nothing against this, but it is as well to know. I find that it is sometimes improved by hanging for a day or so.

Tell the butcher how you want to cook the meat, so that he can advise you as to the best cut.

REASONS FOR FAILURE

If meat is a failure, it nearly always means that it is tough. This is usually because you have chosen the wrong method of cooking for the particular cut of meat, but it can be because you have cooked it too quickly. Meat nearly always wants slow cooking. It often is given fast cooking for the first few minutes, but that is merely to seal the exterior so that the juices and flavours do not flow from it. After that it must have a low heat to cook through.

(1) If it is tough you can sometimes re-cook it very slowly in a casserole and make it more palatable; or you can cut it into small pieces and stew it; or you can serve it minced.
(2) If it is overdone it is sometimes improved if cut into very thin slices and re-heated in thin gravy. Re-heat in a large shallow dish so that it will not receive much more cooking.
(3) If it is underdone it can be re-cooked, sometimes as it is in the joint or by covering with a suet caul (see page 129).

Broadly speaking, those parts of the animal that are exercised and are therefore muscular, need a style of cooking calculated to make them tender—the moist, slow methods which cook the coarse fibre in gentle heat to render it soft and tender. Steaming, stewing, casserole and pressure cooking are all examples of this method.

Such coarser cuts can also very often be boiled or braised with success. These methods subject the food to a high temperature, the one by boiling and the other by frying, but only for a few minutes to seal the juices. After that they both give long slow cooking.

Short fibred cuts, those parts of the animal that are not so muscular, are most suitable for roasting, grilling or frying.

Methods of Cooking

BEEF

Cut	Method	Cut	Method
Ribs, sirloin (best piece)	Roasting or baking	Rounds brisket salted brisket	Boiling
Undercut steak	Grilling and frying	Neck, shoulder	
Rump and round steak	Grilling, frying and braising	Tail, skirt best piece	Stewing and braising

MUTTON AND LAMB

Cut	Method	Cut	Method
Leg, loin, shoulder	Roasting or baking	Leg, neck (middle and best end), head	Boiling
Fillet of leg			
Chops, best end neck chops	Grilling and frying	Breast, leg head, trotters	Stewing and braising

PORK

Cut	Method	Cut	Method
Leg, loin, spare rib	Roasting and baking	Loin chops	Grilling and frying
		Spare rib	Stewing and braising

VEAL

Cut	Method	Cut	Method
Fillet, blade	Roasting or baking	Head, neck, leg, fillet	Stewing, braising
Cutlets from fillet or neck	Grilling or frying		

OFFALS

	Method		Method
Kidney	Braising, frying, grilling	Sheep's head Hearts	Stewing and braising
Liver	Frying, braising and stewing	Tongue	Boiling, braising, stewing

POULTRY

Spring chicken	Roasting, frying	Turkey	Roasting
Chicken	Roasting, boiling, stewing, braising, casseroling	Goose	Roasting
		Wild fowl Duck	Roasting, braising, casseroling

ACCOMPANIMENTS TO THE JOINT

Roast Mutton
Red currant jelly
Onion sauce. Thin gravy

Roast Pork
Apple sauce
Sage and onion stuffing
Thick gravy

Beef
Horseradish sauce. Thin gravy

Roast Lamb
Mint sauce. Mint jelly. Thin gravy

Roast Veal
Thick gravy. Forcemeat stuffing
Garnish with rolls of bacon

Garnishes

Chopped parsley	Breadcrumbs	Nuts. Sliced vegetables
Watercress. Lemon	Grated cheese. Pimento	Piped potatoes
Cucumber	Coloured peppers	Chaudfroid or coating sauce

Artificial colouring and decoration.—It is incorrect to garnish a dish with something that cannot be eaten.

BOILING

When boiling, food is completely covered with liquid, which can be water, stock or milk. This method is particularly good for pickled or salted meats.

FRESH MEAT—is plunged into boiling (212°F.) water to seal in the juices, then it is cooked steadily at simmering point (180°F.) for the allotted time (see below).

SALT MEAT—is placed in cold water, brought up to the boil gradually, and then reduced to simmering point. It is soaked overnight in cold water to extract the salt.

BOILED TONGUE—if salt, wash and soak in cold water for 2 hours. Treat as for fresh meat if unsalted. Place in a pan of cold water and cook as you do other boiled meats, giving it 3 to 3½ hours. If you intend to serve it cold, do not remove it from the water until it has cooled.

Fresh Beef: 18 mins. per lb. for thin cuts	*Mutton:* 25 mins. per lb. for thin cuts
25 mins. per lb. for thick cuts	35 mins. per lb. for thick cuts
Salt Beef: 35 mins. per lb.	*Pork:* 35 mins. per lb.
	Bacon and Ham: 25 mins. per lb.

BOILED FOWL—Truss the bird securely and put it in a large saucepan. Rub the breast with cut lemon and cover with boiling water. Add an onion, a diced turnip and carrot, and cover with a well-fitting lid. Simmer for 1½ to 2 hours, according to size and age. Serve coated with parsley or egg sauce, or cold with salad, when it can be coated with a chaudfroid sauce.

A 5 lb. bird serves six.

All meats can be " boiled " in the oven. In the case of meat that needs to be started in boiling water, put the meat in the fireproof dish and pour boiling water from the kettle over the top, then seal the dish with aluminium foil and a tightly fitting lid. Once the juices are sealed in, the joint can wait in the oven for cooking later in the day.

STEAMING

Food can be steamed by various methods:

(1) In a perforated compartment which is the upper part of a saucepan and is known as a " steamer ". It fits tightly into the rim of the saucepan containing boiling water, and is kept on the brisk boil. A well-fitting lid is used to prevent escape of the steam. This is a good method of cooking meat which might be tough. It can be steamed for an hour or so and then put in the oven with a little fat to give it the appearance of a roast.

(2) On a plate, well covered to retain the heat with greaseproof paper and a saucepan lid or second plate, over a pan of boiling water. Fish is more commonly cooked by this method, but veal cutlets or thin slices of lamb can be done this way and are more digestible for convalescents.

(3) Steak puddings are placed in a basin, covered with greaseproof paper and tied cloth, and either put in a saucepan with sufficient water to come halfway up the sides of the basin, or placed in the steamer. It is very important to keep the water at boiling point and it should be replenished as it boils away.

(4) " Steamed " in the oven (see directions for beefsteak pudding). All steamed puddings can be cooked in the oven by this method and, as they are excellent at any temperature between 375° and 425°, can safely be cooked by the timer with a complete meal.

BEEFSTEAK PUDDING

½ lb. suet pastry (see page 94)	seasoned flour
1 lb. stewing steak	2 mushrooms
1 sheep's kidney	¼ gill water or stock

Grease a fair-sized pudding basin. Roll out the pastry and use two-thirds of it to line the basin. Cut the meat and kidney into slices and dip them into seasoned flour. Slice the mushrooms. Put it all into the lined pudding basin and add the stock. Cut the remainder of the pastry to fit the top of the basin and seal it by pinching it on to the sides. Cover with greased greaseproof paper and finally tie on a floured pudding cloth. Put it in a steamer over fast boiling water and steam for at least 3½ hours. Serve the pudding from the basin wrapped in a folded table napkin. Garnish with sprigs of parsley.

A beefsteak pudding can be " steamed " in the oven. Cover with aluminium foil instead of a pudding cloth and stand the basin on a cutter in a second basin. Half-fill this second basin with cold water and seal with aluminium foil. Place in the centre of the oven and set the timer to cook for 4 hours at 375°. This method has the advantage that you do not have to replenish the water provided the basins are carefully sealed.

STEWING

Very little water is added to the meat so that it is cooking in the released steam and its own juices. Long slow simmering is the secret of successful stewing and it can be done either on a boiling plate or in the oven. The meat should be cut into neat pieces and be free from fat. Allow ½ pint of stock or water to each pound of meat. Bring the liquid to the boil and immediately reduce the heat. Furious boiling would cause toughening and loss of flavour and juices.

Either keep it at a simmer on the hob or put in the oven at a temperature of 300° to 350°. Be sure that the pan or casserole has a well-fitting lid so that the steam does not escape too rapidly.

Sometimes frying is used as preliminary to the stewing of better quality stewing meat; this helps to develop the flavour and colour, and seals in the juices. With tougher meat it is advisable to let these juices flow, as they have a tenderising effect, and pre-frying is not therefore so suitable.

LANCASHIRE HOT POT

1½ lbs. middle neck or scrag	4 medium onions
seasoned flour	¼ turnip
dripping	1 lb. potatoes
4 medium carrots	pepper and salt stock

Wipe the meat and cut it into chops or 1½-inch cubes removing all skin and fat. Roll in seasoned flour and fry until slightly brown. Place layers of meat, carrots, onions, turnip and potatoes in a casserole finishing with a layer of thinly sliced potatoes on the top. Sprinkle with pepper and salt then add stock until it comes halfway up the pot. Cover with a lid and bake at 325°F. for 3 hours, leaving the lid off for the last half hour so that the potatoes brown, floor or centre of oven. *Serves four or five.*

HARICOT MUTTON (*facing page* 73)

6 mutton cutlets or chops	1 stick of celery
4 ozs. haricot beans, soaked overnight	seasoning
3 or 4 tomatoes, blanched and peeled	stock or water
4 medium onions, peeled and left whole	

Trim the cutlets of skin and surplus fat. Into a large fireproof dish, put first the haricot beans and then the tomatoes, cut in half. Lay the cutlets on the top with the onions, celery cut in short lengths and sufficient seasoning. Pour over the top enough white stock or water to cover.

Seal the dish with greaseproof paper or aluminium foil.

Cook at 325°F. for 4 hours, floor or centre of oven.

Serve the chops, etc., on a mound of creamed potatoes, with stock in a separate gravy boat.

Serves four.

TRIPE AND ONIONS

You either like it or you don't—there are no two minds about this dish The most important point is to make it look appetising—badly cooked it can be a nasty pallid mess. Since it is white, make it look very white. Since it is a creamy dish, serve something crisp with it for contrast.

1 lb. tripe	2 onions	pepper and salt
½ pint white stock or water	½ pint milk	parsley
	1 oz. flour	croûtons

Cut the tripe into pieces. Put it in cold water and bring to the boil. Drain. Put it in a saucepan with the stock and the onions cut into rings and simmer for two hours, or cook in the oven at 300° to 350°, closely covering the dish. Make a paste with the flour and milk. Draw the pan off the boiling plate and stir in the paste. Add seasoning—you will require plenty of salt—and cook for 5 mins. Sprinkle with chopped parsley and serve very hot with croûtons or Melba toast and creamed potatoes.

Serves four.

JUGGED HARE

1 hare	cayenne and salt
2 ozs. dripping	1 pint brown stock
1 onion	1½ ozs. flour
1 carrot	1 gill tomato purée
sprig of thyme	1 tablespoonful red currant jelly
bay leaf	1 glass port
2 cloves	2 ozs. forcemeat

Cut the hare into joints and fry them in the dripping. When lightly browned add the vegetables, seasoning and stock and simmer for 1½ hours. Blend the flour in a little more stock and add to the hare with the tomato purée, red-

59

currant jelly and glass of port. Simmer another 45 mins. Dish up the joints.
Boil the sauce, which should now have thickened, and strain it over the meat.
Garnish with forcemeat balls (see page 29) which have been fried in dripping.
Serves six.

FRICASSEES

These should be made from fresh stewing veal but fricassees are often
used as a method of re-heating any white meat. Cut the meat into neat pieces,
and, if it is raw simmer it very gently with an onion, peppercorns, pepper and
salt, and a few mushrooms till tender. Then drain it. If you are re-heating,
simply cut it in neat pieces.

Now make a white coating sauce either from milk or half-milk half-stock
in which the meat was stewed. You will need 1 pint of liquid to each pound
of meat and the sauce should be well seasoned with pepper and salt (see
page 32). Re-heat the meat (and mushrooms if you used them) in the sauce.
Serve on a dish and garnish with fried or grilled bacon rolls, one or two
sprigs of parsley and some shaped slices of fried bread.

STEWED FOWL

1 boiling fowl	1 stick celery (if liked)
1 quart white stock or water	3 tablespoonsful rice
2 small onions	pepper and salt

Cut the fowl into neat joints and place in a saucepan. Add the stock and the
sliced vegetables, and lastly the washed rice with seasoning to taste. Bring
to the boil, then reduce the heat and simmer for 1½ to 2 hours. Stir occasionally to ensure that the rice does not stick. Serve the fowl in a dish bordered
with the rice and garnished with chopped parsley.
Serves four to six, according to size.

BRAISING

Braising is a combination of frying and roasting and is usually applied to
lean meat. Extra fat is added and a good blend of vegetables to give moisture
and flavour. The meat is first fried in hot fat for sufficiently long to brown
and seal the juices. Then it is cooked in the oven in the same pan on a bed of
vegetables known as a mirepoix, the lid being removed for browning for the
last few minutes. The liquid is thickened and served as a sauce. A round of
lean beef, or game, is greatly improved in flavour by this method. It is not
considered strictly correct to serve the mirepoix with the braise, though,
of course, it is often done. One is supposed to save it for a soup or less
important meal.

OXTAIL

Can be casseroled as you would steak but the following braise is excellent:

1 oxtail cut into joints	1 turnip
1 oz. dripping	1 stick celery
2 onions	1 rasher bacon
2 mushrooms	1 bunch of herbs
2 medium size potatoes	paprika and salt
2 carrots	½ gill cooking sherry or stock

Fry the joints of oxtail on all sides in the fat in a strong saucepan, and then remove from the pan.

Prepare the vegetables for the mirepoix by scraping or peeling and cutting in thick chunks. Sauté them with the bacon cut in strips, in the dripping in the saucepan. Now add the herbs and salt and paprika to taste. Arrange the joints of oxtail on top of the vegetables and pour the sherry over the dish. Cover with a well-fitting lid and cook very slowly on the boiling plate, or in the oven for about 1½ hours. Baste the meat frequently during cooking. Serve the meat on a dish with the strained sauce—the vegetables should not be served with it. Stewing steak is excellent cooked by this method.
Serves four.

BRAISED SHEEP'S HEARTS

Clean and remove the veins from the hearts, but leave the flap. Stuff with sage and onion or forcemeat stuffing (see page 29) and fold flaps down, securing with a small skewer, to keep the stuffing in place.

Melt 2 ozs. of dripping in a saucepan and fry the hearts on all sides. Then reduce the heat and cook very slowly with the lid on the pan for an hour, turning the hearts occasionally so that they are evenly browned.

Remove the skewers and serve with thick gravy.

POT ROASTING

This is a good method of cooking when you have only a small joint, especially if you suspect it might be tough. Melt about an ounce of dripping in a strong pan and fry the joint quickly on all sides. Now add ½ gill of water or meat stock, put a tight-fitting lid on the saucepan and simmer very gently until tender. Allow the same times as for roasting.

CASSEROLE COOKING

1. Some joints, like brisket, are apt to be tough if roasted. They are frequently boiled or steamed, and can be cooked in a casserole so that they are tender and have all the appearance of a roast joint. A fowl that you suspect of old age—any meat that might be tough—can be cooked by this method, either whole or in sizeable joints, whichever you think will be more convenient to serve.

Heat some fat in a casserole or a saucepan and fry the food for a few minutes, turning it frequently. Cover the casserole and put it in the oven at 300°F. Give it long, slow cooking—about 40 mins. to the pound. Flavour can be added by putting onion, garlic, cloves or paprika with the meat.

2. The meat is cut into neat pieces and dipped in seasoned flour before frying in the casserole. Then stock and seasoning is added and it is covered and cooked very slowly in the oven, allowing 40 mins. per pound at 300°F.

CASSEROLED STEAK

1 lb. stewing steak	1 stick celery	1 oz. dripping
1 oz. seasoned flour	1 turnip	1 gill stock or
1 onion	1 carrot	cheap red wine

Cut the steak into neat pieces and roll them in seasoned flour. Dice all the vegetables and sauté them in the dripping. Add the steak and fry it lightly on all sides. Turn all into a casserole and add the stock or wine with a little pepper and salt. Cover and cook in the oven at 300°F. for 1½ to 2 hours.

Serves three or four.

CASSEROLED KIDNEYS

4 sheep's kidneys	2 onions	1 oz. dripping
seasoned flour	4 mushrooms	1 gill stock

Cut the kidneys in four, skin them and remove the core. Roll the pieces in seasoned flour. Proceed as for casseroled steak.

Serves two.

CASSEROLED CHICKEN

Cut the chicken in large and meaty joints and dip them in seasoned flour. Now fry them on all sides in 1 oz. of good fat (butter if you can). Cut a clove of garlic and rub it across the bottom of a casserole and place the chicken in the casserole. Put in a bayleaf, about six caraway seeds and a lavish sprinkling of paprika. Mix half a gill of white stock with the fat in which the chicken was fried and pour it over the top; cover and cook in the oven for 3 hours at 325°F.

CHICKEN PAPRIKA

4 onions	salt
a little olive oil	¼ lb. mushrooms
1 small chicken cut in pieces	1 green pepper
flour	½ pint tin tomato purée
1 tablespoonful paprika	½ pint stock

Slice the onions and fry till golden in oil. Roll the chicken in seasoned flour and fry with the onions. Sprinkle with paprika and a little salt. Add the mushrooms and sliced green pepper. Blend the tomato purée with stock and pour over the chicken to cover. Cook in a casserole with a lid on, at 350°F. for 1½ hours, floor of oven.

Serves six.

CASSEROLED RABBIT

Cook exactly as casseroled chicken, but cut up an onion and a rasher of bacon and fry them with the meat. Exclude the caraway seeds and drop in a few cloves and a sprig of rosemary for a change.

GRILLING

Grilling is cooking by exposing food to the direct glow of radiant heat. Turn on the grill for about 3 mins., brush the grid in the grill pan with melted fat, place the food on it under the grill. Fix the grill pan on the runners. Turn the food to cook on the other side. Personal taste decides how well the food should be cooked, but the main point to remember is that it must be cooked quickly to seal in the juices. When meat is done the surface will look brown and puffy and will be springy if pressed with the blade of a knife. Most grilled dishes take 8 to 15 mins.

BACON	3 to 5 mins.—according to thickness
GAMMON RASHER	10 to 20 mins.
CHOPS	7 to 10 mins.—mutton cutlets 10 to 28 mins.—loin chops, etc. 20 mins.—pork, veal or mutton chops
CUTLET OF VEAL	20 mins.
KIDNEYS	6 to 10 mins.
LIVER	6 to 10 mins.—according to thickness
MUSHROOMS	5 to 10 mins.
SAUSAGES	9 to 12 mins.—by size 15 mins.—thick pork
RUMP or FILLET STEAK	15 mins.—2 inches 20 mins.—2½ inches—varying according to degree of cooking preferred

MIXED GRILL (*facing page* 72)

1 sheep's kidney
1 chop
1 rasher of bacon
2 mushrooms
potato straws or chips

1 tomato
1 small piece of fillet or rump steak
1 sausage

Wash and skin the kidney, removing the core, and split without completely severing the two halves. Wipe and trim the chop. Cut off the bacon rind and form the rasher into a roll. Wash and peel the mushroom and cut the tomato in half crosswise. Cook the bacon roll, mushroom and tomato for a shorter time *under* the grid. Put the chop, steak, kidney and sausage (which should be pricked with a fork) on the grid at such a position that they are close to, but not touching the protecting wires beneath the grill. Brush all with melted fat. Turn grill to high and when red-hot fix the grill pan under the grid. Leave 1 min., turn the food on the grid, and cook another minute. Reduce the heat, turn the food frequently, and cook for another 6 to 9 mins., according to its size and how well-done you like it.

Serve garnished with fresh watercress and accompanied by potato straws or chips. *Serves one.*

FRYING

Frying is cooking in hot fat and there are four methods encountered by every housewife:

(1) Dry-frying, or cooking food like bacon in its own grease.

(2) Shallow frying, or cooking food in just sufficient fat to prevent it sticking to the pan. Fillets of fish, liver, chops and cutlets are often cooked by this method.

(3) Deep frying, where the food is completely immersed in boiling fat. Examples of this method are fish coated in batter, chips and doughnuts.

(4) Sautéing, in which the food is tossed in hot fat until the fat is absorbed.

COATING OF FRIED FOODS

The object of coating foods is to protect them against the intense heat of the boiling fat so that they can be cooked through without spoiling the outside, and to prevent the escape of the juices of the food. It also serves to hold the food together while cooking, and being appetising, helps to make a small quantity go further.

With the exception of dry-frying and sautéing, a coating should be used. There are several types, the most common of which are given below:

(1) *Seasoned flour*. This is flour with pepper and salt added in the proportion of ¼ oz. salt and ¼ teaspoonful pepper to every 4 ozs. flour. The food is dipped in the flour.

(2) *Egg and breadcrumbs*. The food is coated with beaten egg and then 'dried off' with breadcrumbs. Repeat this operation a second time to ensure complete coating.

(3) *Batter*. The food is dipped in a batter made in the following proportions: 1 egg, beaten with as much flour as it will absorb and then thinned with water to make batter consistency—beating all the time.

Yeast batter.

1½ gills milk	¼ oz. yeast	¼ teaspoonful salt
½ oz. margarine	¼ lb. flour	

Warm the milk to blood heat and melt the margarine in it. Cream the yeast with a dessertspoonful of milk and then strain into remaining milk. Add all to the warm flour and salt. Beat thoroughly. Stand in a warm (not hot) place for 45 mins.

(4) *Pastry* as in beignets soufflées. These are something like fritters, fruit or vegetables being coated with mixture similar to choux pastry and fried in deep fat.

GENERAL RULES FOR FRYING

(1) Dry the food as much as you can before you start.

(2) Coat it thoroughly, so that the food is completely covered. Then let any excess coating drain or shake off.

(3) Always use clean fat.

(4) Test the temperature of the fat before you start.

(5) Don't try to cook too much at once. A large quantity dropped into the fat sends it off the boil and the food will get 'soggy' unless it cooks quickly.

(6) Drain off excess fat after cooking by laying the food on crumpled grease-proof paper for a few seconds.

FAT TESTS

Temperature °F.	Appearance	An inch cube of bread turns pale brown in	Suitable for
320-360	Fat very " still "	70 seconds	Fritters
340-380	Slight blue haze	60 seconds	Fish
360-390	Haze all over	50 seconds	Meat, réchauffée dishes
400	Haze all over	40 seconds	Whitebait, potato chips

TO CLARIFY FAT

Place the fat in a pan. Cover with cold water and bring to the boil. Then pour it all into a clean basin and leave it to set. You will find that the water will fall to the bottom with any pieces of food and the clean fat will solidify

BAKED HAM: *served with peaches and lettuce*

ROAST DUCK: *garnished with orange slices and wild rice. Apple sauce, duchesse flan with peas, and carrots*

on the top. Lift off the fat, scrape away any crumbs or pieces that may be clinging to the underside, and the fat is suitable for cakes or pastry or for frying. Odours are to a small extent retained, however, and I should not advise you to use for a cake, fat that had been extracted from something strong smelling.

If you overheat fat, it will turn black and get little dark crumbs in it. There is nothing you can do about that and no amount of cleaning will set it right again. You have changed the actual nature of the fat and nothing will change it back. Guard against such waste by never leaving fat on the boil. As soon as blue smoke rises, *do* something—either start cooking, or remove it from the boiling plate.

LIVER AND BACON

| ¾ lb. liver | 6 slices bacon | 1 gill stock |
| seasoned flour | 3 mushrooms | |

Cut the liver into thick slices, wash them and then cover them with boiling water. Leave to stand for 2 or 3 mins. and then drain them and dip in seasoned flour.

Fry the bacon and then put on a dish in the warming drawer to keep hot. Adding a little dripping, if necessary, fry the slices of liver till tender. The mushrooms can be fried at the same time. Remove the pieces, add sufficient more flour to the pan to absorb the fat and cook till brown. Remove the pan from the boiling plate, add the stock and when quite smooth return to the heat and cook for 7 mins. Serve this sauce separately and garnish the liver and bacon with watercress. *Serves three.*

FRIED TRIPE

Cut the tripe into small pieces, blanch it by covering with cold water and bringing to the boil. Drain and then simmer in fresh water for half an hour. Drain and leave to cool. Dip the pieces in batter and fry in deep fat.

FRIED CHICKEN

1 spring chicken	½ pint milk	6 button mushrooms
1 oz. plain flour	pepper and salt	3 tomatoes
1 oz. fat		

Cut the chicken into neat joints and dip them in seasoned flour. Fry them in the fat until they are brown and cooked. Blend the flour with the milk and cook till thick. Put the chicken in the white sauce with pepper and salt to taste, cover and simmer for 20 mins. Dish up the joints on rounds of toast, coat with the sauce and garnish with grilled mushrooms and half tomatoes.

ESCALOPES VIENNOISE

very thin slices of veal cut	butter
from the fillet	slices of lemon
seasoned flour	anchovies
egg yolk	olives and capers
fine white breadcrumbs	chopped hard-boiled egg

Dip the slices of veal in flour, then in egg and finally in the breadcrumbs. Fry in hot butter for a few minutes only. When a golden colour place on a hot dish and garnish with a thin slice of lemon on each escalope, on this place a stoned olive with a boned anchovy around it. The dish is garnished with capers and finely chopped hard boiled egg.

Serve one escalope for each person.

ROASTING AND BAKING

Roasting and baking are dry methods of cooking and short-fibred or tender cuts are therefore most suitable. A suitable meat pan is provided with your cooker but you can, of course, use a different type if more convenient.

Prepare meat for roasting by wiping with a damp cloth or, in cases where it seems necessary, by washing. Dry it thoroughly. Grease the meat pan and put the meat in it. Potatoes can be roasted round the meat if you wish. Put a little dripping on the top of the joint and place it in the oven at the recommended temperature. Do not use water or too much fat in the meat pan.

A few pieces of sliced bacon or carraway seeds, sprinkled over the joint, make a change in flavour. Tiny incisions in a leg of lamb each containing a clove, give a pleasant taste; or, to improve appearance, dust the joint with seasoned flour before coating with liquid fat.

Basting is unnecessary, and only gives additional work while it makes no difference to the cooking.

If you are boning or stuffing the joint, be careful to skewer it thoroughly so that it does not fall apart during cooking and try to send it to the table so that it is easily carved.

The following temperatures must be regarded as a rough guide; with a little experience they can be adapted to suit personal taste.

BEEF	400°	20 mins. to lb.	PORK	400°	35 mins. to lb.
MUTTON	400°	30 mins. to lb.	VEAL	375°	30 mins. to lb.
LAMB	400°	25 mins. to lb.	VENISON	375°	30 mins. to lb.
STUFFED MEATS	350°	30 mins. to lb.			

The meat pan should be placed on floor of the oven.

STUFFED BREASTS OF LAMB

Get two small ones, each roughly the same size and bone them with a sharp knife.

With the proportions to 3 ozs. of breadcrumbs, make a force-meat stuffing (see page 29). Sandwich it between the two pieces of meat, keeping the skin outermost, and tie into a neat, long roll. Place in a greased meat pan and bake at the rate of 30 mins. to the pound. The size recommended here will take about 60 mins. at a temperature of 350°F. Serve hot with onion sauce and thick gravy, or cold.

STUFFED HEARTS

These want careful cooking or they are tough. Steaming or pressure cooking them before baking helps to make them tender.

Clean the hearts and remove the veins and flaps; wash them in cold salt water, and either pressure cook them for 15 mins. or steam them for an hour. Cool slightly and fill the aperture with sage and onion stuffing (see page 29). You will require about 2 ozs. of stuffing for three hearts. Wrap the hearts in slices of fat bacon or in greaseproof paper and bake at 350° for an hour.

This timing is for sheep's hearts. Calves' hearts should be baked for 1½ hours, bullocks' hearts for 2½ to 3 hours, both at 350°F.

Serve one sheep's heart per person.

OVEN BAKED HAM (*facing page* 64)

(*This method is also suitable for boiling bacon.*)

Weigh the ham, soak overnight, then put it in fresh cold water to which carrots, onions, a bouquet garni, 6 cloves, pepper and a little white wine or vinegar have been added. Boil gently for 20 mins. to the lb. When cooked, remove skin and most of the fat, then place in a fireproof dish. Score the top surface and stud with cloves. Brush the top with honey or golden syrup, sprinkle with a mixture of flour and demerara sugar and bake in a moderate oven (350°F.) for about 40 mins. basting frequently with the juices from the ham until the outside is a golden brown.

If to be served hot, place the ham on a serving dish and keep it hot while making a sauce. Add some good stock to the juices in the baking dish. Stir well and season. Boil together for a few minutes and then pour the sauce over the ham.

ROAST CROWN OF LAMB (*facing page* 144)

Get one large or two smaller loins of lamb. The butcher will chine, trim and skewer them into shape if you tell him you want to roast them as a crown.

Place it in a lightly greased meat pan.

Cook at 400°F. for 45 mins. on floor of oven.

Serves six to eight people.

Miscellaneous

Scrag end or middle neck of lamb is a good investment. Get the butcher to chop it carefully and you will find you have at one end three or four chops which are suitable for a mixed grill, a couple or more pieces which would make, say, a good toad-in-the-hole and the remainder for a hotpot. This cut can be used for the recipe for haricot mutton.

TOAD-IN-THE-HOLE (*between pages* 72 *and* 73)

Any small neat pieces of meat will make this dish—chops and cutlets are excellent. Sausage is given below:

½ lb. sausages   ½ oz. dripping
½ pint Yorkshire pudding batter (see page 83)

Skin the sausages. Thoroughly grease a Yorkshire pudding tin and pour in the batter, arranging the sausages in it.

Cook at 400°F. for 30 to 45 mins. towards top of oven.

Serves two.

Small corners of meat, or the mince one gets from the butcher, or the remnants of a joint or fowl can be cooked similarly in batter. (See also the chapter on réchauffé.)

FRENCH LIVER AND BACON (*facing page* 33)

¾ lb. liver
2 ozs. veal forcemeat
6 rashers of bacon

1 gill stock
3 tomatoes
6 mushrooms

Place the slices of liver in a fireproof dish. Cover each slice with veal forcemeat and a rasher of bacon. Pour the stock over the liver. Place halved tomatoes down one side of the dish and mushrooms down the other.

Bake at 375°F. for 30 mins., third runner from top of oven.

Serves three or four.

PIGEON PIE

2 pigeons
½ lb. stewing steak
seasoned flour

1 oz. dripping
4 mushrooms
1 gill stock

10 ozs. rough puff pastry (see page 93)

Split the pigeons straight down through the breast-bone so that they are in two equal halves. Cut the steak into thin slices. Dip both in seasoned flour. Chop the mushrooms into large pieces and sauté in the dripping.

Place the pigeons in a large pie dish and cover with the slices of steak. Arrange them so that the portions will be equal when you cut the pie. Add the stock and mushrooms. Roll the pastry half an inch thick and cover the top of the pie-dish. Trim with leaves of pastry and brush with beaten egg. Flake and knock up the sides in a pattern.

Bake at 400°F. for 45 to 50 mins., centre of oven.

Serves four.

MEAT LOAF

Any meat can be made into a loaf and it can be served either hot or cold with salad. Rabbit, chicken, veal, corned beef, beef, sausage meat, game or lamb are all excellent provided the meat has been trimmed of all fat. The meat can be either fresh or cooked.

1 lb. small-chopped or minced meat
4 ozs. breadcrumbs
½ teaspoonful mixed herbs
2 rashers finely chopped bacon
1 grated or finely chopped onion
3 ozs. grated suet

1 chopped mushroom
grated rind and juice of a lemon
1 egg, and, if necessary a little
  white sauce to bind
pepper and salt

Mix all the ingredients thoroughly together and pack into a well-greased loaf tin. Put one or two small pieces of dripping on the top. Cover with greaseproof paper.

Bake at 300°F. for 1½ hrs. centre of oven.

Serves four.

Turn out of the tin and serve either hot or cold.

You can vary the recipe to suit your taste. Some people add garlic, chopped parsley, tomato pulp or sauce. Hard boiled eggs, shelled and put whole in the centre of the loaf before cooking, give additional flavour and interest.

SHEPHERDS PIE

This, also can be made from any raw or cooked meat which should be free of fat and minced.

1 large or 2 small onions	1 lb. cooked and mashed potatoes
1½ ozs. dripping	pepper and salt
½ lb. fresh or cooked minced beef	margarine

Cut the onion into thin rings, and fry it in the fat. If the meat is raw, just mix with the onions without any further cooking. If the meat is cooked, remove the onions from the pan and make a thin brown sauce with a little flour and the fat left in the pan. Now stir in the meat and onions.

Add, if liked, to either mixture a few drops of Worcester sauce or a teaspoonful of curry powder, a teaspoonful of chopped parsley, and a few peas, beans or a stick of chopped celery.

Season well and put the mixture, which should be moist but not sloppy, in a pie-dish. Cover with mashed potato forked into a pattern and dot with a few small pieces of margarine. Place towards the top of the oven and bake at 375°F. for 30 to 40 mins. or until the potato is browned. Serve with fried bread or toast, and a fresh tomato salad.

Serves three.

LONDON PIE (*facing page* 128)

	⌠ ½ lb. minced raw beef	1 onion grated
Filling	⎨ 1 apple chopped	pepper and salt
	⌡ 1 oz. sultanas	½ gill white or brown stock
	1 lb. cooked mashed potatoes	3 large tomatoes

Mix all the ingredients for the filling together and place in a fireproof dish. Pipe squares of mashed potatoes on the top and garnish with halves of tomato.

Bake at 375°F. for 40 mins. towards the top of the oven.
Serves three.

HAMBURGERS

1 lb. fresh, lean, minced beef	pinch pepper
1 teaspoonful chopped onion	1 teaspoonful Worcester sauce
1 teaspoonful chopped parsley	piece garlic
½ flat teaspoonful salt	1 egg

Cut the clove of garlic and wipe the cut surface round the bottom of the mixing bowl. Put all the ingredients, including the well-beaten egg, into the bowl and mix thoroughly.

Form into square shapes, and fry in very little hot fat.

TO PREPARE A CHICKEN OR TURKEY
FOR THE OVEN

When possible pluck the bird while it is still warm, first from legs to wings and then from the tail towards the head. Then remove all the odd hairs or very small feathers by singeing. Hang at least 24 hours.

Cut the head off, leaving a flap of skin in the front to fold over the cut neck. Loosen the skin at the head end and very carefully draw out the windpipe. Make a slit at the tail end of the bird, crossways, just above the tail and between the tail and vent on the underside, and through this hole loosen the organs at the lower end of the bird, grasp the gizzard, and draw them out, taking care not to break the gall bladder which is attached to the liver. Wipe the bird out thoroughly with a damp cloth. With a sharp knife cut the gizzard up the centre and then remove the bag of grit. Place the gizzard, liver and neck aside for stock.

TO DRAW AND TRUSS

Insert a skewer just below the knee and pull out the sinews. Cut off the feet. Stuff if desired. Place the bird on its back, fold the skin over the opening at the neck end, and tuck it underneath the bird. Fix in place by putting the lower wing joints over it. Push the legs back close to the sides of the bird. Then pass a skewer through the body and the thick part of both legs. Tie with string, catching in the wing tips and drawing the ends through the skewer before knotting across the back. Then bring the ends to the front and tie both tail and legs together.

Place the bird in a well-greased baking tin and lay a rasher of bacon on the breast.

Cook chicken at 400°F. for 1 to 1½ hours, at the bottom of oven.

Cook turkey (10/12 lbs.) at 300° for 2 to 2½ hours, bottom of oven. Above this weight of turkey add 10 mins. per lb.

Remove string, place on a very hot dish, serve garnished with grilled bacon rolls, forcemeat balls, watercress, accompanied by bread sauce and gravy. If sausage-meat has not been used for stuffing, fried sausages can be served.

CHICKEN CHAUDFROID

1 small roasting chicken   1 pint aspic jelly
½ pint béchamel sauce (see page 33)
garnish: truffle, tomato, lettuce, cucumber, watercress, etc.

Roast bird slowly at a temperature of 300°F., well covered with greaseproof paper to prevent browning. Remove skin and leave to cool. Prepare béchamel sauce, strain, cover and leave to cool. Prepare aspic jelly and leave to set. Turn aspic into another bowl leaving sediment behind. Melt half the jelly over a pan of hot water and stir slowly into the sauce. Stand the chicken on a wire tray. When sauce is beginning to set, pour it over the bird to give a complete coating. When almost set, decorate. Leave to set firmly. Melt the remaining jelly and use to coat the chicken, pouring it, when it is almost set but still smooth, over the sauce and decorations with a spoon. Leave to set. *Serves six.*

70

PHEASANTS AND PARTRIDGE

Truss these birds as you would chicken. Keep the tail feathers of a pheasant which are used for decoration.

Cover the breasts with fat bacon.

Cook at 375°F. in the meat pan, floor of oven.

A pheasant will take 40 to 50 mins. Partridges are smaller and will take 25 to 30 mins.

Serve the pheasant garnished with watercress and with the tail feathers stuck back in place. Brown gravy made from the giblets, browned breadcrumbs and game chips are usually served as accompaniments. Make the browned breadcrumbs by frying 2 ozs. of breadcrumbs in 1 oz. of butter.

Serve partridges on fried bread or toast, garnished with browned breadcrumbs and watercress and accompanied by game chips.

GROUSE

Grouse is cooked as you would a partridge.

WOODCOCK AND SNIPE

These birds are plucked and trussed but not drawn. Wipe them with a damp cloth, cover the breasts with fat bacon. Put a meat rack in an oven meat pan, and stand the birds on it with toast below to catch the drippings or trail. Cook for 25 to 30 mins. at 400°F. Serve on the toast garnished with watercress.

TEAL AND PIGEON

Draw and truss the birds and bake at 425°F. for 20 to 25 mins. Garnish with slices of lemon and watercress.

DUCK, DUCKLING AND WILD DUCK (*facing page* 65)

Stuff with sage and onion stuffing, cover the breast with fat bacon and roast at 350° to 375°F. for 35 to 45 mins., floor of oven. If it is a large duck cook for 15 mins. per lb.

Serve with apple sauce or orange salad.

Vegetables

CORRECTLY COOKED and served, vegetables will make an excellent meal in themselves. Today we eat much less meat, and this is by no means entirely due to price. Much more attention is paid to the accompaniments, and there is an increasing interest in vegetarianism. Many households will serve a meal composed entirely of vegetables; they are no humble adjunct, these days, but a very important part of our diet.

REASONS FOR FAILURE

The main complaint against badly cooked vegetables is that they are 'soggy' or watery and tasteless. In the case of boiled vegetables this is caused by cooking overlong in too much water; with frying, it is usually because the fat is not hot enough. Never start cooking vegetables early with the idea of keeping them hot—not only will they be tasteless, but you will lose Vitamin C.

Methods of Cooking

Vegetables can be cooked by a number of methods: *Boiling and Steaming: Baking: Frying: Grilling*.

BOILING AND STEAMING		BAKING	FRYING	GRILLING
potatoes	*beetroot*	*potatoes*	*potatoes*	*mushrooms*
carrots	*cucumber*	*parsnips*	*onions*	*tomatoes*
parsnips	*tomatoes*	*onions*	*aubergines*	
horseradish	*swedes*	*celery*	*tomatoes*	
onions, leek	*cauliflower*	*marrow*	*red and green*	
Jerusalem	*red and green*	*aubergines*	*peppers*	
artichokes	*peppers*	*tomatoes*	*mushrooms*	
globe artichokes	*mushrooms*	*mushrooms*	*cucumber*	
cabbage	*pulses*	*red and green*		
spinach	*celery*	*peppers*		
sprouts	*marrow*			
turnip tops	*peas*			
runner and	*lettuce*			
French beans	*asparagus*			
turnips	*aubergines*			

Many vegetables can also be eaten raw.

Preparation of Vegetables

ROOTS, BULBS, TUBERS, STEMS, need thin peeling or scraping and quick though careful washing. Some vegetables can be scrubbed, and the skin removed after cooking.

MIXED GRILL: *chops, liver, kidneys, sausages, bacon, mushrooms and tomatoes*

TASTY BREAKFAST DISHES

MADE WITH BATTER: *drop scones, pancakes, apple fritters, toad-in-the-hole and Yorkshire pudding*

Haricot mutton

Marrow should be thinly peeled, opened, either by cutting in thick slices (for boiling) or splitting lengthwise (for stuffing) and the seeds removed. Beans should be sliced or broken, and washed. Peas are taken from the shell and washed.

GREEN VEGETABLES. Remove spoiled leaves and wash quickly in cold water. Drain, and with the exception of sprouts and spinach, shred on a chopping board. Cook immediately.

FRUITS. Tomatoes merely require wiping with a damp cloth, although they are sometimes blanched and peeled.

PULSES should be washed, and are usually soaked for twelve hours in cold water before cooking.

TABLE OF COOKING TIMES

	Boiling	Baking	Frying
Green vegetables	7-15 mins.		
Root vegetables according to size and age	20-40 mins.	40-60 mins.	till brown and crisp
Onions	45-60 mins.	60 mins.	till brown
Peas	15-25 mins.		
Beans	15 mins.		
Fruits	10-20 mins.	15-30 mins.	
Stems	15-25 mins.	20-30 mins.	
Pulses	60-90 mins. at a simmer		

BOILING AND STEAMING

BOILING—CONSERVATIVE METHOD: Prepare the vegetables. Have boiling a pan containing a small quantity of water—not more than a teacupful. Put the vegetables in the pan, sprinkle with a flat teaspoonful of salt, and cover with a close-fitting lid. Boil for the time given in the table above.

Many vegetables can be ' boiled ' in the oven. Prepare them in the usual way and put them with seasoning and a little water in a fireproof dish, carefully sealed with aluminium foil. They can be left standing in the oven with the meat and will cook by timer control.

Green vegetables are best if they are not ' boiled ' in the oven for longer than 1 to 1½ hours, but others, such as potatoes, stems, roots, pulses and some fruits can be cooked in the oven for longer. It is therefore possible to prepare them and cook them with a complete meal.

ASPARAGUS (facing page 80)

Scrape the stems and wash. Tie the asparagus into bundles of six or eight, and stand them head upwards in about 1 inch of briskly boiling water. Cover and cook for 20 to 25 mins. according to size and age.

SPINACH

Wash very thoroughly as it is apt to be gritty. Pull off the stem and coarse centre vein and put straight into a dry saucepan. Sprinkle with salt and cover, cooking on a low heat and shaking the pan occasionally, for 15 mins. There is sufficient water on the leaves for cooking.

PEAS

For ½ lb. of shelled peas allow 1 teacupful of water, a sprig of mint and 1 teaspoonful of sugar. Bring the water to the boil, toss in the peas, mint and sugar and boil for 15 to 25 mins. according to their age.

BROAD BEANS

Shell the beans, drop them into boiling water and leave for 2 mins. Drain and remove the skins. Return to the pan with an inch of boiling water and ½ teaspoonful of salt. Cover and boil till tender (about 25 mins.). Drain, toss the beans in melted butter, two leaves of finely chopped mint and a teaspoonful of chopped parsley.

Or serve coated with white parsley sauce.

BEETROOTS

Wash the beetroots, being very careful not to break the skin.

Place in a large pan and cover with hot, not boiling water. Add a teaspoonful of salt. Bring to the boil and then simmer for 1½ to 2½ hours, according to size. Cool and skin. Cut into slices or fancy shapes when cold and serve with a lacing of vinegar.

After cooking, beetroots can be prepared as above, covered with vinegar and sealed in jars, when they will keep for several months.

LEEKS

Wash the leeks very thoroughly, cut into 4-inch lengths, trimming off the tops and the roots. Lay them in a saucepan with pepper, salt and enough milk, or milk and water, to cover. Stew them for about 20 mins. until tender. Remove from the pan on to a suitable dish. Blend enough flour in a little cold milk to thicken the liquid. Boil for a few minutes and pour over the leeks.

Garnish with chopped parsley.

PUMPKIN

Cut the pumpkin into large segments, remove the seeds and peel rather thickly. Boil as you would marrow in slightly salted water. Drain carefully and serve either whole or mashed, coated if liked with a white sauce.

MACEDOINE OF VEGETABLES

Peel and dice an equal number of an assortment of root vegetables (potato, turnip, carrot, etc.). A few peas may be added if available. Cook by the conservative method in salted water.

Serve hot with white or melted butter sauce.

STEAMING

All vegetables can be steamed, though green vegetables are apt to lose colour by this method. Prepare as for boiling and allow double the time for cooking.

74

BAKING OR ROASTING

Potatoes, carrots and parsnips can be peeled or scraped, cut into convenient sized pieces and roasted round the joint. Put in raw, they require 1 to 1½ hours' cooking, according to size.

Another method is to parboil them before baking. Scrape or peel the vegetables, and cook as for boiling (see above) allowing 5 mins. only of cooking time. Then drain and bake. The advantage of this method is that the vegetables can be more easily seasoned and are soft and 'floury' in the centre when cooked.

When vegetables are to wait in the oven before being cooked later in the day by the timer, it is advisable to protect them against discoloration. After peeling, dry root vegetables and then dip them in melted fat so that they are completely coated. When the fat has congealed on the vegetable, dip them a second time. Each vegetable should now be thoroughly coated with a seal of fat which prevents the air from getting to it and causing oxidisation and you can safely leave them in the oven pan with the meat for roasting later in the day.

BAKED ONIONS

Large Spanish onions are more easily cooked if they are parboiled before roasting. Drain them and coat with melted fat or wrap in greased grease-proof paper. Bake at 300° to 350° for about 1 hour.

STUFFED BAKED ONIONS

4 large Spanish onions	1 tomato
¾ lb. potatoes	1 slice of bacon
6 or 8 stoned raisins	pepper and salt
2 ozs. fresh or cooked minced meat	

Peel the onions and parboil in salt water for 10 mins. Cook the potatoes, sieve and cream them and put in a forcing bag. Cool the onions, cut off the tops and scoop out the centre. Chop the raisins and mix with the minced meat, add pepper and salt to taste. If the meat is already cooked, heat this mixture in a small pan with enough stock to moisten; if raw, this is unnecessary. Divide into equal quarters and stuff the onions. Pipe or mash a bed of potatoes in the bottom of a greased fireproof dish, fix the onions in it and decorate the top of each with potato. Garnish with very thin slices of tomato and two or three piles of chopped bacon.

Brush each onion with melted fat or pour a teaspoonful of melted fat over each. Bake at 325° for 45 mins. Garnish with sprigs of parsley and serve with croûtons of bread.

STUFFED BAKED TOMATOES

Wipe the tomatoes, cut off the tops and scoop out a little of the centre and stuff with minced meat, sausage meat or cooked flaked fish. Place the top of the tomato on the stuffing and bake in a greased tin or fireproof dish at 325° for 20 to 25 mins.

Serve on rounds of toast or fried bread and garnish with sprigs of parsley.

STUFFED BAKED AUBERGINES

2 aubergines
1 oz. grated cheese
pepper and salt

breadcrumbs
½ oz. butter or margarine

Parboil the aubergines for 20 mins. and remove from the pan. Split in half, being careful not to break and disfigure the skin. Remove the pulp and either mash it very thoroughly, or better still, press it through a sieve. Mix it with the finely grated cheese and seasoning, and refill the cavities with the mixture. Sprinkle a few breadcrumbs on the top, dot with small pieces of butter and bake at 350° for 25 to 30 mins. until browned.
Serves four.

STUFFED BAKED POTATOES

2 potatoes
1 oz. margarine

1 oz. grated cheese
pepper and salt

Choose large potatoes all the same size and scrub them thoroughly. Prick the skins with a needle in two or three places. Bake at 325° for 1½ hours (or longer if very large).

Cut each potato in half lengthways. Scoop out the centre with a teaspoon and mix with the margarine and grated cheese. Return it to the case and brown under the grill. Garnish with red pepper and chopped parsley.
Serves four.

STUFFED GREEN PEPPERS

3 potatoes
1 stick celery
1 clove garlic
1 oz. grated cheese

1 teaspoonful chopped parsley
pepper and salt
4 green peppers

Cook and mash the potatoes. Chop the celery and garlic very finely and mix into the potato with the cheese, parsley and seasoning.

Cut the tops off the peppers, scoop out fibre and seeds, and immerse them in boiling water. Leave for 5 mins., then drain and fill them with the mixture. Stand on a lightly greased tin and bake for half an hour at 300°.
Serves four.

FRYING

Vegetables contain practically no fat, and cannot therefore be dry-fried, but they are excellent fried in either shallow or deep fat. Roots should be cut thinly if they are to be fried in shallow fat.

The most common example of deep fat frying is the potato. These are either thinly sliced (game chips) or cut into fingers about ½ in. thick (chips). In each case they should be put into a frying basket a few at a time and lowered carefully into smoking fat. Shake them occasionally and remove when pale brown. Stand the basket on a plate and re-heat the fat, then fry the potatoes again until crisp and brown. Drain free of all fat on crumpled greaseproof paper, season and serve very hot.

PUREES AND PIPING

All vegetables can be made into purées and they can be served either as a cream with the main dish or can be used as a foundation for soups. Cook conservative method until soft, drain and rub through a sieve, or press through a ricer.

To make a creamed vegetable add 1 oz. of margarine to each pound of purée and a little milk if required. Beat thoroughly and return to the pan to re-heat.

Root vegetables, particularly potatoes, are the most suitable for piping. Force the creamed vegetable through a large plain or rose pipe.

DUCHESSE POTATOES

1 lb. potatoes	1 egg	a little milk
1 oz. margarine	pepper and salt	

Boil the potatoes, conservative method, until soft. Drain them, and either put them through a ricer or rub through a sieve. Beat in the margarine and the beaten egg, add seasoning and sufficient milk to make them creamy but firm enough to stand in peaks. Force through a piping tube. The potatoes can either be used as a garnish or can be piped in individual portions on a baking sheet. Brown under the grill or in the oven.

DUCHESSE FLAN (*facing page 65*)

Prepare 2 lbs. of potatoes and make as for Duchesse potatoes.

On a plain, greased baking sheet, make a circular platform about 6 ins. across with half the potatoes. Put the remainder in a forcing bag and pipe a decorative edge.

Bake at 350° to 400°F. (to suit the remainder of the meal) for 30 to 40 mins.

When cooked, slide very carefully on to a serving plate and fill the centre with a second cooked vegetable.

This case can be used for a savoury flan.

Pulses

While these foods (haricots, butter beans, lentils, dried peas) are served as a vegetable they do not contain vitamin C and a second vegetable should also be served whenever possible.

All pulses are the better for being soaked in cold water for several hours before cooking. Wash them, cover with plenty of water and leave overnight.

Then simmer in sufficient water to cover for about 2 hours, until they are soft.

They can be drained and served coated with parsley sauce or tomato or cheese sauce and garnished with chopped parsley.

PEASE PUDDING

1½ pints of split peas   2 ozs. margarine   2 eggs   pepper and salt

Soak the peas overnight. Tie them loosely in a pudding cloth and boil them for 2½ hours. Rub them through a coarse sieve and beat in the butter, eggs and seasoning. Turn into a greased pudding basin, tie down and steam for another hour.

This pudding is served with boiled bacon or pork. The peas, while boiling in a cloth, can be cooked in the same saucepan as the pork. The liquid makes an excellent foundation for soups.

Serves six.

Miscellaneous

MARROW FRITTERS

batter: 2½ ozs. flour   1 egg   1 gill milk
1 vegetable marrow

Make the batter by beating the flour into the egg and adding the milk. Peel the marrow, cut into 1-inch slices and remove the seeds. Dip each piece into the batter so that it is thoroughly coated and fry in deep fat.

Serves three or four.

AUBERGINE FRITTERS

Peel and slice the aubergines, coat in batter and fry in deep fat as for marrow fritters.

CORN ON THE COB

Remove the husk and silk and place the cobs in sufficient boiling water to cover. Simmer gently for 30 mins. Drain. Serve hot with melted butter as a savoury or with syrup sauce as a sweet. Or remove the grains and serve cold in a salad.

Serve one corn per person.

EGGS ON SPINACH

1 lb. spinach   2 eggs   croûtons of fried bread

Trim, wash, boil and make a purée of the spinach with a seasoning of pepper and salt. Poach or fry the eggs and fry two croûtons of bread. Put the croûtons on a dish, cover with spinach and lay the eggs on top. Serve very hot.

SPINACH SURPRISE

3 lbs. spinach   3 ozs. of sliced cooked ham
seasoning   1 tomato sliced thinly
1 oz. butter or margarine

Trim, wash, boil and make a purée of the spinach and turn into a basin. Add the seasoning and butter and mix thoroughly. Put half the spinach into a fireproof casserole. Cover with the slices of ham and finally with the remainder of the spinach. Garnish with the thinly sliced tomato. Cover with a lid and cook in the oven for 15 mins. at 300°F. Serve with melba toast.

Serves three.

CAULIFLOWER AU GRATIN

1 large or 2 small cauliflowers   pepper and celery salt
2 ozs. grated cheese   ½ pint white pouring sauce (cold)
          2 tablespoonsful of browned breadcrumbs

Break the cauliflower into sprigs, wash thoroughly and boil till tender. Drain and place in an *au gratin* dish. Beat half the cheese and the seasonings into the cold sauce and pour it over the cauliflower. Mix the remainder of the cheese with the breadcrumbs, sprinkle over the top of the dish, dot with small pieces of butter or margarine and bake for 20 to 30 mins. at 325°F. or brown under the grill. Serve very hot with small triangles of toast.
Serves three.

PUMPKIN PIE

1 pumpkin   1 pinch of ground ginger
½ lb. short pastry   grated rind of a lemon
¼ lb. mixed sultanas and stoned   castor sugar
   raisins   1 egg

Prepare and cook the pumpkin as on page 74. Line a pie-dish with pastry. When the pumpkin is cooked, mash it very thoroughly and stir in the washed and soaked fruit, lemon and ginger. Taste and add a little castor sugar if liked. Leave to cool. Stir in a well-beaten egg.

Pour this mixture into the pie-dish, cover with short pastry and bake at 400°F. for 25 to 40 mins., according to size and thickness of the pastry. Sprinkle with castor sugar and serve hot or cold.
Serves four to six.

Salads and Raw Vegetables

As no nutritional value has been lost in cooking, these are excellent. Ideal catering says that something raw should be eaten at every meal—preferably at the beginning while one's appetite is still keen. One very soon acquires the habit of eating a fresh salad, even with the traditional meal of roast beef and Yorkshire, and it is essential to good feeding.

The most common salad foods are lettuce, tomatoes, cucumbers and beetroot, and many a salad is served with just these four. Many others can be added. Chicory and endive have an advantage in that they appear on the market when lettuce is scarce. Radishes, grated raw carrots, cooked pulses, onions, peas, watercress, cooked sliced potatoes, can also be added to give variety.

Choose salads that are fresh! They are ugly and unappetising when wilted. If you have a lettuce which looks a bit tired, wash it, put it in a basin and cover it with a loosely fitting lid so that there is a slight circulation of air, and keep it in the refrigerator or a cool place for a few hours.

Most important is that the salad should be clean and dry. Wash it thoroughly in cold water and then leave it to drain on a cloth over a sieve. It must also look appetising, and you have a good opportunity to demonstrate your ability to arrange a dish.

Try to avoid colours that clash; the reds of beetroot, radish and tomato can look ugly if they are too close together.

Salads can be served plain or with a coating of French dressing, salad dressing or cream mayonnaise, though the creams are most frequently used to coat a cold food such as fish or eggs or cheese that is being served with it. The easiest method of coating with French dressing is to concentrate on the lettuce or other green foods. Prepare it and put it in a basin. Pour a little of the dressing over the top and toss the lettuce with a wooden spoon till the leaves all have a light coating. Then arrange them with the rest of the ingredients in a salad bowl. For a change, try a few chopped leaves of mint mixed in the dressing before coating.

Recipes for salad dressings, etc., are on page 36.

FOODS SUITABLE TO SERVE WITH A MAYONNAISE

shrimps or prawns	grated cheese	aspics, either of meat,
any cooked fish	hard boiled eggs	fish or vegetables
lobster and crab	cooked pulses	

Each of the above can be served with a fresh mixed salad. Raw vegetables such as hearts of cabbage, grated carrots, small onions, young peas, celery etc. are delicious in a salad.

COLE SLAW

Wash the heart of a firm young cabbage and drain. Shred it finely with a sharp knife and toss it in mayonnaise. If liked add a finely sliced apple, some grated carrot and a few chopped nuts.

FRESH FRUIT SALAD (*facing page* 81)

A mixture of any fruits in season can be used. Peel and core apples, pears etc. Peel oranges and remove pith. Remove stones from cherries, plums etc. Cut into convenient pieces or slices and place in dish. Make a syrup of any fruit juice with sugar to taste and pour over the fruit.

Serve very cold.

ORANGE SALAD

Peel two oranges removing all pith and cut into thin rings. Place them on a bed of lettuce and serve with duck.

PRAWN MAYONNAISE

a few lettuce leaves	2 or 3 radishes
1 pint cooked prawns	slices of cucumber
½ gill mayonnaise (see page 36)	½ gill cooked green peas

Prepare the salad, washing and slicing the radishes or cutting them into roses. Pick the prawns but leave whole.

Arrange the lettuce in a bed on a flat dish and pile the prawns in the centre, keeping one or two aside for decoration. Coat with mayonnaise. Arrange the rest of the salad on the dish, and the remaining prawns on the top of the pile.

Serves two.

A PARTY MEAL: *asparagus, grilled lobster, roast chicken,
green salad, queen of puddings*

FOR A PICNIC: *cold consommé, scotch eggs, veal and
ham pies, salad and fruit salad*

Puddings

Sweet puddings are the climax, the rounding off, of the meal, and great care should be taken with their selection. Very often, bad choice is the main reason for their failure. If the main course has been a heavy one, do not make the mistake, for example, of serving a solid pudding as well; and never, never serve the same method of cooking twice in one meal! Don't have fruit pie following meat pie, or stewed fruit after stewed lamb. Vary the cooking. Make it interesting.

Another failing lies not in the actual pudding but in the sauce served with it. Try to make the accompaniment to a pudding something in the nature of a contrast so that it surprises the appetite. Don't serve a thin custard with very juicy stewed fruit; if you serve custard at all make a stiffly set baked egg custard; or serve short pastry or macaroon biscuits with it; or scatter nuts over it.

When cooking a pudding by timer control you will almost certainly want to cook it for the same length of time as the first course. To some extent it is advisable to select a recipe of roughly the same cooking duration but the following information may be helpful.

Milk and steamed puddings, if cooked for longer than recommended in the following recipes will come to no harm.

Baked puddings will be safe for 15 to 30 mins. longer if placed in the centre of the oven and for yet another 15 mins. if covered with greaseproof paper. If, for example, you refer to the recipe for baked college pudding you will find that you are recommended to bake it at the top of the oven for 60 mins. at 375° or for 45 mins. at 400°. Cover it with greaseproof paper and place it in the centre of the oven and you can delay the cooking so that it will take 90 mins. at 375° or 75 mins. at 400°.

Puddings made with Milk

REASONS FOR FAILURE

Tough skinned baked milk puddings are the result of being cooked in too hot an oven. 'Sloppy' puddings either have the wrong ingredients or were not cooked long enough.

RICE PUDDING

1¾ ozs. rice	flavouring—either cinnamon,
½ to 1 oz. sugar (according to taste)	lemon rind, nutmeg or vanilla
1 pint milk	

Wash the rice and put it in a greased pie-dish. Add the milk, sugar and flavouring. Stir very thoroughly.

Cook at 300°F. for 2 hours or more, centre of oven.
Serves three or four.
Tapioca or sago can be substituted for the rice.

VARIATIONS ON THE ABOVE RECIPE

For added flavour, cook the pudding until the grain is just soft and then stir a well-beaten egg into it.
Or add 1 oz. sultanas or raisins to the recipe.

RICE MOULD (*facing page* 145)

1 egg	½ pint milk
1 flat tablespoonful castor sugar	1 oz. rice

Thoroughly grease a border mould with butter.
Beat the egg and sugar, add to the milk and stir in the washed rice. Pour into the border mould. Cook in the centre of the oven for the time and temperatures given for rice pudding.
When cooked, turn out of the mould and fill with stewed fruit.
Serves two or three.

SEMOLINA PUDDING

1 pint milk	2 ozs. semolina	1 oz. sugar	egg (if liked)

Heat the milk in a saucepan, and sprinkle the semolina and sugar on the top, stirring thoroughly. Cook till the semolina is clear, stirring all the time. Then turn the pudding into a greased dish, stir in a well-beaten egg if liked and brown under the grill or at 350°F. in the oven (about 20 mins.).
Serves three or four.

CORNFLOUR MOULD

½ pint milk	1 oz. cornflour	½ oz. sugar

Blend the cornflour in a little of the milk in a large basin. Boil the remainder in a pan. Then pour it over the cornflour, stirring thoroughly. Return to the pan and cook gently for about 10 mins., stirring all the time. Add the sugar and either turn the pudding into a pie dish and brown under the grill or set in a mould and serve cold.
Serves two.

Puddings made with Eggs

REASONS FOR FAILURE

1. Curdling of egg custards is caused by overcooking. The mixture should not boil, and if cooked on the hob, is best stirred during cooking. If cooked in the oven either cook at a very low temperature or stand in a larger dish containing water.

2. If a soufflé is tough it has been cooked for too long.

3. If batter puddings are 'soggy' or do not rise they did not have sufficient beating or they were cooked in too cool an oven.

4. If a coating batter for fritters is 'soggy' the fat was not at boiling point.

BAKED EGG CUSTARD

½ pint milk   ½ oz. sugar   1 egg

Heat but do not boil the milk with the sugar. Beat the egg in a large basin and pour the milk over it, stirring thoroughly. Strain into the rinsed saucepan and bake in the centre of the oven till the mixture thickens. This custard is less likely to curdle if cooked in a double saucepan over boiling water.
Serves two.

CARAMEL CUSTARD

Caramel	*Custard*
2 ozs. sugar (preferably loaf sugar)	2 eggs
¼ pint water	2 flat teaspoonfuls castor sugar
	½ pint milk

Melt the loaf sugar in the water in a saucepan. Boil without stirring until brown. While still hot, pour it into a tin mould, coating the sides and base.

Beat eggs and castor sugar, add the milk. Pour this mixture into the mould and cover with greased paper.

Put the mould in a steamer or stand it in a saucepan with water coming about halfway up the mould. Steam gently for ½ to ¾ hour.

This pudding can be cooked in the oven. Cover the mould with grease-proof paper and stand it on a cutter in a large pudding basin. Half fill this basin with cold water, and seal with aluminium foil. Cook with a complete meal in the oven.

Cook at 300°F. for 1½ to 2 hours centre of oven.
Serves two.

BREAD AND BUTTER PUDDING

1 oz. sultanas	½ pint milk
1 egg	6 slices of thinly-cut,
½ oz. sugar	buttered, white bread

Clean the fruit; thoroughly beat the egg and sugar together, adding the milk.

Grease a 1-pint pie dish and lay some of the slices of bread in it. Sprinkle the fruit over it and cover with bread. Continue until all the slices are used.

Strain the egg and milk over the pudding, grate a little nutmeg over the top if liked.

Cook at 300°F. for 1½ to 2 hours in centre of oven.
Serves two or three.

YORKSHIRE PUDDING

2 ozs. flour   1 egg   1 oz. dripping or lard
pinch of salt   1½ gills milk or water

Beat the flour and salt into the beaten egg, and then add the milk or water beating all the time. Pour into a very well-greased Yorkshire pudding tin.
Cook at 400°F. for 40 mins near top of oven.
Serves four.

RAISIN BATTER (*facing page* 209)

Add 1 oz. of stoned and cleaned raisins or sultanas to the last batter.

PANCAKES (*between pages* 72 *and* 73)

4 ozs. flour   pinch of salt   1 egg   ½ pint milk

Make a batter as for Yorkshire pudding. In a frypan melt a little lard.

When hot, pour in enough batter to cover the base of the pan, and cook till lightly brown on one side.   Turn with a palette knife or toss and cook on the other side. Sprinkle with castor sugar and a squeeze of lemon juice. Roll up and serve very hot garnished with slices of lemon.

Serves three or four.

APPLE FRITTERS (*between pages* 72 *and* 73)

Make a batter using water instead of milk as follows:

2 ozs. flour   pinch of salt   1 egg   1 gill water

Prepare 2 cooking apples by peeling, coring and cutting into slices about half an inch thick.

Dip them into the batter and fry in smoking hot fat, lowering them into the fat very carefully to prevent splashing.

Dredge with castor sugar and serve very hot.

Serves two or three.

CANADIAN LEMON PUDDING

1 oz. butter   2 eggs   ½ pint milk
5 ozs. sugar   1 lemon   pinch of salt
3 ozs. flour

Cream butter and sugar, add the flour, salt, and egg yolks, lemon rind and juice. Then add milk. Beat egg whites stiffly and fold into mixture. Pour into buttered dish.

Bake at 350°F. for 45 mins. centre of oven.

Serves four or five.

OMELETTES (page 126)

VANILLA SOUFFLE

1 oz. butter, or margarine   1 dessertspoonful castor sugar
1 oz. flour   vanilla essence
¼ pint milk   3 eggs

Grease a 1-pint souffle dish. It is unnecessary to use greaseproof paper.

Make a panada with the butter, flour and milk. Add the sugar and essence. Cool. Add the yolks of eggs, one at a time, and beat well.

Whisk the whites of egg till stiff and fold into the mixture. Pour it into the tin, cover with greased paper and steam for 1 hour, or do not cover and bake in the oven at 400°F. for 15 to 20 mins. Turn into a dish, pour jam sauce round it and serve immediately.

CHOCOLATE SOUFFLE

To the recipe for vanilla souffle add 1 oz. of chocolate or good cocoa. Use this when making the panada adding about 2 extra tablespoonsful of milk. Serve with chocolate sauce.

Puddings made with Suet or Creamed Fat

REASONS FOR FAILURE

Usually these puddings fail by being heavy and over-moist. This is caused by one of the following:

1. Inaccurate measurement of the ingredients.
2. The water under the steamer was allowed to go off the boil once the pudding had started to cook
3. Insufficient cooking

PLUM DUFF

½ lb. flour	3 ozs. sugar
4 ozs. finely chopped or shredded suet	4 ozs. mixed fruit
3 flat teaspoonsful baking powder	water to mix

Grease a pudding basin and prepare a steamer, bringing the water to the boil.

Sift the flour and thoroughly mix into it the other dry ingredients including the suet. Mix to a stiff dough with water. Turn into the pudding basin and then tie down with pudding cloth. Steam for 2½ to 3 hours, taking great care the water never goes off the boil.

Or steam in the oven with the remainder of the meal. Do not cover the pudding basin with a pudding cloth but use aluminium foil. Stand the basin on a metal cutter in a second basin, half filled with cold water. Cover this second basin with aluminium foil.

Cook in the oven for 2 to 2½ hours at 400°F. centre of oven.
Serves four.

MARMALADE PUDDING

Follow the Plum Duff recipe but omit the fruit and stir in 3 tablespoonsful of marmalade.

FRUIT PUDDING. Made with suet pastry (see page 101).

LAYER PUDDING

about ½ lb. jam   6 ozs. suet pastry (see page 94)

Grease a pudding basin and put a good dessertspoonful of jam in the bottom.

Roll the pastry till it is a ¼-inch thick and cut a round to fit over the jam. Put in the basin and spread with jam. Continue till the basin is nearly full, finishing with the suet crust. Cover with greased paper and then tie down with a pudding cloth. Steam for 2½ hours or cook in the oven, following the instructions for Plum Duff given above.
Serves five or six.

CHRISTMAS PUDDING (*sufficient for two puddings*).

½ lb. raisins	a little (½ teaspoonful) mixed spice
¾ lb. sultanas	12 ozs. shredded suet
½ lb. currants	1 lb. sugar (brown if possible)
½ lb. mixed chopped peel	6 eggs
3 ozs. blanched chopped almonds	¼ to ½ pint water
8 ozs. flour	juice 1 lemon
6 ozs. white breadcrumbs	brandy

Prepare the fruit. Mix the flour, breadcrumbs, spice, suet, fruit, almonds and sugar.

Beat the eggs, add to ¼-pint water and stir into the mixture. Add more water if required, to make a stiff dough. Add the lemon juice and stir. Add a little brandy and stir again. Grease two pudding basins and fill with the mixture. Cover with greased paper and tie down with pudding cloths. Steam or boil for 7 hours. Change the pudding cloths for clean ones when cool, and store.

Cook for another 2 hours before serving.

It will sometimes be convenient to ' steam ' the Christmas puddings in the oven by the timer. Cover the basin with aluminium foil, stand it on a cutter inside a larger basin. Half fill this second basin with water and seal with aluminium foil. Cook in the oven for 6 hours at 350°F.—overnight if it suits you!

Each pudding serves six.

EVE'S PUDDING

3 ozs. margarine	4½ ozs. flour
3 ozs. sugar	1½ flat teaspoonsful baking powder
2 eggs	1 lb. apples

Cream the fat and sugar, beat in the eggs one at a time, and fold in the flour and baking powder, which have been sieved together. Peel, core and slice the apples into a greased dish and cover with the sponge mixture.

Cook at 350°F. for 1 hour, centre of oven.

Serves four.

LEMON PUDDING

3 ozs. margarine	½ teaspoonful baking powder
3 ozs. sugar	4 ozs. flour
1 egg	grated rind and juice of a lemon

Cream the margarine and sugar and gradually beat in the egg. Fold in the flour and baking powder. Stir in the lemon. Add a little water, if required, to make a soft consistency. Turn into a greased pudding basin or castle pudding moulds, cover with greased paper and steam for 2 hours if large puddings, 45 mins. if small.

The pudding can be 'steamed' in the oven. Prepare and cook large pudding as instructed for plum duff (page 85).

Small puddings (the above mixture turned into 6 dariole moulds), sealed, should be able to stand in one large deep dish with about 1½ inches of cold water and sealed with aluminium foil. Cook them in the oven for 30 to 45 mins. at 400°F.

Serve four to six.

VARIATIONS ON THE ABOVE RECIPE

Orange Pudding
Substitute orange for the lemon.

Ginger Pudding
Exclude the lemon and add ½ teaspoonful of ground ginger.

Jam or Syrup Pudding (*facing page* 32)
Put a rounded tablespoonful of raspberry jam or syrup in the bottom of the basin before adding the mixed pudding from which the lemon may be excluded if preferred.

BLACK CAP PUDDING

Put a spoonful of golden syrup and teaspoonful currants in the bottom of each dariole before adding the pudding mixture.

TWO-COLOUR PUDDING

Colour half the mixture with ½ oz. of powdered chocolate or cocoa. Put this mixture in the basin first and the white mixture on top.

UPSIDE DOWN CAKE (*facing page* 208)

6 rings of pineapple from a tin	3 eggs
6 ozs. fat	8 ozs. plain flour
6 ozs. castor sugar	2 flat teaspoonsful baking powder

Grease a six-inch square cake tin and stick pineapple rings on the bottom, and half pieces against the side.

Mix the remaining ingredients creaming method as lemon pudding. Pour carefully into the tin.

Cook at 350°F. for 1¾ hours in centre of oven.

Serves four or five.

QUEEN OF PUDDINGS (*facing page* 80)

3 ozs. breadcrumbs	½ pint milk
1 oz. sugar	2 eggs
grated rind of ½ lemon	tablespoonful jam
1 oz. margarine	1 oz. castor sugar for meringue

Put the breadcrumbs, sugar and lemon rind in a basin; melt the margarine in the heated milk and add. Beat the egg yolks and stir into the mixture.

Spread jam at the bottom of a 1-pint pie dish, add half the mixture, spread with more jam and fill with the remainder of the mixture.

Cook at 350°F. for 40 mins. top of oven.

Cool slightly and spread with more jam. Whisk the egg whites till stiff and fold in 1 oz. of castor sugar. Pile this meringue on the top of the pudding and return to the oven with the switch ' OFF ' to set.

Serves three or four.

BAKED COLLEGE PUDDING

3 ozs. plain flour
3 ozs. breadcrumbs
3 ozs. shredded suet

3 ozs. sugar
1 flat teaspoonful baking powder
water to mix

Mix the ingredients and add sufficient water to make a stiff dough. Turn into a well-greased pie dish. Dot the top of the pudding with little pieces of fat.

Bake as instructed for Queen of Puddings.

Puddings made with Gelatine

For proprietary brands of gelatine follow the instructions on the packet. If none is given allow ½ oz. to the pint, dissolving the gelatine in a ¼ gill of warmed liquid taken from the original pint. Make sure it is thoroughly dissolved before straining into the remaining liquid.

Always wet a mould with cold water before pouring in the jelly.

REASONS FOR FAILURE

Provided correct quantities are used the jelly will set, and usual failures are the following:

1. Tasteless. Cold food needs more flavouring than hot. Taste the mixture before setting and ensure that the flavour is decisive.

2. Colourless. Colour is important. It need not be vivid but on the other hand it must not be insipid. Apples, for example, make a pleasant pudding with gelatine but they need colour—either a touch of green or a tinge of pink.

ORANGE JELLY

3 oz. sugar
½ pint orange juice

3 gills water
juice of 2 lemons

½ oz. gelatine

Dissolve the sugar in the fruit juice and water (gentle heat). Dissolve the gelatine in a little of the water and add to the pan. Stir thoroughly and then strain through muslin into a mould. Turn out when set.

Serves two or three.

VARIATIONS ON THE ABOVE RECIPE

Any fruit juice can be used, or milk or port wine. Colouring is sometimes required to improve the appearance.

The jelly can be poured a small quantity at a time into the mould, each pouring being left to set and then covered with raw fruit before more jelly is added. Garnish with fruit and whipped cream.

PRUNE MOULD

½ lb. prunes
½ pint water
1 to 1½ oz. sugar (to taste)

juice of ½ a lemon
¼ oz. gelatine
carmine to colour

Wash and soak the prunes in the ½ pint water overnight; stew till tender

88

and add the sugar. Strain the liquid. Chop and stone the prunes and press them through a sieve. Return this to the liquid, add the lemon juice. Dissolve the gelatine in hot water and stir into the prunes. Add sufficient carmine to make a good colour. Pour into wet moulds.

When set turn on to a dish and garnish with whipped cream and tiny pieces of angelica. *Serves four*.

FRUIT MOULD (*facing page* 128)

You have enough *stewed fruit and custard* for two and want it for four:

Drain the juice from the fruit, add the juice of a lemon if you have it and water to make up to a pint. Melt ½ oz. of gelatine in a little of this juice and return to the remainder.

When nearly at setting point, fold in the fruit and the custard. Turn into a mould and leave to set. Turn out, garnish with halves of walnut.

APPLE MOULD

1 lb. good cooking apples	juice of half lemon
3 or 4 cloves	1 oz. shelled walnuts
½ to 1 oz. of sugar to taste	¼ oz. gelatine

Peel, core and chunk the apples and stew them with the cloves and sugar in just enough water to keep them from burning. Remove the cloves and beat the apples to a pulp. Add the lemon juice and the walnuts, coarsely chopped.

Melt the gelatine in a little hot water and add to the apples, stirring thoroughly. Colour with a few drops of cochineal; do not make the mixture too pink—a faint tinge is all you want. Pour into a wet mould. When set, turn out and garnish with whipped cream.

Any soft fruit can be substituted in this recipe.

Serves four.

CHESTNUT CAKE

1 lb. chestnuts	½ gill milk or cream
¼ oz. gelatine	½ oz. sugar

Cut the skins of the chestnuts with a sharp knife and boil them in water for 30 mins. Drain and skin while still hot. Pass through a sieve.

Melt the gelatine in a little hot water and strain into the milk or cream. Stir into the chestnuts with the sugar. Mix very thoroughly and pack into a plain mould. Leave to set.

Turn on to a dish, garnish with angelica and pour a little caramel sauce round it. *Serves four*.

CHARLOTTE RUSSE

¼ pint lemon jelly	sugar
glacé cherries and crystallised violets	vanilla essence
angelica	a few drops of lemon juice
sponge finger biscuits	½ oz. gelatine
½ pint custard	5 tablespoonsful water
½ pint evaporated milk	

Set a thin layer of jelly in the bottom of a charlotte russe tin. Decorate with cherries, violets and angelica and pour in a little more jelly. When the jelly has set line the sides with the trimmed sponge finger biscuits packed tightly together. Half-whip the custard stir in the evaporated milk, sugar and flavouring and add the gelatine dissolved in the water. When just beginning to thicken pour into the tin. When set, trim the biscuits level with the cream, dip the bottom of the tin in warm water and turn out. Serve with chopped jelly round and whipped cream. This recipe can be varied by using ½ pint of cream instead of ½ pint of evaporated milk.

Serves five or six.

Puddings made with Fruit

STEWED FRUIT

1. When you are serving plain fruit, do not serve pulp. Poach the fruit gently, so that it does not boil to a mash.
2. Taste the fruit before serving and make sure it is sufficiently sweet. Add interest by strewing a few nuts on the surface.
3. Pale fruit, such as apples, must be given colour. Add green or pink colouring, according to your taste.

FRESH FRUIT

Allow ½ pint water and 4 ozs. sugar to each pound of fruit.

Dissolve the sugar in the water and boil for a few minutes, reduce to a simmer and add the fruit. Cook till tender.

Some soft fruits are best not cooked at all. Put the fruit in a dish with layers of castor sugar and stand in a warm place—the warming drawer or the grill chamber for about an hour. This is especially good for ripe raspberries or loganberries.

DRIED FRUITS

Prunes	1 *pint water, 3 ozs. sugar, to each pound*
Apricots	1½ *pints water, 3 ozs. sugar, to each pound*
Apple rings	2 *pints water, 3 ozs. sugar, to each pound*

Wash the fruit and soak in the correct quantity of water overnight. Stew very gently till tender. Add the sugar, stirring till dissolved.

APPLE MERINGUE

1 lb. cooking apples	juice of half a lemon
1 oz. granulated sugar	½ oz. butter
1 egg	½ oz. castor sugar

Peel, core and chunk the apples and stew with the granulated sugar in a very little water. Beat to a pulp, add the yolk of egg, lemon juice and butter and beat.

Pour into a pie dish. Whisk the white of egg to a stiff froth, fold in the castor sugar and pile on top of the apples.

Put in a slow oven (250°F.) or under the grill with switch at low to set the meringue. *Serves three or four.*

APPLE CHARLOTTE

4 ozs. breadcrumbs
2 ozs. shredded suet
3 ozs. sugar

1 lb. cooking apples
juice of half a lemon

Mix the breadcrumbs, suet and sugar, peel and cut the apples into slices and pour the lemon juice over.

Grease a pie dish and line with a little of the crumbs. Alternate layers of apples and crumbs till the pie dish is full, finishing with a layer of crumbs.

Cook at 350° for 1¼ hours in the centre or top of oven.

Serves three or four.

BAKED APPLES

2 large cooking apples
2 teaspoonsful sugar, honey or golden syrup

Wash, dry and remove the core of the apples. With a sharp knife cut a ring through the skin round the apples about 1 inch from the top. This will prevent the skin from splitting. Stand in a dish, and fill the centres with the sugar or honey.

Serves two.

GOOSEBERRY FOOL

1 lb. green gooseberries
1 gill water
juice of 1 lemon

1 gill custard
1 oz. sugar
1 gill cream

Stew the gooseberries with lemon and water and, when soft, press through a fine sieve. Add the custard and sugar and stir. Whip the cream till thick but not stiff and fold into the fruit. Serve in individual glasses.

VARIATIONS ON THE ABOVE RECIPE

Halve the quantity of water and use any soft fruit (raspberries, loganberries, blackcurrants, etc.). With fruit that has a good flavour you may prefer to omit the lemon juice.

SUMMER PUDDING

Line a pudding basin with thinly cut strips of bread from which all the crusts have been cut. Fill the basin with any hot freshly stewed and sweetened fruit, being careful not to add too much juice or syrup. When full cover with a round of bread. Place a saucer or a plate on this with a weight on top and leave for 24 hours. Turn out and serve with a good custard or cream.

Red currants and raspberries can be used uncooked.

Pastry

YOU WANT to make flour rise without the aid of egg or any other raising agent. You do so by entrapping air between the folds of the pastry. The colder it is, the better; for then when it goes into the oven the heat will expand the air and raise the pastry still further.

The *general rules*, then, are as follows:

1. Keep everything cool.
2. Handle lightly.
3. Use freshly drawn cold water for mixing.
4. Sift the flour with the salt and ensure it is dry.
5. Never use baking powder unless particularly stated in the recipe. You can sprinkle a few drops of lemon on the pastry between rolling and this will assist it to be light.
6. Roll with short, sharp, light presses of the rolling pin. Don't be in a hurry or behave like a steam roller. Take your time.

REASONS FOR FAILURE

1. It may be hard. This is caused by insufficient fat, making the pastry too wet or rolling it too heavily. Adhere strictly to the recipe and handle it lightly.
2. It may shrink from the sides of the pie dish and fall into the fruit. This is because you have stretched it as you covered the dish. After rolling for the final time it is a good idea to leave it to relax for about 7 to 10 mins., before laying it across the dish.
3. It may become sodden with fruit juice, which will be because you have added too much water to the fruit so that it boiled over and soaked the pastry. Fruit under pastry only requires enough water to melt the sugar.
4. The jam or syrup in open tarts may boil over. Lay strips of pastry across the jam.

Classification

There are several different kinds of pastry, each of which serves a different purpose. Suet pastry is for steaming and boiling, hot water pastry is for serving as a container for meat and gravy, choux pastry is for cakes. The recipes themselves decide that, but tradition decides also that flaky pastry is to cover meat and short pastry is for sweet things like fruit or jam. It would be perfectly possible to use flaky pastry above fruit (a lot of people do so and very nice it is) but it is not strictly correct.

The difference between the pastries lies in the quantity of fat and in the method of rolling. Opposite is a tabulation of the proportions. Start off with short-crust pastry—it is easiest for a beginner. Don't try puff pastry until you are really efficient.

Type of pastry	Quantity of fat	Quantity of plain flour with ½ teaspoonful salt
short crust	3 ozs. lard and margarine	6 ozs.
rough puff	4 ozs. lard and margarine	6 ozs.
flaky	{ 2 ozs. lard { 2 ozs. margarine or butter	6 ozs.
puff	6 ozs. butter	6 ozs.
suet	3 ozs. suet	6 ozs.
potato	3 ozs. lard and margarine	{ 6 ozs. flour { 3 ozs. potato

SHORT CRUST

6 ozs. flour (plain)
½ teaspoonful salt
1½ ozs. margarine

1½ ozs. lard
water to mix

Sift the flour and salt into a basin. Cut the fat in small pieces into the flour. Then rub them together with the tips of the fingers till the mixture resembles fine breadcrumbs. Mix to a stiff dough with cold water. (Watch that water! The pastry will spoil if you get it too wet.) Turn on to a floured board. Knead into a neat shape, and then roll once only to the required thickness. Try to keep it in a good shape as you roll.

Bake at 400°F. for 15 to 30 mins. Second runner from top of oven.
Sufficient dough to cover a medium pie dish.

CHEESE PASTRY

A variation of the above recipe. It is used for cheese straws, some flan cases and some biscuits.

6 ozs. plain flour
3 ozs. finely-grated cheese
salt, pepper and cayenne pepper

3 ozs. fat (lard, margarine or a mixture of both)
water to mix

Mix as for short pastry and roll once, adding cheese to flour before rubbing in fat. Bake at 400°F. till brown. Second runner from top of oven.
For cheese straws cook for 10 mins.
Sufficient for forty-eight cheese straws.

ROUGH PUFF

6 ozs. plain flour
½ teaspoonful salt
2 ozs. lard

2 ozs. margarine
water to mix

Sift flour and salt into a basin. Cut the fat in pieces about the size of a walnut into the flour and mix with enough cold water to keep the fat in lumps —don't mash it! Turn on to a floured board and roll into a long strip. This isn't easy, as the fat is apt to stick to the board and the rolling pin. Keep both well floured. When the pastry is in a strip fold it in three, give it a quarter turn and seal the edges by pressing it with the rolling pin.

Repeat this rolling and folding three more times. Then for the fifth rolling make it the thickness required.

Bake at 425°F. till brown. Second runner from top of oven.

FLAKY PASTRY

2 ozs. lard   ½ teaspoonful salt
2 ozs. margarine or butter   water to mix
6 ozs. plain flour   lemon juice

Divide the fat into four and rub one quarter into the sifted flour and salt. Mix to a dough with cold water and lemon juice. Leave in a cool place for 15 to 20 mins.

Turn the dough on to a floured board and knead it very lightly before rolling it into a strip. Take tiny pieces of another quarter of the fat and dot them on to two-thirds of the strip. Now fold the strip in three, starting with the end of the strip which has no fat. Seal the edges with a rolling pin, half turn the pastry. Repeat till all the fat is used. Roll to required thickness.

Bake at 425°F. to 450°F. till brown. Second runner from top of oven.

PUFF PASTRY

6 ozs. plain flour   ½ teaspoonful salt   lemon juice
6 ozs. butter   water to mix

Sieve the flour and salt and mix to a soft dough with the juice of a lemon and sufficient cold water. Turn on to a floured board and knead lightly. Leave it in a cool place for 20 mins., and then roll it into a strip.

Place the butter, which should be in a square pat and very cold, in the centre of the strip and fold the pastry so that the butter is inside.

Roll and fold in three till this has been repeated seven times, allowing the pastry to stand in a cool place for 10 mins. between each rolling.

Roll the pastry to the thickness required. Leave it in a cool place for 30 mins. before cutting to shape.

Cook at 425°F. to 450°F. till brown. Second runner from top of oven.

HOT WATER OR RAISED PASTRY

6 ozs. plain flour   3 ozs. lard   ½ gill water
pinch salt   ½ gill milk

Sieve flour and salt into a warm basin. Boil the water, milk and lard together and pour it into the middle of the flour. Mix very quickly and knead till smooth, keeping the pastry warm. Cut off one quarter for the lid and shape the remainder into a deep round case. Lay the filling (see recipe for pork pie) in the pie, cover with the pastry lid and decorate with pastry leaves round a small hole in the centre. Brush with egg or milk.

Bake at 400°F. for 1½ hours, centre of oven.

SUET PASTRY

9 ozs. flour   3 ozs. suet
½ teaspoonful salt   water to mix
½ teaspoonful baking powder

Sieve the flour, baking powder and salt, add the shredded or finely chopped suet and mix with water to a soft dough. Turn on to a floured board and roll to required thickness.

CHOUX PASTRY

4 ozs. plain flour	½ pint water	2 eggs
2 ozs. butter or margarine	pinch salt	

Sieve the flour. Boil the fat, water and salt in a saucepan. Take it off the boiling plate and add the flour, beating all the time. When it is cool, add the beaten eggs and beat till smooth.

Bake at 400°F. for 30 mins., top of oven.

(See recipe for éclairs, page 101.)

POTATO PASTRY

6 ozs. flour	1½ ozs. lard
1 teaspoonful baking powder	1½ ozs. margarine
½ teaspoonful salt	3 ozs. potato

Sieve flour and salt, adding 1 teaspoonful baking powder and rub in the fat. Add the grated raw potato and proceed as for short pastry. Use for hot savoury dishes.

Bake at 425°F. until brown. Second runner from top of oven.

EXAMPLES OF THE USES OF VARIOUS TYPES OF PASTRY

The following recipes may require variation when being cooked with a complete meal. Times are recommended which can be increased by 15 to 30 mins. if you put the pastry in the centre of the oven instead of at the top.

Many of these pastry recipes can be used for packed or cold meals.

Short Crust Recipes

FLAN CASES

Roll the pastry about ¼ inch thick. Put a flan ring on a baking tray and fit the pastry into the ring, being careful not to stretch the pastry. Cut away the edges with a knife and press lightly between the thumb and finger to make a fancy rim if liked. Alternatively, the flan cases can be baked in a sandwich tin.

If the flan case is to be 'baked blind' prick it and lay a piece of grease-proof paper across the bottom with two or three dozen haricot beans in it.

Remove the haricot beans and paper when cooked.

Bake at 425°F. for 20 to 25 mins., top of oven.

FRUIT FLANS (*facing page* 97)

4 ozs. short pastry	1 gill water or fruit juice
suitable fruit, either fresh, stewed or tinned	colouring
1 oz. sugar	1 flat teaspoonful arrowroot
	½ flat teaspoonful gelatine

95

Make the short pastry into a flan case and bake blind. Allow to cool. Arrange the fruit in the flan case. Melt the sugar in the fruit juice, add colouring and thicken with arrowroot and gelatine. Coat the fruit with this, leave to cool and serve cold, garnished with cream.

A flan case approximately 7 inches in diameter will serve four.

MUSHROOM FLAN

4 ozs. short pastry
2 ozs. button mushrooms
1 oz. fat

Sauce:
½ oz. flour ½ oz. fat
1 gill white stock
pepper and salt

Line a flan case and bake it blind.

Clean the mushrooms and remove the stalks, keeping them separate.

Sauté the mushroom heads in the 1 oz. of fat until they are tender, being very careful not to break them.

Sauté the stalks in the ½ oz. of fat. Remove them and make a sauce with the fat, flour and stock, seasoning with pepper and salt.

Fill the flan case when cool, laying the mushroom heads in it and coating with the sauce. Reheat and garnish with sprigs of parsley.

Serves three or four.

JAM, MARMALADE OR HONEY TARTS

The flan case can be filled with jam, marmalade, or honey before baking or with a syrup filling (recipe below). In each case put strips of pastry across the filling which will help to keep it in position, and do not overfill or it is apt to boil over.

Small tarts can also be made with the same pastry. You will require short pastry made with 6 ozs. flour for two 5 in. flan rings or about 18 tarts.

GOLDEN SYRUP OR TREACLE TART (*facing page* 97)

6 ozs. short pastry
3 tablespoonsful golden syrup

3 tablespoonsful white breadcrumbs

Roll the pastry and line a shallow sandwich tin or 9 in. plate. Flour a tablespoon and measure the syrup and breadcrumbs into a basin. Mix thoroughly and pour into the pastry case, spreading it evenly. Cover with a few twisted strips of pastry.

Bake at 400°F. for 40 to 45 mins. Third runner from top of oven.

Serves six.

BAKEWELL TART

4 ozs. short pastry
2 tablespoonsful red currant or raspberry jam
1 oz. margarine
2 ozs. sugar

1 oz. breadcrumbs
2 ozs. ground almonds
1 egg
juice of half a lemon

Line a flan case with the pastry and (very carefully so that you do not tear the pastry) spread the bottom with the jam.

Pork pie made with hot-water pastry

Fruit flan, treacle tart and tartlets

Cream the fat and sugar and add the other ingredients, beating thoroughly. Spread the mixture over the jam. Decorate with narrow strips of pastry, garnish with a few blanched almonds if liked.

Bake at 400°F. for 40 to 45 mins. Second runner from top of oven.

Serves four or five.

MAIDS OF HONOUR *(between pages* 104 *and* 105)

Using the above recipe, make the ingredients into individual tartlets.

LEMON MERINGUE PIE *(facing page* 209)

6 ozs. short pastry

| *Filling:* | **level teaspoonful cornflour** | **½ pint milk** |
| **2 eggs** | **3½ oz. castor sugar** | **juice of 2 lemons** |

Roll the pastry about ¼ in. thick and line an 8 in. plate, saving enough from the cuttings to make a decorative edge.

Separate the eggs, keeping the whites in a cool place.

Blend cornflour with a little of the milk. Heat the remainder of the milk with 1½ ozs. of the sugar. Add to the blended cornflour. When smooth, reheat, stirring all the time until thick. Cool slightly.

Mix in the lemon juice and the yolks of the eggs, beating thoroughly. Pour into the pastry case.

Bake at 425°F. for 30 mins. bottom runner.

Whip the egg whites until very stiff and add the remaining 2 ozs. of sugar. When the pie is cooked pile the meringue on top. Return to the oven for 5 to 10 mins. to set the meringue.

Serves five or six.

Should you wish to cook this pie with a complete meal, place it closely above the meat in the centre of the oven and allow 15 mins. longer cooking time at the temperatures indicated above or 30 mins. longer at 400°F.

PLATE PIE

12 ozs. short pastry   **sugar if required**
sufficient fresh, bottled or tinned fruit to fill

Roll out the pastry about ¼ in. thick and use half to line a 9 in. plate. Be very careful not to stretch or break the pastry. Fill with fruit, adding sugar if necessary and a sprinkling of juice or water. Cover with pastry, moistening the edges with water so that they stick together. Press the edges together between your fingers and thumb or with the back of the blade of a knife to make a decorative finish. Cut three incisions about 1½ ins. long across the centre of the pastry lid. Bake at 425°F. for 60 mins., bottom runner.

Serves six.

FRUIT PIE

6 ozs. short pastry
sufficient fruit (fresh or bottled) to fill a 1-pint or 1½-pint pie dish

Wash and prepare the fruit and put it in the pie dish. Moisten the rim of the dish.

Roll the pastry about ¼ in. thick and cut a narrow strip to fit round the rim of the dish. Moisten this edge of pastry. Fit the remaining pastry over the top, cutting away any surplus. Press the pastry together and make a decorative edge.

Bake at 425°F. for 45 mins. towards top of oven.

(It may be necessary to vary the timing in order to cook various types of fruit.)

Serves five or six.

CUTAWAY PIE *(facing page* 144*)*

Instead of completely covering the fruit it makes a pretty effect if the pastry is cut in rings or fancy shapes.

It is not advisable to use soft fruit for this as the pastry shapes may collapse into the fruit and become sodden.

If the pie is to be served cold the shapes can be decorated with whipped cream.

MINCEMEAT PIE

12 oz. short pastry   1 lb. mincemeat

Roll out pastry and line a plate as for plate pie. Fill with mincemeat. You may like to sprinkle the mincemeat with a little lemon juice which improves the flavour. Cover with pastry.

Bake at 425°F. for 60 mins., bottom runner.

Serves six.

MINCE TARTS

8 oz. short or flaky pastry   4 oz. mincemeat

Roll out pastry and cut twelve rounds 3 in. in diameter and twelve 2½ in.

Lay the larger rounds in patty tins, pressing them slightly. Fill the centre with a teaspoonful of mincemeat and moisten the edge with a little cold water. Cover with the smaller rounds, pressing the edges together to make a fluted edge.

Bake at 400°F. for 30 mins., top of oven.

Sift a little castor sugar over the tops and serve hot or cold. Puff or rough pastry can also be used for mince tarts.

Makes twelve pies.

APPLE DUMPLINGS

1 medium sized cooking apple   1 teaspoonful sugar or golden
2 oz. short pastry   syrup

Peel and core the apple. Roll the pastry very thinly and cut into a square. Stand the apple in the centre, filling it with the sugar.

Lift the corners of the pastry, seal the edges with water and mould round the apple. Stand on a greased tin, brush it with water and sprinkle with a little sugar.

Bake at 400°F. for 35 to 45 mins., centre of oven.

Serves one.

CORNISH PASTY

| 1 small potato | 2 oz. cooked meat | pepper and salt |
| 1 small onion | 3 oz. short pastry | |

Sauté the potato and onion in a little fat and mix with the meat, which should be cut into small neat cubes and free from fat or bone. Leave till cold.

Roll the pastry into a round about 8 in. in diameter, and lay the meat, vegetables and seasoning in the centre. Moisten the edges of the pastry with water and lift two opposite sides so that they meet across the top of the filling. Pinch the edges together, making a fluted top. Brush with egg or milk.

Bake at 400°F. for 45 mins., towards top of oven.
Serves one.

Rough Puff or Flaky Pastry Recipes

MEAT PIE

It is easiest to get good results if the meat has been stewed very gently with the flavourings you select and allowed to get quite cold. Any fat will then come to the top and can be removed; if clarified, it is suitable for making the pastry, as indeed are also fats taken from the top of soups made from bones. Nevertheless, uncooked meat, if lean, can be used.

The pie may want longer baking to ensure that the meat is cooked, in which case put the pie in the centre of the oven or reduce the temperature by 25°.

Vegetables can be stewed with the meat to add flavour and to augment it. The most suitable are mushrooms, tomatoes, carrots and peas as these also give colour to the dish.

Place a pie-funnel in the centre of a pie dish and cover the moistened rim with a strip of rough puff or flaky pastry. You will require 12 oz. pastry for a 1½ pint pie dish. Fill the centre with the meat, vegetables and enough stock to keep moist during cooking. Roll the pastry to ¼ in. thickness. Moisten the rim of pastry already on the pie dish, cover with pastry. Cut a small hole in the centre at the funnel and decorate with pastry leaves. Brush with egg.

Serve either hot or cold with salad.

Bake at 400°F. for 45 mins., towards top of oven.
Serves six.

SAUSAGE ROLLS

| ½ lb. pork sausages | 12 oz. rough puff pastry |

Skin the sausages, flour your hands and roll each sausage between the palms until they have been reduced to the required thickness. This will depend on what you are serving the sausage rolls for. If you want them very small and dainty roll the sausage till it is about ½ in. in diameter and make the finished sausage rolls about 1½ in. long.

Roll the pastry in a strip and about ¼ in. thick. Trim one long side. Lay the sausage on the pastry about $1\frac{1}{2}$ times its own width from the edge. Moisten the edge lightly and fold it over the sausage pressing it on the pastry the other side. Cut away from the main piece of pastry and then slice the roll into short lengths.

Make three incisions in the pastry across the top of each roll and brush lightly with egg. Put them on an ungreased baking sheet.

Continue till all the pastry is used.

Bake at 400°F. for 35 to 45 mins., towards top of oven.

Makes twenty-four rolls.

POLISH TARTLETS (*made from puff pastry cuttings*).

Roll the pastry into thin 2 in. squares, moisten each corner, and fold them over to meet in the centre. Bake at 400°F. on an ungreased baking tray for about 15 mins.

When cooked and cold, put a little raspberry jam on the centre and sprinkle lightly with desiccated coconut.

SARDINE ROLLS

$\frac{1}{4}$ lb. rough puff pastry   1 tin sardines

Roll the pastry thinly and cut it into strips $\frac{1}{4}$ in. wide. Roll each strip around a sardine diagonally.

Bake 15 mins. at 425°F., second runner from top.

Makes approximately five rolls.

VOL AU VENT CASES

$\frac{1}{2}$ lb. puff pastry

Roll the pastry $\frac{1}{2}$ to $\frac{3}{4}$ inch thick and cut it into rounds with a $2\frac{1}{2}$-inch cutter. Then with a 1-inch cutter press into the centre of each round so that the pastry is cut about half through.

Place the rounds on an ungreased baking tray.

Bake at 425°F. for 30 to 40 mins., towards top of oven.

While still warm, lift off the centre which should break away quite easily and scoop out a little of the centre of the case.

Fill with chopped cooked chicken or veal heated in a white savoury sauce, replace the cap of pastry and reheat very gently.

Makes 2 doz. vol au vent cases.

JAM PUFF

$\frac{1}{2}$ lb. puff pastry   1 tablespoonful raspberry or other jam

Roll the pastry $\frac{1}{2}$ an inch thick and cut it into two rectangles of equal size. Spread the jam in the centre of one rectangle, working a thin smear towards, but not right up to, the edge. Slash three or four incisions across the centre of the second rectangle and lay it on top.

Cook on a baking tray.

Bake at 450°F. for 20 to 25 mins., towards top of oven.

Serves six.

Choux Pastry Recipes

ECLAIRS

Put ¼ lb. of choux pastry (see page 95) into a forcing bag with a plain pipe. Force in 3-inch lengths on to a greased baking tray. Bake at 400°F. for 30 mins., towards the top of the oven.

When cooked and cold, cut a short incision along one side and scoop out the interior which may be soft.

Fill the cavity with whipped cream (this can be most easily done through a forcing tube) and coat the top of each éclair with chocolate icing (see page 114).

Makes about twelve, according to size.

Suet Pastry Recipes

FRUIT PUDDING

1 lb. blackcurrants or other suitable fruit   **sugar to taste**
12 ozs. suet pastry (see page 94)

Clean the blackcurrants from the stalks and wash.

Roll the pastry ⅜-inch thick on a very well floured board. Cut off one-third for the lid.

Line a 1½-pint pudding basin with the remainder, greasing the basin thoroughly before you start.

Fill with the blackcurrants and about 1½ ozs. sugar according to taste. Add about ¼ gill of water. Moisten the edges of the pastry and cover with the lid.

Cover with greased greaseproof paper and then tie down with a pudding cloth. Steam for 1½ hours. Or the pudding can be 'steamed' in the oven (see recipe for plum duff, page 85, for method of preparation). Allow a minimum of 1½ hours cooking at 400°F.

Times and temperature can be varied slightly to suit the cooking of the remainder of the meal. Serve hot. Any other fruit can be substituted for the blackcurrants.

Serves six.

STEAK AND KIDNEY PUDDING *(facing page 193)*

Make in the same way as fruit pudding filling the lined basin with 1½ lb. stewing steak mixed with ¼ lb. kidney.

Steam for 4 hours.

Serves six to eight.

ROLY POLY PUDDING

12 ozs. suet pastry   **raspberry jam**

Roll the pastry into an oblong. Spread the centre with jam, leaving ½ in. bare around the edges. Damp this and roll the pudding up folding in the ends. Roll the pudding in greased paper and then in a well-floured cloth. Tie the ends tightly and fasten the edges. Immerse the pudding in boiling water.

Boil for 1½ hours.
Serves six.

Hot Water Pastry Recipes

PORK PIE (*facing page* 96)

½ lb. hot water pastry (page 94)
1 lb. lean pork
½ teaspoonful salt
pinch pepper

hard-boiled egg
milk
a little white stock

Shape the pastry into a case, saving one-third for the lid. Put the pork and seasoning in the case, and arrange a hard-boiled egg in the centre if liked. Cover with the pastry, making a hole in the centre, and decorating with leaves of pastry. Brush with milk.

Pour the stock into the pie through the hole in the top when cooked.

Bake at 400°F. for 1½ hours, centre of oven.

Serves four or five.

VEAL AND HAM PIE (*facing page* 81)

½ lb. hot water pastry
¾ lb. fillet of veal cut in pieces
¼ lb. chopped ham
1 hard-boiled egg
1 teaspoonful salt

pepper
grated rind of ½ lemon
chopped parsley
about ½ pint stock

Make in the same way as pork pie. Bake at 400°F. for 1½ hours, centre of oven.

Serves four or five.

Cakes and Biscuits

CAKES are very easy to make. It is simply a question of knowing a few basic recipes. Once you have these at your finger ends there is no limit to the varied cakes that you can make.

Definition of Terms

The terms in cake-making are simple and self-explanatory. Nevertheless, it will perhaps be useful to go over one or two of them.

CREAMING. Working fat with a wooden spoon or beating until it is soft and the colour and texture of thick, whipped cream.

FOLDING. Cutting a mixture with a metal spoon or palette knife in such a manner that it envelops a second mixture as it turns over.

PREPARING CAKE TINS. This can be done by simple greasing, by brushing with clarified melted fat. Sponges and other soft mixtures are less likely to stick to the tin if it is dusted with dry flour after greasing, and tapped gently to remove any excess.

Provided the tins are seasoned and have been well greased, there is no necessity to line them with greaseproof paper when cooking by electricity.

SHAPING A LARGE CAKE. If you want the top of the cake to be smooth and rounded, put the mixture in the tin and make a well in the centre. If you want it to rise and crack slightly across the top, bring the mixture to a slight point with a palette knife. The shaping is also governed by the temperature of the oven and a cake which might be expected to be iced is given in the recipes at a temperature that will not cause it to rise in a point or crack.

REASONS FOR FAILURE

Cakes will fail for a number of reasons, the most common fault being carelessly weighed ingredients. Don't guess; weigh or measure the ingredients as carefully as you can.

Supposing that you have done this and the cake is still not a success it will probably be for one of the following reasons: ' Heavy,' 'sad' and too moist cakes are caused by oiling the fat, or by insufficient creaming of the fat and sugar to incorporate air, or by adding the eggs too quickly and curdling the mixture. Some cakes are made by rubbing the fat into the flour (see below). Don't be heavy handed with this operation so that the fat becomes oily, and unless the recipe specially directs it, never melt the fat to an oil to make it easy for creaming. Whether you are rubbing in or creaming, your object is to get air into the mixture to make it light. If the mixture curdles the air is lost. You can improve matters by adding a little flour, but it is better to guard against curdling by adding the eggs very gradually.

If a cake falls in the centre it is either because it was slightly under-cooked or for any of the reasons given above. It can also be due to too hot an oven or too liberal a supply of baking powder or other raising agent.

Hard exterior, ugly cracks across the top and the cake rising in unsightly peaks are all caused by an over-hot oven.

If fruit falls to the bottom it may be because the mixture was too wet. Adding the fruit before the flour so that it gets heavy with a coating of fat will also cause it to sink. Always add the fruit *after* the flour and ensure that the fruit is perfectly dry. When cooked, cakes shrink very slightly from the side of the tin. Experienced cooks 'listen' to a cake which makes a singing noise when done; and they can tell by the feel of the top whether it is cooked through. Beginners are advised to thrust a hatpin or knitting needle into the cake; it should draw out perfectly clean with no trace of grease. Don't use a knife for this purpose as it leaves an unsightly gash in the cake.

You will want to cook cakes either by the orthodox method, putting them in a hot oven and removing them when they are cooked or you will want to use the timer. As cakes are eaten cold, it is more likely that you will, when using the timer, put them in a hot oven, leaving it to switch off at the appropriate time for the cakes to cool in the oven. Cakes come to no harm if they cool in the oven and can therefore be cooked overnight in readiness for the following day.

TYPES OF CAKE

These have been divided into three main methods while the less common types are classified under miscellaneous.

Rubbed In Method

1. Sift the flour with baking powder and salt into a basin.
2. Add the fat and cut with a knife.
3. Sift the flour through the finger tips rubbing the fat gently.
4. When the texture resembles fine breadcrumbs and there are no lumps, add the remaining dry ingredients.
5. Add the well-beaten eggs. Mix thoroughly.

FAMILY CAKE

8 ozs. plain flour	6 ozs. sugar
1 flat teaspoonful baking powder	¼ lb. mixed dried fruit
a good pinch of salt	3 eggs
6 ozs. margarine	a little water
½ teaspoonful allspice	

Follow the rubbed in method, mix in the fruit and then the well-beaten egg with sufficient water to make the mixture soft enough to drop from a spoon when shaken.

Bake in a well-greased 8-inch cake tin at 350°F. for 1½ hours. With top of the cake tin in the centre of the oven.

104

Doughnuts, Chelsea buns, Danish pastries and glazed buns

BISCUITS: *Shortbread, macaroons, flapjacks, and tea biscuits made in an assortment of shapes with varied flavours*

CAKES: *gingerbread, mixed fruit cake, walnut cake, butterfly cakes, maids of honour, rock buns, queen cakes coconut cakes and madeleines*

Sponge fruit cake and Genoese fancies

SEED CAKE

Omit the fruit and mix in 2 teaspoonsful of caraway seeds.

WALNUT CAKE

Omit the fruit and mix in 2 ozs. shelled and chopped walnuts.

ROCK BUNS *(between pages* 104-105)

8 ozs. flour	3 ozs. sugar
½ teaspoonful salt	1 egg
2 flat teaspoonsful baking powder	4 ozs. mixed dried fruit
3 ozs. fat	a little milk or water

Follow the rubbed in method. Add the fruit, the egg and sufficient milk or water to make a stiff mixture. Pile in rocky heaps on a greased baking tray. Cook at 450°F. for 10 to 15 mins., towards the top of the oven.
Makes twenty-four buns.

SHORTBREAD

7 ozs. plain flour	6 ozs. margarine	pinch of salt
4 ozs. sugar	few drops of almond essence	

Sift the flour and salt, rub in the fat and then add the other ingredients. Knead the mixture with the hands until it is a stiff dough and binds well together. Work into a flat cake about ½ in. thick and place on a greased baking tin. Pinch the edge to make a pattern.

Prick the shortbread with a fork and mark in triangles by cutting lines with a knife.

Cook at 350°F. for about 30 mins. and leave in the cooling oven until cold, or for 35 to 40 mins., removing from the oven and allowing it to cool in the tin.

Creaming Method

1. Cream the fat and sugar till fluffy and pale.
2. Add the whisked eggs very slowly, beating all the time. If the mixture shows a tendency to curdle, add a little flour.
3. Fold in the sifted flour, salt and raising agent.
4. Mix in the fruit and flavouring.

MADEIRA CAKE

5 ozs. margarine (reduce to 4 ozs. if the cake is to be plainer)	2 flat teaspoonsful baking powder pinch of salt
5 ozs. sugar	juice of 1 lemon
3 eggs (reduce to 2 eggs if necessary)	slice of citron peel
8 ozs. plain flour	

Grease a 6½- or 7-inch cake tin. Follow the creaming method, folding in the lemon juice at the last.

The mixture should be a soft, dropping consistency—add a little water if necessary.

Put into the cake tin and decorate with the slice of citron peel.

Cook at 350°F. for 1½ to 1¾ hours, with the top of the cake tin in the centre of the oven.

VARIATIONS ON THE ABOVE BASIC RECIPE

MIXED FRUIT CAKE

Omit the lemon juice. Add 4 ozs. sultanas, and 4 ozs. currants. Cover the top with blanched almonds.

WALNUT CAKE

Omit the lemon juice. Add 3 ozs. shelled and chopped walnuts, and 2 drops almond essence.

SEED CAKE

Omit the lemon juice. Add 2 teaspoonsful of carraway seeds.

CHERRY CAKE

Add 4 ozs. glacé cherries.

The same recipe is the base for a number of small cakes. The mixture should be made slightly stiffer.

Cook small cakes at 425°F. for 15 to 18 mins., towards the top and bottom of the oven.

QUEEN CAKES (*between pages* 104-105)

6 ozs. margarine	pinch of salt
6 ozs. sugar	2 ozs. currants
2 or 3 eggs	a few drops of vanilla essence
8 ozs. plain flour	water to mix if required
2 flat teaspoonsful baking powder	

Follow creaming method. Mix thoroughly and add enough water to make fairly soft.

Turn into paper cases or well greased patty tins.

Bake at 425°F. for 15 to 18 mins., towards the top and bottom of the oven. *Makes twenty-four cakes.*

VARIATIONS ON THE ABOVE RECIPE

MADELEINES (*between pages* 104-105)

Cook the Queen cake mixture in small dariole moulds and when cool coat them with sieved jam. Roll in desiccated coconut and top with a half cherry.

BUTTERFLY CAKES (*between pages* 104-105)

Cook the Queen cake mixture in paper cases and when cold slice off the top. Pipe butter cream over cut and replace top in two halves to form the wings.

106

CHOCOLATE SANDWICH

4 ozs. fat	2 flat teaspoonsful baking powder
4 ozs. sugar	½ flat teaspoonful bicarbonate of
2 eggs	soda
4 ozs. plain flour	1 oz. cocoa
pinch of salt	about ¼ gill water

Grease two 7-inch cake tins and lay a round of greased paper in the bottom of each.

Follow creaming method adding cocoa with the flour.

Divide the mixture and put half into each tin.

When cooked and cold, sandwich the two cakes together with raspberry jam and coat with chocolate icing.

Bake at 350°F. for 20 to 30 mins., third runner from top of oven and bottom runner.

MOCHA SQUARE *A variation on the above recipe*

Increase the recipe by a half (i.e. 6 ozs. of flour, etc.).

Grease three 6-inch square cake tins and pour one-third of the mixture into each tin.

Cook at same time and temperature. When cold, sandwich the three together with a butter icing (page 115) flavoured with coffee. Ice the top of the cake with chocolate water icing (page 114) and decorate with butter icing.

VICTORIA SANDWICH

4 ozs. fat	pinch of salt
4 ozs. sugar	1 flat teaspoonful baking powder
2 eggs	about ¼ gill water
4 ozs. plain flour	juice of lemon if liked

Follow the creaming method, adding the lemon juice at end.

Divide mixture and put into two 7-inch sandwich tins, well greased.

Any flavouring can be substituted for the lemon, or, if being iced, the sponge is good without flavouring.

Bake at 350°F. for 25 to 30 mins., third runner from top of oven and bottom runner.

VARIATIONS OF THE ABOVE RECIPE

SPONGE FRUIT *(facing page* 105*)*

Allow half the quantities, mix creaming method and pour into a well-greased border mould. Allow same cooking times in centre oven.

Turn out of the tin and when quite cold fill with whipped cream and fresh soft fruit.

ICED FANCY CAKES *(facing page* 105*)*

Grease a rectangular tin about 9 by 6 inches by 1½ inches deep.

Allow full quantity of mixture, mixed creaming method.

Allow same cooking time and temperatures.

When quite cold, cut into fancy shapes, coat with coloured water icing and decorate with crystallised fruit, flaked chocolate, mimosa balls or cachous, etc.

CHRISTMAS CAKE

6 ozs. butter or margarine	6 ozs. raisins
6 ozs. sugar	6 ozs. currants
3 eggs	1 oz. chopped blanched almonds
6 ozs. plain flour	3 ozs. ground almonds
pinch of salt	2 ozs. mixed peel, chopped fine
pinch of bicarbonate soda	¼ gill sherry
6 ozs. sultanas	pinch of spice

Grease a 9-inch cake tin. Follow the creaming method, fold in the flour and then the other ingredients. Mix in the fruit and sherry very thoroughly and put into the cake tin. If the cake is not to be iced, cover the top with blanched almonds.

Cook at 275°F. for 3 hours, bottom runner.

WEDDING CAKE (*facing page* 112)

1¼ lb. butter	1¼ lb. raisins
1¼ lb. sugar	1¼ lb. sultanas
10 eggs	1¼ lb. currants
1 tablespoonful black treacle	10 ozs. chopped glacé cherries
1¼ lb. plain flour	10 ozs. ground almonds
1 teaspoonful powdered mixed spice	wine glass of sherry
½ teaspoonful bicarbonate of soda	

Mix by the creaming method, adding the fruit and sherry last. Turn into a well-greased, well-seasoned cake tin and place on bottom runner in oven.

These quantities will make a cake 12 inches square and 3 inches deep.

Use half the quantities for a cake 9 inches square.

Use quarter the quantities for a cake 6 inches square.

Bake the 12-inch cake at 275°F. for 4½ hours.

Bake the 9-inch cake at 275°F. for 3½ hours.

Bake the 6-inch cake at 275°F. for 2½ hours.

If you want to make round cakes, you can use the same quantities as for the square, but the cakes will be about 1 inch deeper. For each cake therefore add approximately 1 hour to the cooking time.

SIMNEL CAKE

¾ oz. yeast	5 ozs. sultanas
1¼ gills milk	5 ozs. currants
10 ozs. flour (warmed)	½ teaspoonful mixed spice
5 ozs. butter or margarine	4 egg yolks
5 ozs. sugar	1 lb. almond paste
5 ozs. candied peel	

Cream the yeast and add the warmed milk. Pour this into 3 ozs. of the warmed flour and mix into a sponge. Put this to rise in a warm place for 30 mins. Cream the butter with the sugar, add the rest of the flour and the yeast mixture with all the other ingredients except the almond paste. Beat well and put to rise in a warm place for 1 to 2 hours. Grease an 8-inch cake tin and put half the mixture in the tin. Put one-third of the almond paste, rolled thin and cut into a circle, on to the dough and place the other half of the mixture on top. Put to prove for 20 mins.

Bake at 350°F. for 1 to 1½ hours, with the top of the cake tin in the centre of the oven. When cold cover the cake with the rest of the almond paste and decorate the edges. Place in a warm oven for a few minutes to give it a good golden colour.

Whisking Method

True sponge cakes do not contain any fat and depend for their lightness on the amount of air that is beaten into the eggs.

1. Separate the eggs, whisk the whites with a pinch of salt until stiff and fold in the beaten yolks.
2. Fold in the sugar, whisk again.
3. Fold in the sifted flour which should be dry and warm.

SWISS ROLL

3 eggs   3 ozs. dry and sifted plain flour
3 ozs. castor sugar   pinch of salt

Mix the ingredients by the method given above. Turn into a greased and lined Swiss roll tin.

Bake 450°F. for 6 to 8 mins. towards the top of the oven.

Dredge some fine castor sugar on to a piece of paper and turn the Swiss roll on to it. Spread with warm jam and roll up while still hot.

SPONGE SANDWICH

3 ozs. sugar   3 eggs   3 ozs. plain flour   pinch of salt

Whisk by the method given above. Pour into two well-greased 7-inch sandwich tins.

Bake at 375°F. for 25 mins., towards the bottom of the oven.

ANGEL CAKE

Grease a Turk's head mould.

4 egg whites   1 flat teaspoonful cream of tartar
5 ozs. castor sugar   4 drops almond essence
6 ozs. plain flour   4 drops vanilla essence
pinch of salt

Beat the egg whites with the cream of tartar until stiff and then add the sugar, continuing to beat. Fold in the sifted flour, salt and essences.

Turn into the mould.

Bake at 350°F. for 25 to 30 mins., centre of oven.

Turn out and when cold, ice both inside and out with a plain water icing, scattering chopped walnuts over the top before the icing sets.

MERINGUES

2 whites of egg   4 ozs. castor sugar

Cover a baking sheet with a piece of greaseproof paper and grease lightly with melted butter.

Whisk the whites of egg until very stiff. Add a flat teaspoonful of the sugar and whisk again until it is thick. Fold in the remainder of the sugar.

Fit a meringue pipe into a forcing bag, fill with the mixture and force on to the tin in small heaps. Or take a flat dessertspoonful of the mixture and drop it on to the tray in rounded heaps.

Bake at 250°F. till dry but not browned.

Remove from paper when cool and sandwich two together with whipped cream.

COCONUT MACAROONS

rice paper
2 whites of eggs

4 ozs. castor sugar
4 ozs. coconut

Spread rice paper on a baking tray.

Put some hot, not boiling, water in a saucepan and fit a pudding basin over it. Whisk the whites of egg and sugar in the basin until stiff enough to stand in rough peaks.

Remove from heat and fold in the coconut. Drop the mixture in small quantities on to the rice paper.

Bake at 250°F. for about 1 hour towards top and bottom of oven.

COCONUT CAKES (*between pages* 104-105)

1 egg
3 ozs. sugar

6 ozs. coconut
½ oz. flour

Whisk the eggs and sugar until well mixed. Add the coconut and flour and knead. Form into little pyramids and stand on rice paper on a baking tray.

Bake at 350°F. for 15 mins., towards top and bottom of oven, or place in a cold oven, dial 350°F., turn out when oven reaches this temperature and leave to brown (about 4 to 6 mins.).

GENOESE PASTE

3 eggs   4 ozs. sugar   3 ozs. flour   3 ozs. butter

Beat the eggs and add the sugar. Whisk over hot water until thick and creamy. Remove from the heat and whisk until cold. Fold in the flour and melted butter. Pour into a greased, straight sided tin 12 inches by 8 inches by 1 inch high.

Bake at 350°F. for 30 mins. towards bottom of oven.

Turn out and cut up into squares when cold and ice.

Miscellaneous

GINGERBREAD (*between pages* 104-105)

8 ozs. plain flour
2 flat teaspoonsful ground ginger
1 flat teaspoonful bicarbonate of soda
2 ozs. candied peel
1 oz. blanched almonds if liked

3 ozs. margarine
2 ozs. sugar
6 ozs. treacle
¼ pint milk
1 egg

Put the sifted flour, ginger and soda into a basin and add the finely chopped peel and almonds.

Melt the fat, sugar and treacle in a saucepan and add with the milk and well-beaten egg to the flour. Mix very thoroughly.

Pour the mixture into a well-greased 7-inch cake tin or in a 2-lb loaf tin. Bake at 350°F. for 1¼ hours, towards bottom of oven.

MACAROONS (*between pages* 104-105)

2 ozs. ground almonds
3 ozs. castor sugar

1 white of egg
1 flat teaspoonful plain flour

Mix all dry ingredients. Beat the egg enough to cut the white and knead into the mixture.

Roll into small balls and stand them on rice paper on a baking tray, leaving sufficient space between them to spread.

Bake at 300°F. till brown and crisp—about 25 mins.

Biscuits

Biscuits should be light and crumbling when cooked, and of an even colour. Accuracy in following the recipes is important to get good results. Flour should be dry and sifted. The mixture should be rolled carefully so that the biscuits are of uniform thickness, and this is difficult as biscuit mixtures are usually very short and apt to crumble under the rolling pin and the cutter. Dredge a little flour on to the board and rolling pin and dust the mixture with a dry pastry brush dipped in flour. As for the cutters, any shape will do and you *can* use a wine glass or small tumbler or even the lid of a tin. The important thing is to press firmly so that it makes a neat and clean cut—biscuits look a mess if they have a ragged edge. Remove them from the board with a palette knife and place them well apart, so that they will not touch even if they should spread in cooking, on a tin lightly dusted with flour. When cooked but still hot, many biscuits are still apt to crumble; lift them off the tin very carefully and put them on a wire rack to cool. As a rule they are easy enough to handle when cold.

TEA BISCUITS (*between pages* 104-105)

2 ozs. margarine
1 oz. sugar
a few drops of vanilla essence

4 ozs. plain flour
pinch of salt

Cream the margarine and sugar together in a basin. Add the vanilla essence (or any other flavouring you fancy) and beat it some more. Stir in the sifted flour and salt, a tablespoonful at a time. You will find that it will mix together and make a stiff dough without the addition of any liquid.

Turn it on to a lightly floured board and knead gently. Roll out very thinly and cut into shapes and place on floured baking tins.

Bake at 350°F. for 12 to 15 mins., towards top and bottom of oven.

Makes two trays of biscuits, approximately twenty-four to thirty biscuits.

1. Any essence can be substituted for the vanilla.
2. Grate the rind of an orange or lemon into the mixture after the flour is added.
3. Add ¼ ounce of powdered or grated chocolate, ¼ oz. cocoa, or 1 flat teaspoonful of Nescafé sifted with the flour.
4. Add 1½ ozs. of any finely chopped dried fruit, with the flour.
5. Add 1 oz. finely chopped nuts with the flour.
6. Add ¼ oz. mixed spice, cinnamon or carraway seeds to the flour.

MILK BISCUITS

4 ozs. plain flour	½ gill milk
½ teaspoonful baking powder	1 oz. fat
pinch of salt	

Sift flour, baking powder and salt into a mixing basin; warm the milk and fat together until the fat melts. Add to the dry ingredients and mix. The result will be a stiff dough. Turn on to a very lightly floured pastry board. Knead gently to make into a smooth ball. Roll very thin and cut into shapes.

Lift with a palette knife and place on greased and floured baking tins.

Bake at 450°F. for about 10 mins., second runner from top and bottom of oven.

Makes twenty biscuits.

IMPERIAL BISCUITS

2 ozs. margarine	½ teaspoonful cinnamon
2 ozs. sugar	½ teaspoonful baking powder
4 ozs. flour	¼ egg
pinch of salt	

Cream the fat and the sugar and mix in the dry ingredients and egg. Place in a cold place for 15 mins. Roll out thinly and cut into 2-inch rounds.

Bake at 350°F. for 10 to 15 mins., towards the top and bottom of the oven.

When cool sandwich two together with jam and dust the tops with icing sugar.

Makes thirty biscuits.

OAT CAKES

5 ozs. fine Scotch oatmeal	2 ozs. plain flour
½ teaspoonful salt, or double this quantity if you like to taste the salt	1 oz. lard
	½ gill boiling water

Mix the oatmeal, salt and flour; add the fat melted in the boiling water. Well dust a pastry board with oatmeal and roll mixture very thinly.

Cut into triangles or rounds. Dust lightly with oatmeal and place on a greased and floured baking sheet.

Bake at 400°F. for 10 to 15 mins., towards top and bottom of oven.

Oat cakes are traditionally cooked over a fire on a heated girdle till they curl; then they are toasted before the kitchen fire and served fresh with butter, and honey or cheese.

A square wedding cake is easy to cut

Home-baked bread and rolls

CORNFLAKE BISCUITS

2½ ozs. lard
1½ ozs. margarine
3 ozs. castor sugar
half an egg

½ teaspoonful vanilla
5 ozs. self-raising flour
cornflakes
glacé cherries

Cream the fat and sugar. Beat in the egg and the essence and fold in the flour. Make this mixture into one-inch balls by rolling in the palm of the hand. Crush the cornflakes, roll each ball in them. Flatten on a baking sheet, and put half a cherry on the top.

Cook at 350°F. for 15 to 20 mins.

Makes about thirty biscuits.

BRANDY SNAPS

2 ozs. margarine
2 ozs. plain flour
2 flat teaspoonsful of ground ginger
5 ozs. castor sugar

2 ozs. golden syrup
1 flat teaspoonful powdered cinnamon

Rub the fat into the flour with the tips of the fingers and then add the other ingredients, stirring all together until you have a paste. Roll this in long sausages about ½ inch diameter, on a floured pastry board. Cut into 1 inch lengths and place them on a very well greased baking tray.

Bake at 325°F. for 10 to 15 mins., towards top and bottom of oven.

Remove from the oven and leave on the baking tray for 1 minute. Pick up each biscuit and curl round the handle of a wooden spoon. Place on a cooling tray—store in an airtight tin. They are best stuffed each end with whipped cream and eaten the same day they are baked.

FLAPJACKS *(between pages 104-105)*

3 ozs. margarine
3 tablespoonsful golden syrup

8 ozs. rolled oats
few drops vanilla essence

Melt the margarine and syrup, add to the oats and mix well. This will make a stiff consistency. Add the vanilla essence.

Press into a greased tin measuring about 9 by 6 inches (using the palm of the hand or a palette knife).

Bake at 350°F. for 45 mins., towards top and bottom of oven.

When cooked, cut into fingers and leave to cool in the tin.

VARIATIONS

1. Add any other flavouring—lemon is very good.

2. Add 1 tablespoonful of cocoa or chocolate powder to the rolled oats.

Chocolate flavoured flapjacks are ideal for a children's party. Cut into fingers about 3½ by 1½ inches. They can be made more dainty for a tea delicacy by cutting into fingers 1½ by ¾ inches.

CANAPE BISCUITS *(facing page 177)*

Cut bread into slices about ¼ inch thick and then into fancy shapes with a biscuit cutter.

Fry the pieces of bread in hot fat. Fry them quickly and until they are pale golden; then drain them on greaseproof paper.

These 'biscuits' will keep fresh in an airtight tin for 24 hours and can therefore be prepared in advance of a party.

Make a strong aspic jelly. Put a little on the biscuit and then place the cover (a slice of hard-boiled egg, anchovy, shrimps, etc.) on top. Pour more aspic over it to keep it in position and retain its colour. When set arrange on serving dishes.

TEA TIME SPECIAL

Suppose you have no cakes for tea. Try spreading "Ryvita" biscuits with butter. Arrange them on a baking tray and sprinkle liberally with brown sugar and powdered cinnamon.

Bake at 450°F. for 5 mins., towards top and bottom of oven, and serve hot.

Icings for Cakes

The basis for all icing is sugar, and a specially fine white sugar is available for the purpose. For best results, sieve it before use, and if there are lumps in it, crush with a rolling pin.

Never ice a cake until it is quite cold.

Plain water icings are very simple. They are used for biscuits, some small cakes and for sandwich cakes.

WATER ICING

(sufficient for one Victoria Sandwich)

8 to 9 rounded dessertspoonsful icing sugar   **2 dessertspoonsful warm water**

Stir the sugar into the water and continue stirring till the icing is smooth. Spread over the top of the cake with a palette knife. The above icing will be white. You can tint it with a few drops of colouring and flavour with essence if liked. Or you can make the following variations:

ORANGE ICING

Substitute orange juice for the water, and if liked, add a very little of the finely grated peel.

LEMON ICING

Substitute lemon juice for the water.

CHOCOLATE ICING

Mix 1 brimming teaspoonful cocoa or chocolate powder with the water before adding the sugar.

ROYAL ICING

2 egg whites
1 lb. icing sugar
1 teaspoonful of lemon juice

2 drops of blue colouring
1 teaspoonful of glycerine

114

Break the eggs very carefully and put the whites into a basin. Whisk well. Add the sifted sugar a little at a time, stirring all the while. Work it with the spoon till it is perfectly smooth, and then stir in the lemon juice and, to make very white, one or two drops of blue colouring. Finally beat in the glycerine which prevents the icing from becoming too hard.

Spread the foundation icing on the cake with a palette knife. Use the same recipe to force decorative icing on the top.

Sufficient for one eight-inch cake.

ALMOND ICING

8 ozs. ground almonds	a few drops of lemon juice
10 ozs. icing sugar	1 egg white

Knead all together till the mixture is a paste. Smear the surface of the cake with a very little jam to help the paste stick, and spread the paste over it. If you find it easier you can roll it as you would pastry, on a board lightly dusted with castor sugar. To make the top of the paste absolutely level on the cake in readiness for the royal icing, run a rolling pin lightly across the top.

BUTTER ICING

4 ozs. fresh butter	4 ozs. sugar	flavouring

Cream the butter and sugar till soft and white. Flavour with essence, or a little powdered chocolate or coffee essence.

Use as a sandwich cake filling, or this mixture can be piped through a forcing bag and is suitable for final decoration of a cake coated with a water icing.

SEVEN MINUTE FROSTING

1 egg white	2 tablespoonsful cold water
$\frac{2}{3}$ cupful sugar	$\frac{1}{4}$ teaspoonful cream of tartar
few grains salt	

Combine ingredients in top of double boiler. Stir until sugar dissolves, then place over boiling water. Beat until stiff enough to stand in peaks (7 to 10 mins.). Flavour as desired. Beat until thick enough to spread. Use for a sandwich cake, or to coat an angel cake.

Bread and Scones

BREAD has the reputation of being very difficult to make, though it is really nothing of the kind. It takes time. One cannot really hurry over the job and making large quantities is hard work because of the kneading; that is what has probably given it its reputation; but in point of fact, provided that one follows a few simple rules and instructions one can't go wrong.

Definition of Cooking Terms

Bread-making is a very old art; attached to it are some terms and definitions which are generations old. As you are unlikely to come across them except in bread-making it might be as well to tell you what they mean.

First of all, yeast or leavening. Yeast is a living growth. When you buy it, be sure it is fresh. This you can tell by appearance. It should be pale fawn in colour and rather moist with a heavy fruity smell. Like plants, it does not grow in the cold; keep it in a cool place. Like mould, it contaminates other food; wrap it carefully and try to keep it apart, and thoroughly wash your mixing bowls and your kitchen table after using it. Your object is to make the yeast grow inside some flour so that it makes it increase in bulk. Then, if you kill the yeast by putting the mixture in great heat the flour will set in its larger bulk thus being aerated and light.

So, having procured your fresh yeast you put it in a warm basin or a cup with a teaspoonful of sugar. Now it has warmth and food and will grow. Stir it (this is called ' creaming the yeast ') and it will very quickly change in appearance. It will look like a thick brown cream.

Meanwhile the flour, which should be dry and warm, is sifted into a warm basin. Make a well in the centre, add tepid water to the creamed yeast. Strain it into the well and sprinkle it with a little of the flour. Put it in a warm, but not hot, place to ' sponge '. This means leaving the yeast to grow. You will soon see why the operation gets its name because the top of it will look like a sponge after about 10 to 15 mins.

Knead it with the hand. After about 5 mins. the mixture will change in appearance. It will be dry and firm and leave the bowl clean. Continue to knead for about another 10 mins. Get it into a tidy shape and cut a cross about an inch deep right across the dough. This is called ' letting the devil out ', and helps to prevent a hard skin from forming.

Cover the basin with a damp cloth and ' set the dough to rise '. This means putting it in a warm room temperature until the yeast has grown and made the dough double its original size. See to it that it is in a basin large enough to allow for this growth without touching the damp cloth. The rising should take about an hour.

Take the dough out of the basin and put it on a well-floured board. 'Knock it back'. In other words, knead it again until, if you cut a little slit in the dough, there are no large holes. This takes about 5 mins.

Shape it into loaves and 'set them to prove'; that is to say, leave them in a warm place to rise till they are double in size. Now you want to kill the yeast so that it will not rise any more. Great heat does that at once. Put your loaves in a very hot oven.

REASONS FOR FAILURE

1. Bread should look and smell *good*. It should have a well-rounded surface free from cracks or wrinkles, should be a golden brown in colour and feel firm and slightly 'crunchy' in the crust as you squeeze the loaf gently in your fingers. Insufficient kneading or rising will spoil the appearance.

2. It should feel light. If it feels heavy it is because you either did not 'rise' it for long enough or for too long. It should double in bulk—neither more nor less.

3. If the bread is streaky when cut it is because you did not mix and knead sufficiently.

4. If you knock it with your knuckles it should sound hollow. If it does not, cook it for longer.

5. If the loaf has large holes in it you failed to 'knock it back'.

6. Appearance is improved by a slight crack in the top or at the side of the loaf, but if this is too pronounced you did not put the bread in a sufficiently hot oven.

7. Don't use self-raising flour—it is apt to upset the rising.

8. Salt gives the flavour. About 1 rounded teaspoonful to the pound of flour is right for most palates.

9. Fat. A small quantity of fat in the recipe helps to keep the bread moist and fresh.

10. Instead of water, some people use skim milk or potato water, as they say it improves the flavour.

WHITE BREAD (*facing page* 113)

3½ lb. plain flour	1 oz. yeast
3½ rounded teaspoonsful salt	1 teaspoonful sugar
1 oz. margarine	about 2 pints tepid water

Sieve the flour and salt into a warm basin. Rub in the fat until very fine and stand the basin in a warm place. Cream the yeast with the sugar and add 1 pint of tepid water, mixing thoroughly. Make a well in the centre of the flour and strain in the yeast and water. Sprinkle a little of the flour over the liquid and leave in a warm place to 'sponge'.

Mix the flour into the liquid with your hand adding more tepid water as you need it, until the mixture is a firm dough. Knead thoroughly but with light fingers for 5 to 10 mins. Cut a cross in the dough, cover the basin with a damp cloth and put it in a warm place to rise. If you use the warming drawer for this process, do not leave it switched on for the whole time or it will be too hot. Switch on for 5 mins. and off for 20.

When the dough has doubled in size, which will be in about an hour, knead slightly, shape it into loaves, place in greased and floured tins and leave in a warm place till each loaf has doubled in bulk.

Bake at 475°F. for 5 mins. Three loaves on floor, two in centre of oven. Reduce heat to 425°F. and cook for 50 mins.

Switch off, take the loaves out of the tin, brush the tops with melted fat and stand them on the rod shelves in the oven for a few minutes for a final crisp. *Makes five 1 lb. loaves.*

WHITE BREAD

Quick Method without ' Sponging '

4 lb. plain flour	1 oz. yeast
4 rounded teaspoonsful salt	1 teaspoonful sugar
1 oz. margarine	about 2½ pints tepid water

Sieve warm flour and salt, rub in the fat. Cream the yeast and sugar, add 1 pint of the water. Strain into the flour and mix, adding more water as required. Knead thoroughly.

Set to rise till doubled in size, knead again and shape into loaves.

Set to rise again and then bake as above.

Two loaves in centre, three on floor of oven.

Either of these recipes can be used for small rolls, which will take 15 to 18 mins. to cook at the same temperature.

Makes five 1-lb. loaves.

BROWN BREAD *(facing page 113)*

2 lb. plain white flour	1 oz. yeast
2½ teaspoonsful salt	1 teaspoonful sugar
1¼ lb. wholemeal flour	1½ pints tepid water

Sieve the white flour and salt and add the wholemeal. Cream the yeast and proceed as for white bread. The dough should be slightly more moist than white bread and is a little sticky as you knead it—you will find it easier if you sprinkle flour on your hands.

Bake at 475°F. for 5 mins. Two loaves in centre, two on floor of oven. Reduce heat to 425°F. and cook for 45 mins.

Makes four loaves.

BAKING POWDER BREAD

2 lb. flour	1 flat teaspoonful salt
2 heaped teaspoonsful baking powder	milk and water to mix

Sieve the dry ingredients and mix to a stiff paste with milk and water. Knead lightly and quickly and form into loaves. Place in greased and floured tins. Bake at 425°F. for 45 to 50 mins. in centre of oven.

Baking powder bread can also be cooked on a griddle or the boiling plate.

MILK ROLLS *(facing page 113)*

1 lb. flour	1 teaspoonful salt
2 flat teaspoonsful baking powder	milk to mix

Sieve dry ingredients into a basin, and add sufficient milk to mix to a soft dough. Work very quickly, shaping the dough into small rolls. Place them on a floured baking tray, brush with milk.

Bake at 500°F. for 10 mins. on second runner from top.

Makes eighteen rolls.

SALLY LUNNS

¾ lb. flour
1 oz. margarine
1½ gills milk

½ teaspoonful salt
1 egg

½ oz. yeast
1 teaspoonful sugar

Sieve the warm flour and salt. Melt the fat in a saucepan, add the milk and heat till tepid. Stir in the beaten egg and add to the creamed yeast. Strain the mixture into the flour.

Knead thoroughly, and form the dough into two pieces. Put them into greased sally lunn tins, and set them to rise till they are doubled in bulk. This will take about 45 mins.

Bake at 450°F. for 15 mins. in centre of oven.

Remove the loaves from the tins, brush the tops with egg or milk and return to the oven for a few minutes to glaze.

Makes two loaves.

DOUGHNUTS (*facing page* 104)

½ oz. yeast
1 oz. sugar

½ gill milk
½ lb. flour

2 ozs. margarine
1 egg

Cream the yeast with a little of the sugar and add the tepid milk. Add it to the sifted flour and set to sponge. Break the margarine into small pieces and add to the flour with the sugar and beaten egg. Mix with your hand until it forms a dough, then leave it to rise for about 70 to 80 mins.

Knead the dough lightly, turn it on to a floured board and roll into a flat cake about ½ an inch thick. Cut rounds of the dough with a 1½-inch pastry cutter and put a very small quantity of raspberry jam in the centre of half the rings, covering each with a plain ring. Roll the doughnuts very gently in the palms of your hands to shape them and then prove them for 15 mins.

Fry them in a deep fat till golden brown; do not fry too many at once or the fat will go off the boil. Drain the doughnuts on crumpled kitchen paper and roll them in castor sugar.

Makes twelve.

DANISH PASTRIES (*facing page* 104)

8 ozs. plain flour
salt
½ oz. yeast
1 oz. castor sugar

1 gill milk
2½ ozs. butter or margarine
2 ozs. lard
2 ozs. almond paste for filling

For Glaze: 2 ozs. castor sugar
a few chopped blanched almonds

1 tablespoonful hot milk

Sift flour with salt. Cream yeast with sugar. Warm the milk and ½ oz. of butter until melted and add to the creamed yeast. Pour into flour and mix to a smooth dough. Cover the bowl with a clean damp cloth and place in the

119

warming drawer or a warm place to rise for 1 hour. Turn on to a floured board and knead lightly. Roll out into an oblong strip.

Divide rest of butter and lard into two, and dab small pieces of one half on to two-thirds of the dough. Fold up into three, seal the edges of the dough with the rolling pin, turn once and roll out again into an oblong. Repeat this process with the remaining butter. Place in a cool larder or a refrigerator for 30 mins. Roll the dough into a ¼ in. thick square. Cut out triangular pieces. Put a little almond paste in the centre of each triangle and fold the point over the top of it pressing down firmly. Then twist the other two points round. Place on a greased baking tray. Cover with a cloth and put in a warm place to prove for 15 mins.

Bake at 375°F. for 25 mins.

Remove from the oven and brush over with glaze while the buns are still warm. Decorate with blanched almonds.

Makes eighteen pastries.

CHELSEA BUNS (*facing page* 104)

Ingredients for dough	*Filling*
1 oz. yeast	4 ozs. lard (melted)
4 ozs. sugar	3 ozs. castor sugar
3 gills warm milk	3 ozs. currants
1¾ lb. plain flour	3 ozs. chopped peel
4 ozs. margarine	
1 teaspoonful salt	
2 eggs	

Cream the yeast with a teaspoonful of sugar and add the milk. Pour into 8 ozs. of the flour and stir thoroughly. Set this to rise, covered with a damp cloth, in a warm place for about 1 hour. Rub the fat into the remainder of the flour and mix in the remainder of the sugar and salt. Add this to the sponged mixture and beat in the eggs. Beat with the hand for 5 mins. Cover and leave to rise again for 1 hour. Turn the dough on to a well floured board. Roll out into a square, brush with melted lard, and sprinkle with sugar, currants and peel evenly all over the surface. Roll up and cut into slices across the roll about 1½ ins. thick. Place on a greased baking tray.

Leave to prove for about 10 to 15 mins.

Bake at 475°F. reducing heat immediately to 425°F. for 10 to 15 mins.

Glaze while the buns are still warm with 1 tablespoonful of sugar mixed with 1 tablespoonful of warm milk.

Makes thirty-six.

GLAZED BUNS (*facing page* 104)

1 oz. yeast	½ teaspoonful mixed spice
4 ozs. sugar	4 ozs. sultanas
3 gills lukewarm milk	2 ozs. chopped candied peel
1¾ lb. flour	2 eggs
4 ozs. margarine	

Glaze: 1 flat tablespoonful of castor sugar
      1 tablespoonful of milk

Cream the yeast with a teaspoonful of the sugar and add the milk. Strain the liquid into 8 ozs. of the flour and stir thoroughly. Set this batter to rise, covered with a damp cloth, in a warm place for about an hour.

Rub the fat into the remainder of the flour and mix in all the dry ingredients and fruit. Add this mixture to the sponged batter and beat in the eggs. Beat with the hand for 5 mins. Cover and leave it to rise again for another hour.

Now make the mixture into small round buns and leave to prove for 15 mins.

Bake at 475°F. reducing at once to 425°F. for 10 to 15 mins. on second runner from top and bottom of oven.

When cooked, brush the tops with glaze, returning the buns to the oven (which should now be switched off) for a minute or two to dry.

Makes thirty-six buns.

HOT CROSS BUNS

Follow the above recipe but mark with a cross after proving for 15 mins. and before baking.

FRUITY MILK BREAD

4 ozs. margarine	pinch allspice
1 lb. plain flour	3 ozs. castor sugar
3 ozs. currants	½ oz. yeast
1 oz. sultanas	1 egg
1 oz. candied peel	½ pint warm milk

Rub the fat into the flour, and then mix in all the dry ingredients and fruit. Cream the yeast in a little of the sugar. Beat the egg and add to the milk; add this to the creamed yeast. Strain into a well in the centre of the mixture. Mix and knead. Shape into two one-pound loaf tins.

Bake at 425°F., reducing the temperature to 375°F. immediately you close the oven door. Centre of the oven for approximately 30 mins.

Scones

PLAIN SCONES

1 lb. flour	2 flat teaspoonsful salt
1 flat teaspoonful bicarbonate of soda	2 ozs. margarine
2 flat teaspoonsful cream of tartar	milk to mix

Sift the dry ingredients into a mixing bowl and then rub in the fat with the tips of the fingers. When the mixture is entirely free of lumps, make a well in the centre and add sufficient milk to make a soft dough.

Flour the hands thoroughly and turn the mixture on to a well-floured board. Knead lightly and then press with the palm of the hand into a flat cake about 1¼ in. thick. Cut into rings or triangles and put on a lightly floured baking tray

Bake at 475° for 10 to 15 mins. according to size, on second runner from top and bottom of oven.

Makes twenty to twenty-four scones.

SOUR MILK SCONES

1 lb. flour
1 flat teaspoonful bicarbonate of soda
1 flat teaspoonful cream of tartar

2 flat teaspoonsful of salt
2 ozs. margarine
sour milk to mix

Proceed as for plain scones.

AFTERNOON TEA SCONES

½ lb. flour
3 flat teaspoonsful baking powder
pinch of salt
1 oz. margarine

1 egg
1 oz. sugar
1 oz. sultanas or currants
milk or water to mix

Sift the flour and salt and rub in the margarine. Add the remaining dry ingredients and fruit, mixing thoroughly, and finally the beaten egg with sufficient milk to make a soft dough.

Proceed as for plain scones.

DROP SCONES (*between pages 72 and 73*)

½ lb. flour
1 flat teaspoonful bicarbonate of soda
2 flat teaspoonsful cream of tartar

a pinch of salt
2 ozs. castor sugar
1 egg
between ½ and ¾ pints of milk

Sift the dry ingredients. Mix in the beaten egg and sufficient milk to make a very stiff batter.

Turn a solid boiling plate to full heat, use a griddle on a radiant plate, or, alternatively, heat a frypan. Grease lightly. When hot, reduce heat, and drop the mixture a tablespoonful at a time on to it. Leave cooking till little bubbles appear on the surface of the scones, then turn with a palette knife and cook till brown.

Serve hot or cold with butter.

Makes thirty-six scones.

Breakfasts

MANY dishes that are served for breakfast have been dealt with in other chapters. Methods of cooking haddock and kippers, for example, are in the chapter on Fish, and there are several ideas for breakfast in the section headed Réchauffées. This chapter contains those dishes which do not so naturally come into another place.

• When planning breakfast you should bear in mind two important points. First it is essential to start the day with a good meal; a cup of tea and a piece of toast are not enough. Second, you should have a well-proportioned meal. If you reckon to include some fruit juice, milk and something cooked, you cannot go far wrong.

Many breakfast dishes can be prepared overnight and cooked by the timer, so that it is ready to put on the table when you get up in the morning.

Fruit

Citrus fruits, such as grapefruit or oranges, are good sources of Vitamin C. Dried fruits such as figs or prunes, while they contain the necessary minerals, are lacking in this valuable vitamin, but it can be supplied by serving them with a lacing of fresh lemon juice.

It is simple enough to cut and prepare a fresh grapefruit but in winter some people object to cold fruit. Try cutting it in half and smothering the top with brown sugar after preparing, and putting it under the grill for a couple of minutes.

It can also be baked.

BAKED GRAPEFRUIT

Cut the grapefruit in the usual way and stand it on a baking tin. Smother with brown sugar and bake for 30 mins. at 400°F. or put in a cold oven and set the timer to cook for 45 mins. at 375° or 400°F.

Canned fruit juices are good, and can be served either hot or cold.

Porridge

There are several methods of making it; in fact every household seems to have its own recipe.

SCOTCH OATMEAL PORRIDGE

4 tablespoonsful of medium or coarse oatmeal
1 pint water   salt to taste

Cook in a porringer for 1 to 1½ hours, stirring occasionally. It can be cooked at night and reheated for breakfast.

Or bring to the boil in a saucepan on the boiling plate. Turn off when fast boiling, stir occasionally until simmering, then cover and leave overnight. Bring to the boil for breakfast the following morning.

Serves three or four.

ROLLED OATS PORRIDGE

1 pint water   4 to 5 tablespoonsful rolled oats   salt to taste

Heat the salted water in a saucepan and stir the oats into it. Bring to the boil, stirring all the time, and cook till thick. Serve at once.

This porridge can be cooked in the oven. Put the rolled oats in a fireproof basin, add the boiling water and salt. Stir and cover with aluminium foil. Put in the oven overnight. Set the timer to suit the remainder of the breakfast —the porridge will cook at any temperature between 350° and 400°F. in any time between 30 and 45 mins.

Serves four.

MY FAVOURITE PORRIDGE

½ pint milk   2 teaspoonsful sugar
2 flat tablespoonsful rolled oats   pinch of salt

Boil together, stirring all the time, till it thickens. Serve hot with cream.
Serves two.

MUESLI

This is a dish for the summer.

1 oz. rolled oats   1 apple   juice of a lemon
1 dozen raisins   1 teaspoonful sugar

Wash and stone the raisins and add them to the rolled oats with ½ gill of water or fruit juice. Leave soaking overnight.

Peel and core the apple and grate it into the oats, mix in with the lemon juice and serve with cream. *Serves two.*

Toast

Cut the bread to the thickness you like. Turn the grill to ' FULL ' for 2 to 3 mins. Place the bread on the grid at the highest position in the grill pan and fix in the runners under the grill. Forty to 50 seconds will be sufficient for each side. Trim off crusts before serving.

MELBA TOAST

This must be cooked in the oven. Cut very thin slices of bread and place them on a baking tray. Put in the oven at 450°F. and leave about 6 mins. or till brown.

Melba toast can be stored for a day or two in an airtight tin and it is a good idea to make it after you have been using the oven for other cooking. Put it in the oven and switch off—there will be sufficient heat to toast it.

SPLIT TOAST

This is another method of making Melba toast.

Cut a slice of bread $\frac{1}{4}$ inch thick and toast it on both sides. Take a sharp knife and cut the slice in half and toast the other sides.

Hot Dishes

EGGS AND BACON

Method 1. Trim the rashers of bacon of rind and, to prevent them from curling, snip the lean side in one or two places with a pair of scissors. Place the rashers in a dry frying pan and cook quickly, turning them frequently until they are done. Serve on a hot dish.

Sufficient fat will be left in the pan to fry the eggs. Cook them separately, or at any rate, drop them one at a time into the frypan or you will have difficulty in dishing them up. Crack them into a cup and pour them gently into the hot fat, leaving them to cook for 2 to 3 mins. until they are set. Lift carefully with a slice and serve on the dish with bacon. A slice of bread fried in the bacon fat adds to the meal.

Method 2. Some people prefer to grill rather than fry bacon and eggs. It is an easy method, saves washing up, and is more economical. Trim the bacon and place it in the grill-pan in position and grill 2 mins. each side (longer if you like it well done). Remove the grill-pan and put the bacon on a serving dish. Crack an egg into a cup and pour into the corner of the grill-pan, keeping it tilted. There should be sufficient bacon fat to cook the egg. Hold the grill-pan, still tilted, under the grill for half a minute, until egg is just set; then fix under the grill and leave till it is cooked.

Method 3. Arrange some chippolata sausages, rolls of bacon and tomatoes in a large fireproof dish that has been lightly greased with bacon fat. Crack some eggs in a cup and pour them into the dish.

Cook at 375°F. for 30 mins., bottom runner in oven.

EGGS AND TOMATOES

Cut the tops off enough tomatoes and scoop out the centre. Allow 1 egg for each 2 tomatoes, beat the egg with the pulp from the centre and spoon into the cavities. Stand in a fireproof dish.

Alternatively, crack an egg in a cup and pour it, whole, into the cavity in the tomato.

Stand in a fireproof dish.

Cook at 350°F. for 30 mins., centre of oven.

KIDNEYS, BACON AND MUSHROOMS

Skin the kidneys, removing the tubes but leaving them whole. Cut the rind from the bacon rashers and peel and clean the mushrooms. Place all in a fireproof dish that has been greased with bacon dripping.

Cook at 375°F. for 30 to 40 mins., centre or bottom of oven.

SAUSAGE AND TOMATOES

In a greased fireproof dish make a bed of sausage meat about $\frac{1}{4}$ to $\frac{1}{2}$ an inch thick. Cut the tops off some tomatoes, and wrap a rasher of bacon round each one. Stand these in the sausage meat.

Cook at 375°F. for 60 mins., centre or bottom of oven.

SAUSAGES AND PANCAKES

Prick the sausages and put them in a baking tin in the centre of the oven.

Make some thin pancakes (see page 84) and lay each one as it is cooked on a saucer inverted on a plate. When sufficient are cooked, cover with a damp cloth and put them, on the plate, in the warming drawer.

Set the timers to switch on both oven and warming drawer in time for breakfast. Cook at 400°F. for 30 mins., centre of oven.

When cooked, wrap each sausage in a pancake which has been heated in the warming drawer.

CROÛTES

Melt some dripping (from previous fryings of bacon if you have it) by placing in the grill-pan under the grill. When hot lay a slice of bread in the fat and turn it till it is well soaked with the fat. Now place it back under the grill and brown each side.

POOR KNIGHT'S FRITTERS

1 egg	2 slices bread	2 tomatoes
pepper and salt	$\frac{1}{2}$ oz. fat	2 rashers bacon

Well beat the egg, adding pepper and salt. Cut three or four half slices of bread and remove the crust. Coat them with the egg.

Melt the fat in the grill-pan and when very hot, lay the bread in the fat, turning almost immediately to set the egg on both sides. Then brown under the grill.

Alternatively the fritters can be fried in shallow fat.

Garnish with grilled halves of tomatoes and chopped and grilled bacon.

PLAIN OMELETTE

2 eggs   2 tablespoonsful water or milk   pepper and salt

Well beat the eggs, add and beat in the other ingredients. Heat an omelette pan which should have been well greased, but contains insufficient fat to leave more than a film on the pan. When hot, pour in the mixture and cut through the omelette with a palette knife or a spoon until it is set underneath. Whilst it is still moist on the top fold the omelette over three or four times according to size. The easiest way is to hold the pan, handle towards you, in your left hand with your palm above and fingers below the handle. Tilt the pan away from you. The omelette will slide towards the lower end of the pan and you can fold it with a palette knife quite easily. This folding must be done quickly and immediately the omelette is set on the underside; if the operation is made too lengthy the omelette will be tough. After folding, hold in the side of the hot pan for a few seconds to set, then dish on to a hot plate and serve at once.

Omelettes can be made with a number of flavourings and fillings.

Chopped parsley or a pinch of herbs or a little grated cheese can be mixed with the ingredients, or minced ham, cooked meat or fish, or chopped kidneys, heated separately, can be placed in the centre of the omelette before folding. It is usual to sprinkle a few pieces of the filling on the top of the folded omelette, to indicate the contents.

SOUFFLÉ OMELETTE

2 eggs
1 dessertspoonful of fine sugar

2 dessertspoonsful jam, fruit jelly or marmalade

Separate the yolks and white of the eggs. Whisk the white to a stiff froth. Beat the yolks and sugar together and cut them into the egg white with a metal spoon until well mixed. Do not beat the mixture.

Turn into a prepared and hot omelette pan and cook for a few seconds until it is just set underneath. Pour the jam, which should have been heated in a saucepan, on to the centre, fold the omelette in half and serve immediately.

BAKED OMELETTE

2 eggs
pepper and salt

2 tablespoonsful chopped cooked ham, or shelled shrimps

Separate the yolks and whites of the eggs. Whisk the white to a stiff froth. Beat the yolks and stir in the pepper, salt and ham or shrimps. Fold the yolks into the whites and pour into a well buttered soufflé mould.

Bake for 15 mins. at 450°F. centre of the oven.

SCRAMBLED EGG

2 eggs
2 tablespoonsful water

pepper and salt
a small nut of butter

Beat the eggs and add the water, season, and pour into a saucepan. Add the butter. Cook on a medium heat, stirring all the time and, immediately it shows signs of setting, remove the pan and stir vigorously. Serve at once on hot buttered toast. Chopped parsley, chopped cooked ham or bacon or chopped cooked mushrooms can be added to the mixture before cooking.

BOILED EGGS

Take a pan that fits the boiling plate and put enough water in it just to cover the bottom. Put in the eggs, cover with a closely fitting lid and turn to full heat. Leave for 6 to 7 mins. according to how well set you like them.

POACHED EGGS

Have boiling a shallow pan of water containing a few drops of vinegar. Crack each egg into a cup and either slide them very gently into cutters standing in the water or into poaching rings. Cook until lightly set. Lift out, drain and serve on buttered toast.

GRILLED OR FRIED SAUSAGES

Wipe the sausages with a cloth and prick them thoroughly with a fork.
Melt ½ oz. of dripping in a fry-pan or the grill-pan, roll the sausages in it
till they are thoroughly coated and either grill or fry them, turning frequently
until they are brown and crisp.

SCOTCH EGGS (*facing page* 81)

3 hard boiled eggs	½ lb. sausage meat
1 raw egg	breadcrumbs

Shell the eggs, keeping them whole. Cover them with the sausage meat.
Coat with beaten egg, dry with breadcrumbs and fry till brown in hot fat.
Serve cold and cut in half.

WELSH RAREBIT

2 to 3 oz. grated cheese	1 tablespoonful milk
1 teaspoonful made mustard	seasoning
1 tablespoonful melted butter	1 slice buttered toast

Mix all the ingredients and spread on the toast. Place in the grill-pan with
the grid in the lowest position and grill for about 10 mins. Garnish with
parsley and slices of grilled tomato and serve very hot.

BUCK RAREBIT

Put a lightly poached egg on the top of a welsh rarebit.

BACON AND TOMATOES IN CHEESE SAUCE

4 tomatoes	grated cheese
8 rashers bacon	white breadcrumbs
½ pint cheese sauce (see page 33)	

Halve the tomatoes and wrap each half in a rasher of bacon. Place in a
fireproof dish and pour cheese sauce round. Sprinkle the top with a mixture
of grated cheese and breadcrumbs. Place under the grill until brown.

RECHAUFFE DISHES: *Roman pie, fruit mould, London pie,*
fish pie, rice rissoles and duchesse flan

Vol-au-vent of chicken

Réchauffées

RÉCHAUFFÉES are made from food that is already cooked. All they need is preparation for reheating.

REASONS FOR FAILURE

The *main reasons for failure* nearly always point to unimaginative serving and the following points should be remembered:

1. Reheated foods lose colour and are unattractive in appearance unless extra care is given to garnish and serving.

2. They have lost moisture or juice and are dry and therefore flavourless. Something must be done to replace this moisture and to give additional flavour.

3. Many foods, particularly fruit and vegetables, lose nutritional value. Try to put it back. Serve something fresh, either newly cooked or raw, with a réchauffée.

Meat

The family joint, cut one day, can often be reheated in the following way:

SUET CAUL

For a joint weighing three pounds make a suet pastry using 6 ozs. flour (see page 94).

Roll ¼ inch thick. Put the joint in the greased meat pan and cover with the pastry. Cover with a few small dabs of dripping.

Cook at 350°F. for 45 mins., bottom of oven.

HASH

To each pound of cold meat, allow 1 pint of brown sauce (see page 32). Cut the meat into neat chunks or slices and add to the sauce. Cover with a lid and heat without boiling for 20 mins.

Turn on to a dish, garnish with a narrow border of cooked rice, macaroni, or creamed and piped potatoes. Scatter the border with chopped parsley and finish with a few croutons of fried bread.

SHEPHERD'S PIE *(see page 69)*

CURRIED LAMB *(facing page 48)*

Make a curry sauce (see recipe page 38), and add to it the slices or chunks of cold, cooked lamb. Heat through before serving. Other kinds of cold meat may be used.

RICE RISSOLES (*facing page* 128)

4 ozs. cold meat	cayenne pepper and salt
2 ozs. cooked rice	a little curry powder, if liked
1 oz. dripping	a little stock
1 oz. white breadcrumbs	

Mince the meat and add to the strained rice. Mix thoroughly adding the fat, breadcrumbs and seasoning, and a little stock if necessary to make it hold together. Cool.

Shape with the hands into rissoles, or make cutlet shapes if preferred. Coat with beaten egg and dry with breadcrumbs and fry in hot fat. Drain carefully, serve very hot, garnished with parsley.

FRICASSEE (*see page* 60)

CURRIES (*see page* 38)

PLATE PIES, PASTIES AND PATTIES

1 small onion	1 lb. cooked meat, minced
dripping	a little brown sauce
1 tomato	seasoning
12 oz. quick flaky or short pastry	

Cut the onion into thin rings and sauté in a little fat. Peel and slice the tomato. Add both to the minced meat with seasoning and enough sauce to make moist but not wet.

PLATE PIE

Roll the pastry about ¼ inch thick. Line an 8- or 10-inch plate with half the pastry and moisten the edges.

Put the meat in the centre, cover with another round of pastry, knock up the edges and brush the top with beaten egg.

Cook at 425°F. for 40 to 50 mins., any position. *Serves six.*

PASTIES

Cut circles of pastry about 7 inches in diameter, moisten the edges, put some of the meat in the centre and fold the circle together across the top of the meat. Brush with egg or milk, place on a floured baking tray.

Cook at 425°F. for 30 to 40 mins., any position. *Makes three.*

PATTIES

Line some 4-inch flan rings with pastry. Put meat in the case, cover with pastry, moistening the edges and folding them together.

Cook at 425°F. for 25 to 30 mins., any position. *Makes four.*

ROMAN PIE (*facing page* 128)

4 ozs. short pastry	1 dessertspoonful grated onion
brown breadcrumbs	½ gill of cheese sauce
6 ozs. mixed cooked vegetables	½ to 1 oz. cooked macaroni
1 mushroom, chopped	pepper and salt
1 tomato, chopped	

Line with pastry a 5-inch cake tin which has been greased and coated with brown breadcrumbs saving enough pastry to make a lid.

Fill with layers of vegetables, sauce and macaroni. Season. Cover with the lid. Cook at 425°F. for 40 to 45 mins., centre of oven.

Serves three or four.

SAVOURY PANCAKES

Filling: **2 onions**
    1 oz. butter
    1 oz. flour
    1 tablespoonful tomato purée
½ pint batter (see page 84)

½ pint stock
¾ lb. minced cooked meat
1 clove garlic
pepper and salt
½ pint tomato sauce (see page 38)
grated cheese

Fry the onions in the butter. Add the flour and cook it with the butter. Add the tomato purée and stock to make a binding sauce. Heat the meat in the sauce with a finely-chopped clove of garlic. Season.

Make very thick pancakes with the batter. Fill each one with the meat mixture and roll it up. Place on a fireproof dish. Pour tomato sauce round and cover with grated cheese.

Place under the grill and cook until brown.

Serves four.

Fish

FISH PIE (*facing page* 128)

½ lb. any cooked white fish
1 gill white sauce
seasoning
1 lb. cooked potatoes

½ oz. margarine
½ oz. grated cheese
2 tomatoes

Flake the fish and remove bones and skin. Mix it into the sauce with the seasoning.

Put it in a greased dish. Pipe a border of the potatoes creamed with the margarine. Sprinkle the whole with grated cheese and decorate with half tomatoes.

Cook at 350°F. for 45 mins. centre of oven.

Serves three or four.

FISH CAKES

½ lb. cooked fish
½ lb. mashed potato
seasoning
flavouring of grated onion or
    lemon juice
anchovy essence

½ oz. dripping
½ gill thick white sauce
egg
breadcrumbs
fried bread
tomatoes

Mash the fish and mix with the potato and seasonings. Melt the dripping and add with enough sauce to bind. Shape into 8 round flat cakes; coat with egg and breadcrumbs and fry in hot fat.

Serve on slices of fried bread and garnish with fried halves of tomato.

FISH SOUFFLE

1 oz. flour	½ lb. cooked white fish	lemon juice
1 oz. butter	3 eggs	seasoning
1 gill milk		

Make a panada with the flour, butter and milk and leave to cool.

Press the shredded fish through a sieve. Thoroughly mix the fish, panada and egg yolks with a few drops of lemon juice and the seasoning.

Whisk the egg whites till stiff and fold into the mixture. Turn into a greased soufflé tin with a round of greased paper in the bottom. Cover with greased paper and steam for 45 mins. Turn the soufflé on to an entrée dish, coat with white sauce and garnish with thin slices of lemon.

Serves four.

PRAWN BATTER

1 pint of cooked prawns or shrimps   ¼ pint yeast batter (see page 64)
seasoning

Pick the prawns and put them in a basin. Season. Add the batter. Drop a spoonful of the mixture into well-greased patty tins.

Cook at 450°F. for 10 to 15 mins., any position.

Serves four.

Miscellaneous

MACARONI CHEESE

3 ozs. macaroni	seasoning
½ oz. margarine	3 ozs. grated cheese
½ oz. plain flour	parsley
½ pint milk	fried bread
½ teaspoonful made mustard	potato

Break the macaroni and cook (see opposite). Make a sauce with the margarine, flour and milk, add the macaroni, seasonings and half the cheese.

Turn into a greased dish, scatter with the remaining cheese, and brown under the grill. Garnish with parsley, little triangles of fried bread and, if liked, pipe a border of creamed potato. *Serves three.*

CAULIFLOWER CURRY

1 dozen chestnuts	4 tomatoes
½ a cooked cauliflower	3 to 4 ozs. rice
½ pint curry sauce (see page 38)	1 oz. blanched and toasted almonds

Cut the chestnuts to pierce the skin and boil them for 25 to 30 mins. Remove the skins while still hot, keeping the chestnuts whole.

Break the cauliflower into sprigs and reheat in the curry sauce. Blanch and peel the tomatoes, keeping them whole. Put the curry in the centre of a dish, place tomatoes at each end and the chestnuts along the side. Border with the plain boiled rice (opposite) and scatter the nuts over the top as a garnish. Serve with fresh watercress.

Serves three or four.

PLAIN BOILED RICE

1 oz. Patna rice per portion

Wash the rice in cold water. Drain and sprinkle it into a saucepan of fast boiling water; add a little salt and a teaspoonful of white vinegar to keep the rice a good colour. Boil until the rice is tender. This takes about 11 mins.

Pour the rice into a fine sieve, or a colander in which a piece of muslin has been laid, and allow cold water to run through to wash out any free starch. This prevents the rice grains from sticking together. Put the rice into a shallow vessel and place in a warming drawer or cool oven to dry it. This takes about 20 mins.

If the rice is not wanted for a longer period of time it is quite safe to leave it drying until such time as it is required. Stir the grains with a fork to separate them.

PLAIN BOILED MACARONI

Break the macaroni into short lengths and rinse them under the tap. Drop into boiling salted water and boil for about 30 mins. or until tender.

Not Enough Left

You've had the freshly cooked meal and what is left is not quite sufficient for the following day. Somehow it has to be stretched. The following recipes may give you some ideas on how to augment and make it enough.

ENOUGH COLD MEAT FOR TWO AND REQUIRED FOR FOUR

KROMESKIES

2 ozs. cooked meat	½ oz. margarine	fried bread
1 rasher of fat bacon	½ oz. flour	parsley
2 mushrooms	¾ gill yeast batter (see	tomato sauce
½ gill stock	page 64)	

Mince the meat with the bacon and add the chopped mushrooms. Make a panada with the stock, margarine and flour and add enough to the minced meat to make soft. Mix thoroughly.

When cool form into four large or eight small cakes. Dip each one in batter and fry in deep fat till brown.

Serve on fried bread, garnish with parsley and serve with tomato sauce.

CASSEROLE OF COOKED MEAT

2 ozs. or less of cold meat	white stock
1 stick celery	1 small vegetable marrow
2 raw tomatoes	6 ozs. plain boiled rice
a small onion	4 eggs

Mince the meat, celery, tomatoes and onion and mix well. Put it in the bottom of a good-sized casserole with sufficient white stock to make very moist.

Peel the marrow, cut lengthwise and remove the seeds. Lay the two halves on the meat

Cover with the rice, packing it round the marrow so that you have a flat surface. Crack the eggs in a cup and slide them carefully on to the top of the rice so that they are equally spaced. The eggs should more or less cover the rice. Put a lid on the casserole

Cook at 350°F. for 40 mins. Any position.

ENOUGH HOTPOT OR STEW FOR TWO
AND REQUIRED FOR FOUR

4 ozs. haricot beans	1 carrot
the remains of the stew	2 pork sausages
2 small onions	1 oz. fat
3 tomatoes	1 oz. plain flour
2 potatoes, medium sized	cayenne and salt

Soak the haricot beans overnight and boil until tender (about 45 mins.). Keep hot.

Strain the stew and remove any bones from the meat, saving the stock. Put the meat, onions, potatoes, tomatoes and carrot through the mincer.

Grill the sausages, cool, skin and add to the mixture. Mix thoroughly. Make a roux with the fat and flour and add 1 pint of the stock. Cook until thickened. Add the mince and heat without boiling. Season.

Strain the haricot beans and border them round an entrée dish. Fill the centre with the mince.

DUMPLING STEW

the remains of a stew	stick of celery
3 ozs. suet pastry	1 oz. dripping
2 tomatoes	1 oz. flour
1 onion	seasoning
2 potatoes	

Take the meat from the stew and remove it from the bones, cut into cubes and cover these with the suet pastry to form small dumplings. Slice and sauté the vegetables in dripping and remove from the pan. Use the dripping to make a brown roux, with flour and stock (see page 32). Add the liquid from the stew to the roux and bring to the boil, then add vegetables and seasonings and bring back to the boil, add the dumplings then simmer for 1½ hours. *Serves four.*

HARICOT MUTTON

1 onion	½ pint brown sauce
2 tomatoes	paprika and salt
1 oz. haricot beans soaked overnight	chopped parsley
½ lb. cooked mutton cut into small, neat chunks	

Slice the onion, cut the tomatoes in four and sauté in a very little dripping. Cook the haricot beans and drain.

Put all the ingredients in a casserole, cover and put in the oven. When cooked garnish with chopped parsley, wrap the casserole in a napkin and serve.

Cook at 300°F. for 40 mins. Any position.
Serves four.

HOT MEAT LOAF

You have 2 lamb cutlets, 2 ozs. mushrooms, a kidney and some rashers of bacon and unexpectedly want supper for four people:

Remove all bone from cutlets, and put the meat, kidneys, mushrooms, an onion, and two or three rashers through a mincer. Hard boil one or two eggs.

Add 3 ozs. of white bread to mince. Season well and bind with beaten egg.

Grease a 1-lb. loaf tin (or a round 5-inch cake tin) and then coat it with browned breadcrumbs. Pack the mince into this and put the hard-boiled eggs in the centre. Cover with greaseproof paper.

Cook at 375°F. for 35 to 40 mins., centre of oven.

Turn on to a meat dish, garnish with grilled halves of tomato and duchesse potatoes.

LEEK AND MEAT PIE

You have the remains of some stewed steak enough for two, and want to provide a meal for four:

Lift the meat out of stock, cut it into pieces and put in a pie dish. Take 6 large or 8 smaller leeks, clean them carefully and split them lengthways into four. Lay these on top of the meat. Add a little of the stock—enough to keep it moist during cooking—and season with pepper and salt.

Cover with flaky or rough puff pastry.

Cook at 425°F. for 25 to 30 mins., any position.

The CARCASE OF A CHICKEN with enough meat on it for two is required for four.

VOL AU VENT OF CHICKEN (*facing page* 129)

remains of chicken	1 large vol au vent case or
½ pint white sauce	4 vol au vent cases (see page 100)
seasoning	¼ lb. mushrooms

Cut the meat away from the carcase and cube it. Reheat in the white sauce, being careful not to boil, season and fill the vol au vent cases. Cook the mushrooms in a little butter and use to decorate the top of the filling.

MAYONNAISE OF CHICKEN

¼ pint of mayonnaise	½ oz. gelatine dissolved in ½ gill
chicken cut into small cubes	of stock
potato salad	

Mix all together with a little chopped parsley and seasoning. Turn into four small wet moulds and leave to set. Serve on a bed of potato chopped and tossed in mayonnaise, and with a colourful salad.

MOCK CRAB

You have enough white fish for two, but it will make a *mock crab* for four:

white fish	oil, vinegar	salad
1 small tin of crab	pepper and salt	mayonnaise
2 ozs. white breadcrumbs		

Free the fish of bone and skin and press through a sieve with the crab Mix with breadcrumbs and seasoning.

Put in the centre of individual salads, dress with mayonnaise, chill and serve.

SURPRISE TOAD

You have a little cooked fish and a few tomatoes, and require a meal for two:

2 ozs. flaked white fish   4 sound tomatoes   ½ pint Yorkshire batter

Flake and mash the fish. Cut the tops off the tomatoes and remove some of the interior. Stuff with the fish. Grease the Yorkshire pudding tin liberally, pour in the batter and add the tomatoes.

Cook at 425°F. for 30 mins., top of oven.

POTATO SOUFFLÉS

1 lb. hot boiled potatoes   **a good pinch pepper**
2 eggs   **flat teaspoonful salt**
¼ pint hot milk   **3 ozs. grated cheese**
2 ozs. margarine

Rice the potatoes or press them through a sieve. Add the well-beaten egg yolks and all the other ingredients, except egg whites. Beat very thoroughly until soft and creamy.

Whip the whites of egg till stiff and fold into the mixture. Turn into a one-quart soufflé dish—sprinkle with paprika.

Cook at 425°F. for 20 mins., top of oven.
Serves four.

EGG AND CHEESE PIE

You have 2 eggs, a little cheese and want to make supper for four:

1 or 2 ozs. grated cheese   **2 hard-boiled eggs**
½ teaspoonful made mustard   **1 gill white sauce**
pepper and salt   **2 mashed potatoes**
7 or 8-inch flan case baked blind

Stir half the cheese and the seasoning into the sauce, cut the hard-boiled eggs into thin slices. Lay the eggs in the flan case when cold and coat with the sauce. Garnish with a piping of mashed potato, sprinkle with the remainder of the cheese and brown in the oven or under the grill.

QUICK PATTY CASES

Suppose you want patty cases and have no ingredients for pastry. Cut slices of a sandwich loaf about ¼ in. thick and remove the crusts. Lightly grease some patty tins and line each with the bread so that the corners of the slice form four points. Press into the tin. Bake at 350°F. for about 20 mins. till pale brown. Alternatively, cut slices of bread about 2½ to 3 ins. thick. Scoop out the centre so that you have a square case, and fry.

Puddings made with Leftovers

APPLE SNOW

1 sponge cake
¼ pint custard
sugar to taste

lemon juice
¼ pint apple pulp

1 white of egg
glacé cherries

Put cake in a sundae glass, pour custard over. Add sugar and lemon juice to apple pulp. Whip the egg white until stiff and add the pulp while whisking. Pile on top of the custard and decorate with cherries.

TIPSY TRIFLE

4 sponge cakes or any stale cake
a little stewed fruit
1 tablespoonful brandy
1 tablespoonful sherry

½ pint custard
cherries and whipped cream
to decorate

Place sponge cakes in a glass dish and pour over the stewed fruit, brandy and sherry. Make a good custard and pour over the top. When set decorate with cream and cherries.

BREAD PUDDING

Pieces of stale bread and cake
milk
2 ozs. sultanas

2 ozs. mixed peel
½ teaspoonful mixed spice

Soak the bread and cake in milk. Squeeze out excess liquid and mix in the dried fruit and mixed spice. Grease a pie dish with butter and put the bread mixture into the dish. Place dots of butter on the top and bake at 375°F. for 40 mins.

RICE CONDÉ

1 orange
sugar

redcurrant jelly
cold cooked rice pudding

Slice the orange and place it in the bottom of sundae glasses. Sprinkle with sugar. Cover with cold rice pudding. Melt 1 tablespoonful of redcurrant jelly and pour over the top of each.

Preserving and Pickling

THERE are various methods of preserving food and the simple ones are given here, it being assumed that with the more specialist work, such as canning and freezing, the manufacturer's instructions would be followed.

Drying

This most frequently applies to fruits, though herbs and some vegetables can also be dried. The main point to remember is that they should dry in a free circulation of warm, not hot, air.

APPLES

should be peeled, cored and cut in rings about $\frac{1}{4}$ in. thick. Drop them into salt water (1 oz. to each quart). Thread them on a stick and place across the rod shelves, leaving a space between each ring. Dial 150°F. and leave them till they feel soft and look like chamois leather. This will take about 6 hours. Then hang them in a warm, dry cupboard for 24 hours. Store in screw top jars.

PEARS

should be peeled, cut into quarters and the core removed with a spoon. Soak them for a few minutes in brine. Stand them on a wire rack and dry for about 6 hours in the oven at 150°F. or in the warming drawer. Leave them on the rack in a warm cupboard for another 24 hours, then store in screw top jars.

Bottling

All fruit can be preserved by bottling, provided it is sound and not over-ripe. Some that is of a delicate flavour when fresh is apt to be tasteless by the time it is bottled; strawberries are, for example, not very successful. Some need great care if they are not to become a bad colour and peaches are difficult although not impossible; it is for this reason that apples and pears are dropped into a brine.

JARS

Patent caps for jam jars or one of the patent screw-top type jars are all suitable. Make sure the jars are not cracked or chipped, that the lid fits snugly, and that the rubber rings are pliable and unperished.

REASONS FOR FAILURE

1. Nothing is more irritating than to go to the trouble of preserving the

138

fruit only to find that some jars have not sealed. Make sure that they will seal before you start with this simple little test: light a piece of paper and drop it, flaming, into the jar. Cover and screw or clip down. If it is not sealed by the time the jar is cold (a few seconds) it is faulty and never *will* seal—change the rubber ring and examine for a chipped lid or jar.

2. Fruit rises to the top of the jar either because you made too strong a syrup or because the fruit was loosely packed or because you heated it too quickly. It does not necessarily mean failure, but is unsightly.

3. Mould forming on the top of the fruit shows that it was not sterile. Another indication is when the fruit smells fermented and like wine. Either you did not get the fruit hot enough or did not process it for long enough. You are advised not to use the fruit.

4. Plums and other stone-fruit sometimes taste of bitter almonds. This is caused by the stone and is particularly noticeable when the fruit is bottled without sugar. It is harmless but if you object to the flavour, either stone the fruit before bottling or bottle in a syrup.

Methods of Bottling

Pick over, remove stalks and if necessary wash the fruit. Pack it tightly into the jars, allowing an extra jar full for filling if the fruit shrinks during sterilisation.

WATER-BATH METHOD

Pack the clean jars with cold fruit and fill to the top with water or syrup if necessary. Cover with the lid and clip or screw down. With the screw type *un*screw a half turn. Stand on a wooden trivet or several folds of cardboard in a pan that will hold sufficient water to cover the jars so that they are completely immersed in cold water at least one inch above the lid. The jars should not touch each other.

Bring very slowly to simmering point, taking about 1 hour to raise the water to this temperature. When it is simmering gently, time it and leave another hour at the simmer. Lift out the jars and stand them on a wooden tray to cool. Screw down as they cool.

Unscrew and test them twenty-four hours later to make sure they are sealed and for ease of removing the screw at a later date, smear a very little fat on the threads.

OVEN METHOD

You can pack and fill the jars with water or syrup as above and sterilise them in the oven.

Put in a cold oven, dial 200°F. and leave 2 hours. Proceed as above.

Alternatively, pack dry fruit in dry jars and put in a cold oven. Dial 225°F. and leave for 1½ hours. Remove the jars one at a time, stand on a wooden tray, cover the fruit with boiling water and screw down immediately.

You will find the first oven method or the water-bath method best for wet or juicy fruit. The second oven method is excellent for fruits that are being bottled in the skin, such as plums or tomatoes.

Select good fruit and place it in a saucepan with just enough water to prevent burning and bring to the boil. Cook thoroughly and while still boiling, pour immediately into very hot jars. Seal at once with hot lids. Place the bottles in pans of hot water, bring to the boil and boil for 5 mins. Tighten the lids as soon as the jars are removed from the steriliser.

This method is excellent for using up windfall apples. Cut out any bad part of the fruit, cut up and cook to a pulp. Put through a sieve to remove pips and skin. Reheat the pulp to boiling and bottle in the same way as above.

Tomato purée can be made in the same manner.

APPLES AND PEARS

should be peeled, cut into quarters and cored. Drop them into a brine made from 1 oz. salt to each quart of water. Drain pears and plunge them into boiling water, stew gently for a few minutes.

Pack the fruit into the bottles, cover immediately with a syrup of 4 ozs. sugar to each pint of water, adding a few drops of cochineal to make it pink. Use the water-bath method (see page 139).

Since bottled apples are always served cooked you may find it an economy in space and time to pulp them. Peel and core them in the usual way and cut them into chunks. Put them in a pan with enough water just to prevent them boiling dry and boil them fast, stirring occasionally, till they are a soft pulp. Leave to stand until cool and add sugar to taste; or they can be bottled without sugar and this can be added before serving.

When cool fill the jars and sterilise by the water-bath method.

PEACHES

should be peeled very carefully with a silver knife to prevent discoloration. Cut them in half and remove the stone. Drop into brine. Make a syrup of 4 ozs. sugar to the pint of water, and for each pint, stir in 1 ascorbic acid tablet which helps to prevent discoloration.

Pack the peaches into jars, cover immediately with syrup and sterilise in a water bath (see page 139).

RHUBARB

is a useful fruit and although not enjoyed as a dessert by many people it is worth storing for mixing with other fruits. It is rich in pectin and if added to jams and jellies made from fruit that has a deficiency of it, such as strawberries, will assist setting; and it has the happy knack of subduing its own flavour. Provided you do not actually encounter its unmistakable appearance which is easily hidden by pressing through a sieve, it cannot be detected when mixed with other fruits.

To preserve, wipe the stalks and cut them into lengths slightly shorter than the jar. Cover with water or syrup and sterilise in a water bath (see page 139).

PLUMS AND DAMSONS

can be packed into jars and sterilised by the oven method. With large plums, when you can only pack a few into each jar, it is frequently an economy to remove the stones. Cut each plum through to the stone, open and remove the stone and fold together again. Pack the stoned fruit in jars and proceed by the oven method (see page 139).

TOMATOES

1. Simply pack the tomatoes in jars and proceed by the dry oven method, adding a teaspoonful of salt when you fill with water.
2. Blanch and peel the tomatoes, cut them in half and pack them in the jars with a sprinkle of salt. Press them down well so that with their own juice they completely fill the jar. Proceed by wet oven method or sterilising in a water bath.

Jams

Choose sound, just ripe fruit; it should never be over-ripe, as it then has a reduced pectin content and may not set. Always cook the fruit thoroughly first; you will have difficulty in getting it tender after the sugar has been added. Simmer gently until the fruit is soft, add the sugar and stir till it dissolves. Then boil rapidly until it is ready to set. Use a preserving pan or large shallow saucepan with a solid base.

TO TEST FOR SETTING

Put a little of the jam in a saucer and leave to cool. When you tilt the saucer, the surface of the jam should wrinkle.

REASONS FOR FAILURE

Mould forming on the top of the jam is an indication of either insufficient sugar in the recipe, of covering or tying down the jam before it was cold, or of storing in a damp or warm pantry.

Crystals on top of the jam indicate over-cooking or too much sugar.

Broadly speaking, the basic recipes for jams are as follows:

HARD FRUITS

3 lbs. fruit   ½ pint water   3 lbs. sugar

SOFT FRUITS

3 lbs. fruit   juice 2 lemons   3 lbs. sugar

BLACKCURRANT JAM

2 lbs. blackcurrants   1½ pints water   3 lbs. sugar

Clean the fruit and let it simmer in the water until tender. Add the sugar and stir till it is dissolved. Boil rapidly for 3 to 5 mins. Test for setting, pour into warm, dry jars. Seal when cold.
Makes about five pounds.

CHERRY JAM

juice of 6 lemons (1½ gills)   1½ lbs. stoned morello cherries
3 lbs. stoned black cherries   3½ lbs. preserving sugar

Strain the lemon juice on the fruit and pour the sugar over. Leave for a night then dissolve the sugar in the mixture over a low heat. When all is dissolved bring very gently to the boil then reduce the heat and simmer until thick and syrupy—about ¾ hour. Pot and cover when cold.

DRIED APRICOT JAM

1 lb. apricots   juice of 1 lemon
3 pints water   3 ozs. blanched almonds
3 lbs. sugar

Soak the apricots in the water overnight. Simmer gently until tender, which will take about ½ hour, add the sugar, lemon juice and almonds and stir till the sugar is dissolved. Boil rapidly for 5 to 10 mins. Test for setting, pour into jars and seal when cold.

Makes about five pounds.

MARMALADE

5 seville oranges   1 lemon   4 lbs. sugar
2 sweet oranges   2 quarts of water

Wipe the fruit and cut in half, removing the pips and tying them in a muslin bag. With a sharp knife, cut the fruit into thin shreds and drop into a preserving pan with the water and the pips.

Leave it soaking for 24 hours.

Bring to the boil and simmer for 30 mins. By then the rind should be tender but simmer longer if necessary.

Remove the bag containing pips, and add the sugar, stirring till dissolved. Boil rapidly for 10 to 15 mins. Test for setting, pour into hot, dry jars and seal when cold.

PLUM JAM

3 lbs. plums   ½ pint water   3 lbs. sugar

Put the fruit with the water in a pan and stew gently, removing the stones as the fruit cooks and they come to the surface. If you crack the stones and add the kernels to the jam it improves the flavour, or you can add a few blanched almonds. Add the sugar, dissolve, and boil the jam rapidly for 20 mins. Test for setting, pour into jars, and tie down when cold.

QUINCE MARMALADE

6 lbs. quinces   6 lbs. sugar   juice of 2 lemons
2 pints water   ½ lb. coarsely chopped   ½ lb. stoned raisins
              walnuts

Peel the quinces and cut them into chunks, removing the hard centre. Drop into water and boil till tender, stirring and mashing with a wooden spoon.

When all the fruit is pulped, add the sugar, stirring till dissolved. Boil for 10 mins., add the nuts, lemon juice and raisins and boil for another 5 mins. Pour into hot, dry jars and cover when cold.

STRAWBERRY JAM

| 6 lbs. strawberries | 1 gill of redcurrant juice | 6 lbs. sugar |
| juice of 1 lemon | or purée of rhubarb | |

Put the strawberries with the fruit juice in a pan and heat slowly till the strawberries are on the point of softening. Add the sugar and stir till dissolved. Boil rapidly for 3 to 5 mins. Test for setting, pour into warm, dry jars. Seal when cold.

Jellies

Allow sufficient water to break down the fruit while cooking. Measure the strained juice and add 1 lb. of sugar to each pint.

REASONS FOR FAILURE

A jelly sometimes will not set, despite reducing by boiling, if too much water is added. More frequently it is due to insufficient boiling.

If a jelly ferments it is an indication that it was insufficiently set.

BRAMBLE JELLY

| 4 lbs. blackberries | ½ pint water |
| juice of 2 lemons | 1 lb. sugar to each pint of juice |

Boil the fruit, lemon juice and water, mashing the fruit with a wooden spoon till tender.

Strain through a jelly bag, letting the juice drip through slowly. If you try to hurry the operation by pressing the bag, the jelly will be cloudy.

Measure the juice, heat it without boiling and add 1 lb. sugar for each pint. Boil rapidly for 10 mins. Test for setting, pour into jars and cover when cold.

PLUM JELLY *(to serve with mutton)*

| 2 lbs. of plums | 1 lb. sour apples | 1 gill measure of leaves |
| 1½ pint water | about 1½ lbs. of sugar | of mint |

Stew the plums till soft in half the water. Cut the apples in large pieces but do not peel and boil in the remaining water. When both are cooked mix the two together, stir and strain through a jelly bag. Measure the liquid.

Add sugar at the rate of 1 lb. to the pint of liquid. Tie the mint in a muslin bag and hang in the liquid while it boils briskly for about 15 mins.

Test for setting; pour into hot jars and seal.

LEMON CURD

| ½ lb. sugar | the juice and finely grated rind of 2 lemons |
| 3 ozs. butter | 3 egg yolks |

Cream the sugar and butter, add the lemons and beaten egg yolks and heat in a double cooker, stirring with a wooden spoon until it thickens.

Put the curd in jam jars and cover.

MINCEMEAT

1 lb. suet	1 lb. sugar
1 lb. currants	grated rind and juice of 3 lemons
1 lb. raisins	1 teaspoonful mixed spice
1 lb. apples	¼ pint white wine ⎱
1 lb. candied peel	¼ pint brandy ⎰ mix together
¼ lb. almonds	

Chop the suet. Wash and dry the fruit. Remove stones from the raisins. Peel, core and mince the apples. Chop the peel and nuts. Mix all the ingredients together and store for a month in an earthenware jar, carefully covered with a well-fitting lid. Alternatively the mincemeat can be put into jam jars and covered.

Chutneys and Pickles

GREEN TOMATO CHUTNEY

4 lbs. apples	3 pints malt vinegar
1 lb. shallots	juice of 2 lemons
4 lbs. green tomatoes	3 ozs. salt
1 lb. brown sugar	¼ oz. ground ginger
1 lb. sultanas	1 oz. mixed spice
½ lb. raisins	

Peel, slice and core the apples, peel the shallots and cut the tomatoes in half. Put them through a mincer with the dried fruit. Boil the sugar and vinegar and add the lemon juice, seasoning and minced ingredients. Simmer very gently for about 3 hours till the mixture is thick. Pour into hot jars and seal.

ONION PICKLE

1 lb. minced onions	1 pint wine vinegar
2 large chopped cooking apples	a good pinch cayenne pepper
½ lb. brown sugar	2 flat teaspoonsful salt
1 flat teaspoonful dry mustard	a small piece chopped horseradish

Boil all the ingredients together for 45 mins., stirring occasionally. Pour into hot jars and seal.

PICKLED EGGS

1 doz. eggs	1 oz. salt
½ oz. mixed pickling spices	2 bay leaves
½ grated nutmeg	vinegar

Boil the eggs for 20 mins., and shell them. Place in a jar and add seasonings. Cover with boiling vinegar. When cool seal the jar.

TO PRESERVE EGGS

Waterglass is bought at a chemist's and should be prepared as given on the packet. Place the eggs in a bucket or large crock and pour the prepared waterglass over to cover them. Cover the top with a cloth to keep out dust and help delay evaporation. The eggs must be new laid.

Roast crown of lamb, mint sauce and cut-away fruit pie

Fish pie, roast pork with accompaniments, rice mould with stewed plums and apple charlotte

Complete Meals

THE following menus may help you at some time when you are wondering what in the world to have for dinner, or, when you have already decided on the main dish, what to give for the accompaniments and other courses.

The page number where you will find instructions for preparation or mixing is given in parenthesis after each dish, and below each menu all the instructions on where to put it in the oven, how long to cook it and at what temperature are given. When it applies I have also told you how you can cook the complete meal, all of it together in the oven, by the timer.

MENU I   **roast crown of lamb** (67)
(*facing page* 144)   **mint sauce** (38):   **gravy** (34)
                    duchesse potatoes (77):   **new potatoes**
                    peas (74):   **buttered carrots**
                    cut-away plum pie (98)

Place lamb on floor of oven, pie second runner from top, duchesse potatoes in centre. Cook for 45 to 50 mins. at 400°F., removing pie after the first 35 to 40 mins. Cook the new potatoes, peas and carrots on the hob. Drain carrots after they are cooked and toss in butter adding a little chopped parsley to improve the appearance.

To cook the complete meal by the timer, put the carrots and peas in casseroles with water and seasoning and seal with aluminium foil. Toss the new potatoes in melted butter or margarine until thoroughly coated; place them in a casserole, add cold water and salt, and seal with aluminium foil. Put these three casseroles and the duchesse flan on one rod shelf as close above the meat (which should be in the meatpan on the floor of the oven) as you can. Put the pie on the third runner from the top of the oven. Set the timer on your cooker to switch on at the appropriate time to allow 45 mins. cooking. Dial 400°F.

MENU II   **haricot mutton** (59)
                    creamed potatoes (77)
            carrots in white sauce (32):   **peas** (74)
                    baked college pudding (88)

Place haricot mutton on the floor of the oven and cook for 4 hours at 325°F. Put college pudding at the top of the oven for the final hour; do not increase the temperature. Cook the vegetables on the hob.

To cook a similar meal by the timer putting everything in the oven, select a steamed pudding instead of the college pudding and omit the peas. Place the haricot mutton on the floor of the oven. Mix the pudding and put it into a greased pudding basin, sealing it with aluminium foil. Stand this on a cutter in a second, much larger, basin, add cold water to come nearly to the top of the outer basin and seal across the top with aluminium foil; place in the centre of the oven. Toss the vegetables in melted margarine or butter, place in fireproof casseroles, add a little cold water and seal with aluminium foil. Put them wherever they can go in the oven—probably on the floor with the haricot mutton. Set the timer to switch on at the appropriate time to allow 4 hours cooking at 325°F.

MENU III   **stuffed soles (49)**
(facing page 32)   **roast loin of lamb (66)**
              onion sauce (34):   gravy (34)
                       roast potatoes (75)
       sprouts: carrots: peas (74)
              steamed jam pudding (87)

Put the loin of lamb and potatoes in the meat pan on the floor of the oven and cook for 1 hour at 400°F. Put the sole in the centre of the oven and cook for 40 mins. Cook the remainder of the meal on the hob.

To cook by the timer, thoroughly coat the potatoes by dipping in melted fat, prepare the vegetables by sealing in a casserole as instructed in Menu I, and the steamed pudding as in Menu IX. Place the pudding immediately above the meat, with the stuffed soles in a dish sealed with aluminium foil beside it, and the casseroles above. Set the timer to start cooking one hour before you want to serve the meal. Make the gravy and onion sauce as you dish up.

MENU IV   **vegetable soup (42)**
(facing page 208)   **roast rib of beef (66)**
       Yorkshire pudding (83):   gravy (34)
       roast potatoes (75):   green beans
              pineapple upside down cake (87)

Put the meat and potatoes in the meat pan on the floor of the oven, and cook at 400°F. for 1½ hours or according to the size of the joint of meat. Bake the upside down pudding in the centre of the oven for 1¼ hours at the same temperature. Put the Yorkshire pudding towards the top of the oven and cook for the final 40 mins. Cook the soup and make the gravy on the hob.

To cook this meal by the timer, select a piece of beef weighing not more than 3½ to 4 lbs. Place it with the potatoes well coated in fat in meat pan on the floor of the oven. Put the Yorkshire pudding and the upside down pudding immediately above the meat and the beans and soup (both sealed with aluminium foil) in casseroles towards the top. Set the timer to cook for 1½ hours at 400°F. Make the gravy and thicken the soup while you are dishing up.

MENU V   **roast duck (71)**
       orange salad (80):   apple sauce (36):   gravy (34)
                       duchesse potatoes (77)
       roast potatoes (75):   green peas (74)
              charlotte russe (89)

Place the duck and roast potatoes in the meat pan on the floor of the oven and the duchesse potatoes in the centre. Cook at 375°F. for one hour or according to size of the duck. Cook the remainder of the meal on the hob—except, of course, for the charlotte russe.

To cook this meal by a timer, select a duck requiring 60 to 75 mins. cooking. Place in meat pan with potatoes well-coated in fat. Make a duchesse flan and place in the centre of the oven; put the peas with a little water and seasoning in a fireproof dish and seal with aluminium foil. Place both these in the centre of the oven. Prepare the apples for the sauce, place in a fireproof dish with sugar and water, and seal with aluminium foil. Set the timer to cook for 1¼ hours at 375°F. Make the gravy and orange salad and finish the apple sauce when you dish up the meal.

MENU VI   **fish pie (131)**
(*facing page* 145)   **roast leg of pork (66)**
apple sauce (36):   **sage and onion forcemeat (29)**
creamed potatoes (77):   **green peas (74)**
rice mould (82)   **stewed plums (90)**

Place the meat in the pan on the floor of the oven. Allow 35 mins. to the lb. and cook at 400°F. Put the rice mould in the centre of the oven for a minimum of 1½ hrs. Cook the fish pie at the top of the oven for 45 mins. The forcemeat stuffing can be cooked in the meat pan or in a separate dish for 45 mins. Cook the vegetables and plums on the hob.

MENU VII   **French liver and bacon (68)**
leeks (74) with white sauce (32)
creamed potatoes (77)
queen of puddings (87)

Put the dish containing the liver and bacon on the floor of the oven and cook for 30 mins. at 375°F. Put the queen of puddings near the top of the oven and cook for the same time. Cook the leaks and potatoes on the hob.

Reduce the temperature and increase the time, in order to allow for the vegetables, if you want to cook the whole of this meal by the timer. Put the vegetables with a cupful of water (first having tossed the potatoes in butter or margarine) in casseroles and seal them with aluminium foil. Place these in the centre of the oven. Set the timer to cook for 45 mins. at 350°F. Make the white sauce for the leeks and mash and cream the potatoes while you are dishing up.

MENU VIII   **London pie (69)**
cauliflower with white sauce (32)
buttered carrots
stewed fruit (90):   **baked egg custard (83)**

Place the egg custard in the centre of the oven and the London pie above it. Bake for 1 hour at 350°F. Cook the vegetables and stew the fruit on the hob.

To cook the complete meal by the timer, cut the carrots into rings and put in a casserole with seasoning and water; cover with aluminium foil. Stand the cauliflower, head upwards in a deep dish, add a cup of water and seal with aluminium foil. Place both these casseroles on the floor of the oven and position the remaining food as above. Prepare the fruit for stewing and put in a casserole with sugar and water or syrup; seal with aluminium foil. Set the timer to cook for 1 hour at 350°F. Make the white sauce for the cauliflower while you are dishing up.

MENU IX   baked grapefruit (123)
                            chicken paprika (62)
                  green peas (74):   creamed potatoes (77)
                            steamed syrup sponge (87)

Place the casserole containing the chicken on the floor of the oven and cook
at 350°F. for 1½ hours. Put the grapefruit in the oven at the top for the final
½ hour and cook the vegetables and steamed pudding on the hob.

To cook this meal by a timer, make individual puddings in small moulds.
Seal the top of each pudding with greaseproof paper or aluminium foil and
stand them on a trivet in a large basin. Put cold water in the basin so that it
comes at least half-way up the sides of the moulds and seal the basin with
aluminium foil. Place it in the centre of the oven, immediately above the
chicken (which should be on the floor) with the peas prepared as in Menu V
and the potatoes as in Menu VII beside it. Set the timer to cook for 1½ hours
at 350°F. Grill the grapefruit while you are creaming the potatoes and dishing
up.

MENU X   baked stuffed haddock (49)
                      buttered potatoes: peas (74)
                      bread and butter pudding (83)

Place the haddock in a fireproof dish on the floor of the oven, and the bread
and butter pudding in the centre. Cook at 350°F. for 45 mins. Cook the
vegetables on the hob.

Cook this meal by the timer by putting one vegetable beside the fish and
the other by the pudding (both vegetables should be sealed with aluminium
foil in casseroles as described in Menu I). Set the timer to cook for 45 mins.
at 350°F.

MENU XI   baked ham with peaches (67)
                  boiled new potatoes: Brussels sprouts
                      fresh fruit salad and cream (80)

Cook on the hob, baking the ham at 375°F. for the final 40 mins.

MENU XII   cream of tomato soup (44)
                            roast chicken (70)
                      bread sauce (37):   gravy (34)
                  roast potatoes (75):   peas and carrots macedoine (74)
                            fruit pie (97)

Put the chicken and potatoes in the meat pan on the floor of the oven and
cook for 1 to 1¼ hours, according to size, at 400°F. Put the fruit pie at the top
of the oven for the final 40 mins. Cut the carrots into small cubes, mix with
the peas and cook on the hob with the soup. Make the sauce and gravy at the
last minute.

Cook the meal by the timer by putting the chicken and potatoes (coated
in fat) in the same position but put the pie in the centre of the oven. Put the
vegetables in a casserole with the seasoning, add a cup of water and seal with
aluminium foil; place them beside the pie. Prepare the tomatoes and put with
stock in a casserole; seal with aluminium foil and place above the pie. Put
onion in milk for bread sauce in fireproof dish and leave in warming drawer

148

to infuse. Set the timers to cook for 1 hour at 400°F. Before serving, add roux to strained soup and leave to boil on the hob while you are making the gravy and finishing the bread sauce.

MENU XIII

steak and kidney pie (see Meat Pie, page 99)
spring cabbage: creamed potatoes (77)
fruit fool (91)

To cook this meal by a timer place the pie on the third runner from the top and the vegetables in casseroles with water and sealed with aluminium foil on the floor of the oven. Set the timer to cook for 45 mins. at 400°F.

Fruit fool is served cold, but it might be convenient to have a hot pudding and cook it in the oven with this meal. I suggest a Canadian Lemon Pudding (make it according to the recipe on page 84, but cover it with greased grease-proof paper). Place in the centre of the oven and cook with the remainder of the meal.

MENU XIV   Lancashire hot pot (58)

cauliflower: Jerusalem artichokes
lemon meringue pie (97)

Place the hot pot on the floor of the oven and cook at 325°F. for 2 hours. Increase the temperature to 400°F. and cook the lemon meringue at the top of the oven. Cook vegetables on the hob.

MENU XV   cream of mushroom soup (43)

roast loin of pork (66)
apple sauce (36):   gravy (34)
roast potatoes (75):   peas (74)
treacle tart (96)

Place pork and potatoes in meat pan on floor of oven and cook at 400°F. for a time to allow 35 mins. to the lb. Put the treacle tart at the top of the oven for the final 45 mins. Cook the soup, vegetables, sauce and gravy on the hob.

To cook this meal by the timer get a piece of pork that will cook in 1½ hours. Place in the meat pan with the potatoes well coated in fat, and put on the floor of the oven. Prepare the mushrooms and put in stock in a casserole sealed with aluminium foil. Place this immediately above the meat with the treacle tart on the same runner. Put the peas in a casserole with half a cup of water and seasoning; seal with aluminium foil. Prepare the apples and place in water in a fireproof dish sealed with aluminium foil. Set the timers to cook for 1½ hours at 400°F.

Sieve the soup, add a roux and bring to the boil while you finish the apple sauce and gravy as you dish up.

Refrigeration

BY ANN SMITH

As TIME marches on and fades away into the hazy past we must look forward and not back as so many people are apt to do. How many times do we hear – what was good enough for my grandfather or grandmother is good enough for me ! The sooner this idea is stamped out the better, particularly when considering the safe keeping of perishable foods.

How can anyone compare the slow tempo of life some 50 years ago with the speed at which we live to-day? Gone is the pony and trap ambling leisurely along the quiet country lanes of Britain. The horse and cart no longer stands at the garden gate with a delivery of coal, milk or the goods from the railway. This comfortable life has disappeared for the sake of speed, the speed of the modern world of to-day, for the motor car and motor lorry, the fast new trains, and aeroplanes which are jet propelled.

NEED FOR PRESERVING FOOD

The need of some means of preserving perishable foods has been foremost in people's minds ever since man inhabited the earth. Throughout the ages man has experimented to invent methods of preserving the quality and freshness of food for human consumption.

In days gone by people did not realise what caused food to spoil, although they understood that illness often resulted from something that had been eaten. With the progress of time they learnt that many perishable foods quickly deteriorated and became uneatable in warm weather. Then came the vague realisation that flies, dust, changes of temperature and dampness also caused food spoilage. This is true, but not the whole story.

Modern science has taught us that the real danger to food lies in the decay caused by bacteria and moulds, a decay completely invisible to the human eye in its first stages. After about 36 hours these moulds sprout grey furry looking whiskers, when these appear we throw away the food as unfit to eat. But what we do not realise is that while the mould is growing, before the grey furry whiskers appear, it is giving off spores and contaminating other foods stored near it.

Flies also cause a great deal of food spoilage through contamination and they have a persistent way of penetrating to the safest of larders. However, to-day we have many modern means of getting rid of vicious looking bluebottles. A much more serious problem is the decay caused by temperatures and dampness, because temperature has such a great effect on the increase rate of bacteria.

Mould is the outward sign of living bacteria. It is a plant which, given moisture and warmth, will grow rapidly, causing decay to food which becomes dangerous to eat.

Many people have the impression that a larder is a very cold place, so it should be, but for perishable foods to be safe they must be kept below 50°F. So often cellars and larders have a damp spot somewhere, which makes them unsuitable for storage of perishable foods as mould thrives on damp and varying temperatures.

Some bacteria are necessary to life itself but there is a type that causes food spoilage and injures health. This type of bacteria is to be avoided in the life of a healthy nation.

TEMPERATURES AND HUMIDITY

On 1st July, 1956, it became law in England that all catering establishments must store their perishable foods either above 145°F. or below 50°F., to safeguard them from rapid decay.

If this is law in the catering world surely it is important to the housewife whose whole aim is to feed the family on a good variety of healthy wholesome food. Once this need is appreciated the housewife will realise that makeshift methods of storage will not help.

Why not be safe and invest in a refrigerator which can take care of all these needs for safe storage? It will help you in your daily work by safeguarding the family's health, save money on food bills and save time and energy; it will also be an aid to producing a variety of new menus. A refrigerator is not designed as a means for producing elaborate cold dishes, but if the housewife has a refrigerator she can practise making the most exotic cold dishes to her heart's content. The object of a refrigerator is to store food at a safe temperature, the everyday food eaten by every family in the country, so ensuring good health. In addition it can help with economy on food bills by eliminating wastage of food, time, energy and endless trips to the shops, which often involve transport costs; not to mention getting wet on rainy days.

THE USE OF A REFRIGERATOR

A refrigerator is a dry, cold and sealed cabinet designed for use in the winter months as well as the summer, which enables the busy housewife to buy her fresh produce once a week, very often when prices are favourable, and store it safely at a temperature below 50°F., so eliminating the risk of rapid food decay.

Some people are under the impression that a refrigerator is of no use in the winter months. Kitchen temperatures are often as high in the winter, when the house is heated, as in the summer, and the weather in winter months is often very very damp.

Quick-frozen foods are rapidly becoming popular and are ever increasing in variety and quantity. And so, every modern refrigerator keeps up with the times and allows ample storage space for these commodities in the Freezer Compartment, which, not so long ago had room only for the ice cube tray !

A refrigerator is easy and safe to use. Every type of perishable food can be stored in it, not only just the fats and milk which up to very recently seemed to be the popular idea, but also the meat, vegetables, fruit, made-up sweet dishes as well as savoury ones, the potted paste or the home-made paté, cheese, bacon, a week's supply of raw pastry, and those 'left-overs' which, with the aid of a refrigerator, can be served up under a new name.

HOW TO CHOOSE A REFRIGERATOR

It is essential to choose a refrigerator of ample size to suit the family's needs. Nothing is more annoying than to find that the model chosen is too small almost right away. The motto is—Be Brave !—and choose the largest model that money will stretch to, an act which will never be regretted. The refrigerator can be put to so many uses to aid the busy housewives.

A refrigerator will bring speed, economy, cleanliness, health and energy into everyone's lives. Refrigeration is a 'must' in the life of to-day.

Provided there is floor space a refrigerator can be placed anywhere that is convenient. Usually there is ample room in the kitchen but so many people do not seem to realise how little space a modern refrigerator requires. Why not put it in an airy cupboard or larder, under the stairs, or in the dining room ? Even 'to a bed-sitting room' dweller a refrigerator will prove a boon.

An electric refrigerator does not affect the atmosphere, so dry goods stored near it are perfectly safe. It is not affected by draughts, and does not spoil the radio or television programme.

When choosing a site for a refrigerator ensure sufficient space round it to allow for the free movement of air and a point somewhere handy for plugging into.

A refrigerator can be built in to a modern kitchen assembly or stand under a draining board. It can match the colour scheme of the kitchen by bringing gaiety and freshness into the home. And there are models made to open either to the left or to the right.

HOW TO USE A REFRIGERATOR

When the refrigerator has been delivered and connected, the first thing to do is to give the interior a good wash. This is best done with warm water which has a little bicarbonate of soda dissolved in it. Whilst cleaning the interior the shelves should be removed and cleaned, not forgetting the ice cube trays, the freezer compartment and all the shelves and compartments on the inside of the door.

The exterior of the cabinet must also be cleaned. It can be washed with warm soapy water and polished with a soft dry cloth or cleaned with special polishing materials available for the purpose.

The refrigerator is then ready for use. The COLD CONTROL DIAL must be turned to the setting recommended by the manufacturer for normal daily storage use to maintain a temperature for the safe keeping of perishable foods. This information will be found in the book supplied with the refrigerator. The ice cube tray is filled two-thirds full of cold water and replaced in the freezer compartment. The refrigerator should be left to work for a few hours prior to putting in the first load of fresh food. It will then reach the required safe storage temperature below 50°F.

The doors must be kept closed to ensure an even temperature inside. After taking food out of the cabinet the door must be closed immediately. The less the temperature inside fluctuates the better the food will keep.

The average sized mechanical electric refrigerator uses about 1 unit of electricity a day (24 hours). As the cost of running is so economical so everyone can afford to keep it working for 12 months of the year. The motor is very consistent in operation and keeps the cabinet at a steady temperature throughout the year.

HOW TO USE THE COLD CONTROL

The Cold Control is usually a combined switch and thermostat control. This serves a dual purpose of turning the electricity ' ON ' or ' OFF ' to the refrigerating unit and also for regulating the temperature inside the cabinet. The thermostat controls the temperature constantly at a perfect level for safe food storage.

Usually the Cold Control Dial is marked with an 'off' position, a 'defrost' position and numbers, the highest number giving the coldest temperature. For daily use the dial should be set at a normal setting suitable for everyday purposes. Sometimes, but this is an exception, owing to the varying conditions surrounding the refrigerator this normal setting has to be adjusted as it may prove to be too cold. This is detected by milk freezing and frail vegetables, such as lettuce or watercress, becoming stiff, then the setting must be turned to a warmer one.

Once the setting on the Cold Control Dial is established, it should not be altered except when ice cream is to be made. The dial is then turned on to the coldest setting, but only for the duration of making and storing of the ice cream. Afterwards it must be returned to the normal.

DEFROSTING AND CLEANING THE REFRIGERATOR

While using the refrigerator, moisture from the air, which is let in every time the door is opened, and some of the moisture from the food stored in the refrigerator settles on the coils of the freezer unit (in simple words it settles on the walls of the freezer compartment), in the form of frost. This frost acts as a heat insulator, preventing efficient working results, also wasting electricity.

The inside of the cabinet should be cleaned out once in two or three weeks, but it may have to be defrosted more often than that, a factor which depends mainly on the atmospheric conditions around the refrigerator. Excess moisture in the air is usually caused by too much rain but sometimes it is helped on by the clouds of steam rising from saucepans left to boil too hard.

A refrigerator should be defrosted when the build-up of frost on the walls of the freezer compartment is about $\frac{1}{4}$ in. thick, which is about a pencil thickness.

Provided there is no quick-frozen food stored in the freezing compartment, the dial can be turned to the ' defrost ' setting, and the food may be left in the refrigerator for a few hours or overnight. The door must be shut. The temperature inside the refrigerator will be maintained at about 50°F. which is much colder than the larder or kitchen shelf.

Quick-frozen food should not be allowed to defrost, as once the food has become completely defrosted it should *never* be re-frozen again, so if such foods are being stored the cabinet has to be defrosted quickly.

The quick-frozen food should be taken out of the freezer compartment, wrapped in plenty of newspaper and placed in a cool place. The refrigerator is then switched off and a bowl of warm water is placed inside the freezer compartment. The frost will start melting in a few minutes. A wooden cooking spoon or a spatula can be used to scrape off the frost, but on no account must any *sharp implement be used*. With a clean cloth dipped in hot water, and well wrung out the walls of the freezer compartment must be cleaned, then wiped over with a dry cloth, the current is switched on and the quick-frozen food replaced. The defrosting process should take about 15 minutes in a small refrigerator and 25 minutes in a big one.

Whichever way a refrigerator is defrosted it is important to make sure that the drip tray is under the freezer compartment prior to starting the defrosting. To clean the refrigerator the food and shelves must be taken out and the cabinet given a good wash as described in HOW TO USE A REFRIGERATOR. Never use soap to clean the interior of a refrigerator but a small quantity of scentless detergent may be substituted for the bicarbonate of soda.

If there is no 'defrost' setting on the Cold Control of the refrigerator it has to be defrosted by switching off the electricity, opening the door, taking out all the food and storing it in a cool place. By placing a bowl of warm water in the freezer compartment of refrigerator, the defrosting process can be speeded up. The interior of the cabinet is cleaned in the usual way, the electricity switched on and the food replaced.

WHEN GOING AWAY

When going away for four or five days most foods can be left safely in the refrigerator with the exception of the very perishable foods such as fresh fish, minced steak, poultry, offal, custards, milk puddings, cream and custard fillings for cakes and pies, egg salads and stuffed eggs. As the door of the refrigerator will not be opened and closed during the above mentioned period the temperature inside will not fluctuate and so the Cold Control Dial can be set to a warmer temperature.

When going away for longer periods the refrigerator is emptied and switched off, and it is important to leave the door wide open for ventilation, otherwise, it acquires a 'musty' smell inside.

Should the refrigerator be switched off for longer periods than two or three weeks, or if it has to be moved, it is advisable to contact the manufacturer's local dealer for advice.

STORING FOOD

It is important not to overload the refrigerator as free air circulation round the food is necessary for perfect preservation.

The leading manufacturers of refrigerators supply books with pictures showing the approximate positions where foods can be stored on the shelves, in the interior of the cabinet and on the door. Sometimes there may be a few extras to store such as prepared grapefruit, small moulds and sundae glasses, etc. These can be placed between other items of food provided there is still air circulation.

COVERING FOODS

To cover food in a refrigerator is an asset. It has a two-fold function. Uncovered foods have a tendency to dry out a little and so lose the moisture content of the natural juices, and some of the taste. Moisture extracted from uncovered food adds to the excess build-up of frost on the freezer compartment. Strong tasting food may taint other food in the refrigerator.

There are plenty of good containers available for use in a refrigerator as well as a variety of plastic bags, aluminium foil and waxed paper. Often the use of these saves valuable shelf space.

With the exception of quick-frozen food, containers must not be sealed. A little air must be allowed to penetrate round fresh food to allow it to breath. In the case of the very strong smelling foods such as fish, pineapple, melon, strawberries, etc., the containers must be closed tightly to prevent other foods such as milk, butter, fats, cheese, acquiring their taste. Usually strong foods are not kept longer than 24 hours, but if it is required that they be kept longer than this, they should be taken out once in 24 hours and left to breathe for a couple of minutes. The container is then closed again and replaced in the refrigerator.

HOT FOOD

It is not advisable to put hot food into the refrigerator. It should be cooled to room temperature first, then covered and stored as described. Warm food creates more frost and tends to slow down the cooling process, however, if necessary, it can go into the refrigerator when slightly warm.

Moulds and jellies can be quickly cooled in making to room temperature, by packing ice cubes round them in an outer basin, or ice cubes can be substituted as part of the liquid content and stirred till melted.

ICE CUBES

The temperature inside the freezer compartment is below freezing point and is very much colder than the temperature in the body of the refrigerator so there is no need, unless in a hurry, to alter the setting of the Cold Control Dial to make ice cubes. The trays must only be two-thirds filled with cold water to allow for the expansion of water in the formation of ice.

Ice cubes can be made for gay festive occasions in a variety of ways. Some cubes can be made coloured and some garnished. When using garnish first fill the tray one-third full of cold water and freeze. Then take the tray out and add to each compartment some garnish which can be a glacé cherry, slices of orange or lemon or thin strips of orange or lemon rind, mint leaves, thin slices of cucumber, etc., then add another one-third of cold water and freeze.

Flowers can look very lovely frozen in ice cubes but these cubes can only be used for decorative purposes as many flowers must not be eaten.

Cubes can also be made of tomato juice and a variety of fruit juices.

155

ICE CREAM

Manufactured ice cream should not be kept in a freezer compartment for longer than the day of purchase, unless you have one of the large refrigerators with the specially constructed freezer chest which runs right across the top of the refrigerator.

The secret of good home-made ice cream is to make it as quickly as possible so as not to separate the solid from the liquid content such as often occurs when ice cream is frozen too slowly. This is detected by the formation of large ice crystals on top of the ice cream.

The Cold Control Dial of the refrigerator should be set on the coldest setting for about half an hour before the mixture is put in. When the ice cream is made, the time depending on the mixture and the make of the refrigerator, it is important to return the Cold Control on to the normal setting again. If this is not done the extra cold in the freezer compartment will freeze up other food stored in the refrigerator.

A housewifely tip for making ice cream. Prior to pouring the mixture into the ice cube tray take out the grid for making the cubes, line the tray with a piece of Polythene, large enough to hold the mixture, and freeze.

When the ice cream is ready it is easy to take out and cut, using a fruit knife or wrong side of a tea knife, so as not to cut the Polythene which can then be washed and used again. Similarly, by using this lining, some mixtures of ice cream can be frozen in various shapes and sizes. With the help of bowls, and cartons and a little imagination a variety of fancy shapes can be made, such as a snowman, flower pot, basket, a boat with a wafer sail and even a small house!

Food Preservation by Freezing

Preserving food by freezing is a century-old practice which was used in the far north parts of the world as a natural method of food preservation. To-day, with the aid of scientific research, mechanical refrigeration for preserving perishable food by freezing for long term storage has become possible.

It is important to remember that a FREEZER and a REFRIGERATOR are two very different electrical appliances. No mistake should be made regarding the use of an ordinary household refrigerator and a freezer. The freezer must operate at a temperature of 0°F. and lower. It is therefore much colder than the temperature in the body of a household refrigerator which operates above freezing point at 34°F. to 42°F.

FREEZERS

These can be divided into three groups.

The chest type freezer. Is the most popular. It is more economical on electrical consumption, more practical for storage purposes and need only be defrosted once a year. It is like a large box, usually designed with one tank for freezing and storing pruduce. The smaller models are usually set to work at 0°F. and the larger ones often have a dual temperature control which can be set so that the freezer will operate at about minus 20°F. to minus 30°F. This means that larger quantities can be frozen at a time.

It is important never to overload a freezer with fresh, room temperature, produce at the time of freezing. Too much fresh food will cause defrosting to the already frozen food stored in the cabinet. For the cabinets set to work at one temperature, the rule for quantities of fresh produce to be frozen at one time must not exceed one-tenth of the storage capacity of the cabinet, *i.e.*, if the freezer can store 200 lb. of food, then the load of fresh food must not exceed 20 lb. This load will take approximately 24 hours to freeze, and it is advisable to wait for another 24 hours before freezing another fresh load of food.

The upright freezer. This type of freezer is like a cupboard with shelves. However, it is usually much more expensive than the similar size chest type freezer and is much heavier on electrical consumption. It is a great asset when floor space is limited and it is much easier to pack, though often space is wasted. It has to be defrosted about four times a year. Some people find the upright freezer more convenient to use but not as practical as the chest type. The quantity of fresh produce that can be frozen at a time is the same as for the chest type.

The built-in freezer or small cold room. This type of freezer is mainly designed for the small poultry keeper or market gardener who intends to sell produce.

CHOOSING A FREEZER

Choosing a freezer is very important. So often people choose one much too small for their requirements. The freezer must pay for itself, so it is economy which has to be considered first prior to choosing the size. With a freezer advantage can be taken of favourable market prices to preserve surplus produce in its prime.

Large quantities of poultry, which must be fed at vast expense if there is no market for them, can be stored safely in the freezer. Large quantities of meat and game need not be given away any more, it can be stored in the freezer. The surplus fruit and vegetables from the garden and orchard can be stored in the freezer. Quantities of made up dishes can be stored in the freezer. The more favourable-priced food stored in the freezer the more money is returned when the produce is used and the more money is saved, therefore the quicker the capital outlay on the purchase of the cabinet is returned.

The larger the freezer the cheaper it is per cubic foot of storage space. So the larger the freezer, the quicker will be the money return, not to mention the pleasure derived from using a variety of 'out of season' produce for twelve months of the year. Above all it represents an enormous saving on food bills.

SELECTION OF FOOD FOR FREEZING

The main object of storing food by freezing is to preserve it in its prime condition as freezing retains the natural flavour, colour, texture and nutrient value.

Only the best quality produce in its prime is worth freezing. Poor quality produce such as old tough meat, old poultry and game, over-ripe or bruised fruit and vegetables will not rejuvenate in the process of freezing. Freezing arrests all growth of life by the formation of the moisture content into ice crystals in the food. The food will come out of the freezer in the same state as it went in. So the best results are obtained by careful selection of prime quality produce.

Owing to the very low humidity in a freezer, produce, unless properly packed and sealed in moisture-vapour-proof containers, will lose some of its moisture by dehydration. With the loss of moisture the food will lose its colour, texture and taste.

Those who freeze produce for the first time may try to make do with ordinary greaseproof paper or ice cream cartons. Experiments have proved that it pays to spend a little extra money on the proper containers to avoid spoilage of food which results in financial loss.

It is important never to refreeze produce which has completely thawed out. If the produce has partially thawed out but still contains some ice crystals it can be cooked and refrozen in a cooked state. If only the surface of the produce is defrosted it can be refrozen, but in both cases the food must be used as soon as possible. Prepared dishes must never be refrozen.

HOW TO FREEZE

All food should go into the freezer ready for use. Meat must be butchered to the size joint required, poultry and game must be plucked, drawn and trussed. In the case of game it must be hung prior to freezing and not after. Vegetables and fruit must be cleaned. When two or more chops or steaks are placed in one container two pieces of greaseproof paper must be put between each portion to prevent them freezing together. This enables a quantity to be put into one container and some can easily be taken out without having to defrost the lot. The same applies to jointed poultry and fish.

Vegetables. All vegetables must be prepared ready for use and blanched prior to freezing to arrest the growth of enzymes, that is to protect the colour and texture. The vegetables should be packed in quantities required for the table. Seasoning should not be used although mint can be added to peas. All vegetables are cooked from the frozen state and seasoned during cooking. Lettuce class vegetables do not freeze well. Tomatoes can be frozen in purée form.

Fruit: The choice of fruit is important. It must be firm, ripe, freshly picked and in perfect condition. If necessary fruit should be washed quickly in ice cold water. Sugar must be added to fruit prior to freezing to protect the colour and the texture. It can be added in syrup form or dry.

When using syrup the minimum strength must not be less than a 10 per cent solution and can only be used when cold. Dry sugar must not be used in quantities less than 4 ozs. to the pound of fruit. In both cases the quantity of sugar can be increased according to taste.

When using sugar syrup it is important to leave about $\frac{1}{2}$ in. headroom between the surface of the syrup and the lid to allow for the expansion of ice.

Fruit with a very high content of water such as melons do not freeze well. Lemons can only be frozen as lemon juice. Grapefruit and oranges can be frozen, peeled and skinned, but it is easier to freeze the juice.

Meat. Meat is one of the easier foods to freeze. Freezing does not improve its texture or quality so it is best to select young animals. Unskilled butchering spoils and wastes meat. Those who are not skilled in butchering should get an experienced butcher to cut up the carcase. Joints, steaks, chops, etc., must be packed in moisture-vapour-proof containers and sealed. Particular care should be taken when freezing more than one piece of meat in the same container to separate each portion with two pieces of greaseproof paper.

All meat should be defrosted prior to cooking. After it has completely thawed out it must be used within 24 hours. All meat should be defrosted in its original sealed container. This eliminates any loss of moisture by evaporation and the meat will retain its full flavour and taste.

Offal. Hearts and liver freeze well but should not be kept longer than three months.

Whole Poultry. Birds should be selected when in their prime. Birds must be hung in the normal way after killing, the plucked bird is then drawn and trussed. Should there be any sharp edges where the legs are severed the stumps must be overwrapped with greaseproof paper prior to packing the bird in the moisture-vapour-proof container. This protects them from piercing the container from the inside. Once the container is pierced much of the natural juices of the poultry meat will dehydrate and the cooked bird will be dry and tasteless. Giblets must be overwrapped separately and put by the side of the bird in the same container.

Jointed Poultry. The jointed bird should be packed either on special trays or each piece overwrapped with greaseproof paper and stored in one container. This enables the user to take out any quantity required without having to defrost the lot.

Game. Game must be hung prior to freezing for the usual time and then treated in the same way as poultry.

Fish. It is important to know that the fish is really fresh. No one should freeze fish bought from the local fishmonger as it might have been frozen before for transport purposes.

Fish must be gutted and prepared for cooking prior to freezing. Small fish can be overwrapped with greaseproof paper and several can be placed in one container.

In the case of large fish, such as salmon, it can be cut up into portions, two pieces of greaseproof paper placed between each piece, and the whole fish sealed in one container. Once again, any quantity can be taken out at a time without having to defrost the whole fish.

All fish should be defrosted before cooking.

DEFROSTING FOOD

The same method applies to defrosting Meat, Poultry, Game and Fish.

The best way is to place the frozen food, in its sealed container, to defrost slowly in a household refrigerator, allowing about five hours per pound weight. The quicker produce is frozen and the slower it is thawed out the better is the result.

By leaving the food, still in its sealed container, to thaw out at room temperature. As the temperature of every kitchen varies, the time allowed should be two to three hours per pound weight.

By placing the food, still in its sealed container, in a draught, allowing 45 minutes per pound weight.

Storage time. Meats, poultry, game and fish can be stored from nine months to a year in a freezer operating at O°F., and for longer periods in the low temperature freezers.

Fruit and vegetables from six to nine months in the O°F. and nine months to a year in the lower temperature freezers.

Dairy produce will keep well for six to nine months if stored at O°F. Made up dishes should not be kept for longer than two to three months when stored at O°F.

CLEANING A FREEZER

The chest type freezer need only be cleaned once a year when the stock of frozen produce is at its lowest. The best way to clean it is to take out all the food, over-wrap it with plenty of newspaper or hay, and store it in a cold place. The electricity is switched off and the lid is opened wide. A bucket of warm water can then be placed in the freezer. In about half an hour the water can be changed and the walls of the tank scraped with a wooden cooking spoon or a plastic spatula. On no account must a sharp implement such as a knife or fork be used to clean the freezer. Then with a clean tea cloth wrung out in hot water, the sides of the tank are wiped down, the bits of frost scooped up from the bottom, the tank wiped over with a dry cloth, the electricity switched on and the food replaced.

Cold Food Recipes

ICE CREAM SNOWMAN (*facing page* 160)

½ lb. marshmallows
1 lb. crushed pineapple (fresh or tinned)
½ pint synthetic or real cream
1 oz. sugar
2 teaspoonsful vanilla essence
6 currants, and one small piece of glacé cherry

a small broomlike twig
a paper tricorn hat (aluminium foil makes a nice one)
2 pieces of Polythene paper or a Polythene bag cut in half

Cut the marshmallows into small pieces and cover with crushed pineapple and juice. Cover tightly and store in refrigerator for at least 24 hours.

Whip the cream adding sugar and vanilla essence. Fold whipped cream into the marshmallow and fruit mixture until pieces of marshmallow have nearly disappeared.

Line two small bowls with the Polythene and spoon the mixture in putting one-third into one and two-thirds into the other. Gather up the edges of the Polythene until the mixture forms a ball shape. Tie the ends very firmly, remove the tied up mixture from the bowls and put them in the freezer compartment of the refrigerator.

When making ice cream the Cold Control Dial of the refrigerator must be set on the coldest setting.

When the ice cream is made, take out both portions, unwrap them, join the

REFRIGERATED FOOD: *ham and egg salad, ice cream snowman, prawns at play, fruit flowers in jelly, and charlotte russe*

BASKET OF FLOWERS: *fruit cake decorated with royal icing as a basket filled with marzipan flowers*

head to the body—a couple of cherry sticks help. Using the currants and cherry, give the snowman eyes, nose, mouth, three buttons for his coat, stick in the broom and put his hat on. Now replace the snowman into the freezer compartment, standing him on a small cake stand or plastic plate.

After he has been served it is important to return the Cold Control of the refrigerator to the normal setting.

VANILLA ICE CREAM

6-oz. tin evaporated milk
1½ ozs. sugar
½ oz. cornflour

½ pint fresh milk
1 small teaspoonful vanilla essence (or more if liked)

Chill the evaporated milk in the refrigerator for at least 12 hours.

About 1 hour before starting to make the ice cream in the freezer compartment of the refrigerator, turn the Cold Control on to the coldest setting.

Line an ice cube tray with a piece of plastic or foil paper (such as a plastic bag cut in half or a piece of aluminium foil) and chill in the refrigerator.

Mix sugar and cornflour with a little cold milk. Bring the rest of the milk to the boil and pour it on to the cornflour and sugar stirring well all the time. Transfer to a clean saucepan and bring the mixture to the boil, then allow to simmer for 2 to 3 mins., stirring all the time. Pour into a bowl to cool till quite cold.

Whip the evaporated milk in a mixing bowl, till quite stiff. Add the cold cornflour mixture very slowly and whip it vigorously.

Add vanilla essence and mix it well. Pour the mixture into the lined and chilled ice cube tray, turn up the ends of the lining to cover the surface of the mixture and place in the refrigerator freezer compartment.

The time taken to freeze the mixture will depend upon the type of refrigerator and will vary between 1½ to 3 hours.

When the ice cream is frozen return the Cold Control on to the normal setting or one advised by the manufacturer of the refrigerator for storage of ice cream.

As the ice cream is wrapped it can be taken out of the tray, the ice cube grid replaced and ice cubes made. The ice cream must be left in the freezing compartment until required for use.

CHARLOTTE GLACE

½ lb. fresh or quick-frozen strawberries in dry sugar*
2 tablespoonsful castor sugar
1 pint cream

½ level tablespoonful gelatine
4 tablespoonsful cold water
18 lady fingers

Add sugar to strawberries and mash them well till the sugar has melted. Add gelatine to cold water and dissolve over heat. Whip mashed strawberries and sugar, add the dissolved gelatine in water and whip again. Fold in cream and whip vigorously.

Line a cylindrical mould, cake tin or round waxed carton with a piece of plastic paper or aluminium foil, smooth out the creases, fill with the ice cream mixture and place in the freezer compartment of the refrigerator, set on the coldest setting. Freeze.

* When using quick-frozen strawberries in dry sugar there is no need to add the extra sugar.

To serve, turn the ice cream out on to a plate, unwrap and surround it with lady fingers and decorate the top with a little whipped cream.

PURE RASPBERRY ICE

1 lb. raspberries	1 tablespoonful lemon juice
¼ lb. sugar	pinch of salt
¼ pint hot water	¼ pint double cream

Sieve the raspberries. Cook sugar and water for about 5 mins. till all the sugar is dissolved, add the sieved raspberries, lemon juice and salt and stir well. Allow to cool. Pour the mixture into an ice cube tray and start freezing. When the mixture is fairly thick but not quite frozen take it out and whip it very quickly till it becomes really light. Having washed the ice cube tray, line with a piece of plastic or aluminium foil, pour in the mixture, and finish freezing it.

To serve, whip the cream. Turn out the raspberry ice into a plate and decorate with the whipped cream.

FROZEN APPLE CREAM

½ pint fresh double cream or tinned cream	¼ teaspoonful of cinnamon
2 tablespoonsful sugar	1 pint apple purée

Whip cream until it reaches a custard-like consistency, stir in sugar and cinnamon until it is well mixed. Gently fold in the apple purée.

Take the cube grid out of the ice cube tray, line it with a piece of Polythene and spoon in the mixture. Freeze.

The ice cream must be taken out of the freezer compartment 15 mins. before serving.

MARSHMALLOW CAKE

½ lb. marshmallows	½ cupful chopped red and green glacé cherries
3 tablespoonsful milk	
1 teacupful condensed milk or double cream	3 cups biscuit crumbs (sweet)
	a little grated chocolate
½ cupful chopped walnuts	

Cut marshmallow into small pieces, pour milk over them and let them stand for about an hour.

Add the condensed milk or cream, chopped nuts, glacé cherries and biscuit crumbs, blend thoroughly together.

Roll into the shape of a 'Swiss roll', wrap in a piece of Polythene waxed paper, or aluminium foil, and chill in the refrigerator over night.

To serve, remove the covering and cut into slices and garnish with a little grated chocolate.

CHOCOLATE FRIDGE CAKE

4 ozs. plain chocolate	1 teaspoonful vanilla essence
1 large tin condensed milk	½ lb. sweet biscuits, square or oblong in shape
3 tablespoonsful water	

Melt the chocolate in a double saucepan. When it is all melted stir in condensed milk, keeping it stirred for about 5 mins. until the mixture thickens. Add the water and vanilla essence, and stir again.

Line an oblong cake tin with waxed paper, Polythene or aluminium foil, spoon in carefully a layer of the chocolate mixture, then a layer of biscuits, repeat this until the mixture is used up, ending with a layer of biscuits. Cover over with the lining material and store in the refrigerator.

This dish can either be served chilled or frozen. When served chilled it must be kept in the refrigerator for at least 12 hours and longer if time is available.

For serving turn out carefully on to a plate, remove the covering and decorate according to the seasons, for Christmas, with Christmas decorations. In the summer, small flowers made with glacé cherries and angelica look very pretty.

CHARLOTTE RUSSE (*facing page* 160)

18 lady fingers	1 heaped tablespoonful powdered sugar
½ oz. gelatine	1 to 2 teaspoonsful vanilla essence
2 tablespoonsful cold water	(according to taste)
2 tablespoonsful milk	¾ pint cream

Line a cake tin with lady fingers trimmed at the ends. Pieces of plain cake may be used, these should be cut uniformly and about ½ inch thick.

A charlotte can be made with a variety of fillings using cream and any flavouring required such as vanilla, chocolate, coffee, raspberries, etc.

Soak gelatine in cold water and dissolve over boiling water. To the milk add the sugar and gelatine and mix well, add the vanilla essence. Leave to cool until it begins to thicken. Whip the cream, add the sugar and gelatine mixture and whisk to a stiff froth. Fill the mould lined with lady fingers and put in the refrigerator to set. The charlotte must be really well chilled before serving.

Turn out very carefully and decorate on the top with a little whipped cream and fruit in season, or grated chocolate.

FRUIT FLOWERS IN JELLY (*facing page* 160)

Dissolve 1 pint of lemon jelly and let it cool.

Chill a mould or flat dish about 1½ inches deep. Spoon in a layer of jelly about ¾ inch thick, and let it congeal in the refrigerator. When firm arrange a design of flowers, or any other subject, using fruit or nuts or both. Angelica can be used for flower stems, leaves and grass. Put a couple of drops of jelly on to each piece to hold the design and leave to chill in the refrigerator. This will take about 5 mins.

Gently spoon in another layer of jelly to cover all the design and when this layer is congealed, pour in the rest and let it set.

To serve turn out the jelly and decorate the plate round it with any left-over fruit and nuts.

A light coloured jelly is best to use as it shows up the design, which can be made in several layers.

PRAWNS AT PLAY (*facing page* 160)

½ lb. shelled peas
aspic
½ cucumber

salt
12 large cooked prawns
parsley

Cook the peas very lightly, drain and cool. Then set them in aspic in a ring mould.

Slice the cucumber, sprinkle on some salt and chill in the refrigerator for at least 1 hour.

To serve. Drain the excess water off the cucumber and arrange the slices round the dish. Turn out the aspic in the centre of the dish. Put 2 prawns to dance in the middle of the ring mould and the other 10 dancing in a ring outside the mould.

Garnish with small sprigs of parsley.

HAM AND EGG SALAD (*facing page* 160)

5 hard-boiled eggs
5 medium-sized, firm tomatoes
1 lettuce
1 medium-sized, cooked beetroot
4 slices cooked ham

½ tin mandarin oranges (about 20 pieces)
½ cucumber
12 radishes
a little cream cheese

Shell the eggs and trim the tops and bottoms so that they stand firmly. Cut about a quarter off each tomato and scoop out the inside, leave them to drain.

Shred the lettuce very finely. Chop up the beetroot into tiny pieces, and slice the cucumber leaving the skin on.

Put a layer of cucumber round the dish then line the dish with the shredded lettuce, place one egg in the centre and the other four in each corner, put the tomato hats on. Roll each slice of ham and arrange between the eggs.

Decorate the dish with four little heaps of chopped beetroot on the lettuce, the radishes cut as flowers, the mandarin slices, and slices of egg on the cucumber, and put little spots of cream cheese on the tomato hats.

Store in the refrigerator until required for the table.

STEAK RISSOLES WITH PRUNES AND TOMATOES

2 ozs. stale white bread
1 lb. minced fresh steak
1 teaspoonful grated onion
pepper and salt
1 egg
brown breadcrumbs

5 fairly large tomatoes (not too ripe)
10 stewed prunes
1 lb. potato salad
a little parsley
1 cucumber

Cut crusts off bread and soak it in a little cold water. Mix the minced steak and onion with the bread squeezed free of water. Season well and bind with the egg.

Roll out 10 rissoles on a board well covered with brown breadcrumbs and fry them or bake them in the oven at about 375°F. for 25 to 30 mins. Cool and chill in the refrigerator.

Cut the tomatoes in half and scoop out the centres. Make a slit in the prunes and remove the stones.

164

To serve line a dish with potato salad, cut each rissole to about half-way down and put the prune in. Place the half tomatoes on the dish and stand a rissole in each one. Sprinkle a little chopped parsley over each prune and serve with a well-chilled cucumber salad.

SAVOURY RICE WITH CABBAGE

1 pint tomato juice
pepper and salt
1 teaspoonful sugar
a little grated lemon rind
1 clove garlic
2 rashers lean bacon
½ lb. onion

½ lb. mushrooms
¼ lb. tomatoes
pinch mixed herbs
1 oz. raisins or sultanas
nutmeg
2 cupfuls rice (slightly undercooked)
1 small firm cabbage

Season well the tomato juice with pepper, salt, sugar, grated lemon rind, and the crushed clove of garlic, and let it stand for a short while.

Cut up the bacon into thin strips and cook gently, then add the onion very finely chopped and cook till it is lightly browned, add chopped mushrooms, peeled tomatoes, herbs, raisins or sultanas, nutmeg, seasoning and cook slowly for about a couple of minutes stirring well. Mix with the rice.

Shred the cabbage thinly as for a salad. Into a deep casserole type of dish put a layer of cabbage, then a layer of rice mixture, and so on until filling the dish three-quarters full. Pour over the seasoned tomato juice and cover the dish.

Cook in a very low oven for about two hours. Then cool and put it in the refrigerator to chill.

SWEET BAVARIAN RICE PUDDING

1½ pints milk
a little lemon rind
½ cup rice
pinch of salt
1 teaspoonful vanilla essence

½ cup sugar
1 oz. gelatine
½ cup cold water (⅛ pint)
1 cup double cream (¼ pint)
1 lb. strawberries

Put the milk and a few thin strips of lemon rind into a double saucepan. When hot stir in the well washed rice and salt. Cook until the rice is quite tender. The milk should be nearly absorbed leaving the rice very moist. Add to the hot cooked rice vanilla essence, sugar and gelatine soaked in cold water, and mix very carefully. When the mixture is beginning to set, fold in the cream whipped stiff. Pour into a mould and chill in a refrigerator. Serve with sweetened sliced strawberries.

This dish looks very pretty when the rice is set in a ring mould and the sliced berries are arranged over it for serving.

PINK CONSOMME

2 lbs. tomatoes
1 lb. minced fresh steak
3 pints meat stock or water
2 egg whites

1 small onion
1 small clove of garlic
2 bay leaves
pepper and salt

Skin the tomatoes, put all the ingredients into a saucepan, bring to the boil and simmer gently for about 1 hour. Strain through a thin muslin, cool and chill in a refrigerator.

Prior to serving skim off any fats settled on the top. The consommé can be served garnished with a little chopped parsley, or spring onion, or plain.

The cooked meat and tomato can be stored in the refrigerator and used as a sauce with spaghetti or mixed with a little cooked rice as a stuffing for marrow or green peppers.

COLD SHRIMP SOUP

Fish stock:

½ lb. white fish	3 tablespoonsful white breadcrumbs
1 small onion	1 pint cooked shrimps or prawns
herbs	juice of ½ lemon
lemon peel	pinch nutmeg
pepper and salt	1 egg yolk
1½ pints water	¼ pint milk or cream

Prepare the fish stock by simmering the fish and shrimp or prawn shells, onion, herbs, lemon peel, salt and pepper in 1½ pints of water for about 20 mins. Strain through a thin muslin and add the white breadcrumbs. Pound or mince up the shrimps or prawns, add the lemon juice and nutmeg, and gradually add the fish stock with breadcrumbs stirring well until the mixture is creamy. Heat it up in a saucepan for about 5 mins., and strain it.

Whip up together the yolk of egg with the cream or milk, stir in 2 or 3 tablespoonsful of hot soup then mix it all into the remaining soup in the saucepan, stirring well all the time until the soup is hot but *not* boiling.

Cool it and chill in a refrigerator.

When serving the soup must be really cold and garnished with some chopped cucumber, watercress and slices of lemon.

Wine

BY AMBROSE HEATH

IN THE last 25 years or so the attitude of British people towards wine has undergone a very considerable change. The period between the two world wars saw a gradual resuscitation of interest in good food and drink, but it was confined to a comparatively small proportion of the general public. Since the last war, however, a far wider interest has been aroused, in particular so far as the relationship between food and wine is concerned.

There are two main reasons for this, I think. The first is the larger knowledge of wine-drinking that has been fostered by the much increased facilities for foreign travel. Many people who normally would never have strayed beyond our own shores have ventured much farther afield, and with a taste for new foods has grown up a taste for wine. The second reason is that once having enjoyed a bottle while they were abroad the foreign traveller feels that this enjoyment could well be repeated at home. It has rightly been said that in no country but Britain can you buy such a large and varied range of foreign wines, and it is the ability to do this which has still further added to the public interest in them and the desire to drink them at a comparatively modest cost.

The presence of this considerable variety of wines in the merchants' shops has helped to alter the attitude of the man in the street toward wine-drinking which, I am glad to say, has for this reason now been shorn of much of the rather fake mysticism that made many ordinary people shy of embarking on what seemed to them so costly and erudite a subject.

A quarter of a century ago the wine-drinker (and I speak here of the man of good living) was able to indulge his tastes at a considerably lower price than today. He dined in an aura of *crus* and vintages, and his dishes were nicely attuned to the particular wine he was enjoying. I am not saying that this is not so nowadays, but the people fortunate enough to do it have shrunk to the barest minimum. In those days much stress was laid upon vintages and the older wines. The times were leisurely and domestic labour was cheap; you could linger and enjoy. Today the whole tempo of life has changed. There is no time to delay over meals, and no inclination to do so; and for economic reasons the vintage bottle is getting scarcer and scarcer and more and more expensive.

I do not say that this is a bad thing in its way. Each generation must live the kind of life that the present thrusts upon it, and eating and drinking habits must follow suit and adapt themselves to the standards of the times. One of the results of the change in our habits has been a wider dissemination of wine. More people are drinking it, and the wines they drink are young wines, freed from the shackles of the cult of the vintage and, as I have said, easily obtainable from nearly all the wine-growing countries of the world. It is more important than ever, therefore, that a little guidance should be available for those to whom this pleasant habit seems so far a mystery, though indeed it is, actually, far from that.

WINE AND FOOD

In writing about wine in a cookery book, it is obvious that one should be thinking about the relationship between wine and food, for in the main it is as a partner to the meal that wine should be considered. Sherry as an apéritif and port, sherry or Madeira with the dessert are simple matters with which the novice can easily deal. Here the taste lies in the wine itself, and not in the relationship which a glass of wine with a dish of food implies.

I would like to say this at once, however. Many people seem to have the idea that in order to drink wine with a meal you have to eat some sort of unusual and possibly elaborate dish often described vaguely as French cooking. Nothing is further from the truth. Naturally certain wines will appear to better advantage when drunk with a dish that specially suits them, but for the fresh young wines that are coming more and more to our tables, any of our familiar native dishes can very happily be eaten, and there is nothing to stop anyone from drinking a claret with a pork chop, a Burgundy with roast beef or even a white wine with a dish of tripe. This is done and enjoyed abroad every day. And when I say claret or Burgundy, I am not insisting on French wines in particular, but include all those similar table wines from other countries of which I shall speak later.

There are, nevertheless, certain types of wine that are better with certain types of dishes than others, and there is general agreement on this, so that in most books on the subject you will find a comparative list of much the same sort as the following:

With the *Hors d'Oeuvre:* a dry white wine.

With *Oysters:* Chablis or Muscadet are particularly suitable.

With *Soups:* Sherry or Madeira.

With *Fish and Shellfish:* white wine, usually dry, though the richer the fish, the sweeter the wine can be. With fish like cold trout for example a pink wine (*vin rosé*) is always pleasing.

With *Poultry and White Meat:* generally a claret and sometimes a white Burgundy.

With *Red Meat and Game:* a red wine from a claret to a rich Burgundy, depending on the richness of the meat to be eaten with it.

With *Sweets and Dessert:* a sweet white wine of a Sauternes type, a rich Hock or a special sweet wine of other countries than France such as the Portuguese Moscatel de Setubal and the better-known Hungarian Tokay Aszu.

I have said nothing about Champagne, for this is a wine which can be drunk with almost anything with the exception of red meat and game, dry in the earlier courses of the meal, sweeter as the meal progresses, but a sweet champagne such as is drunk in France is uncommon here (though it can be got) and I do not think it appeals a great deal to the British palate, which is very dry for this kind of wine.

I have also omitted to mention cheese, because lately the relationship between cheese and wine has been much insisted upon in connection with the advertisement of English cheeses, and as cheese and wine parties have been enjoying some popularity, the following special notes may be useful for those who are thinking of having one.

In general, more or less any wine will go with cheese, but a mild or medium mild cheese will like a dry white wine, the fuller cheeses call for something more vigorous. Here, at any rate, are some recommendations for wines to drink with English cheeses, and from this list comparisons can easily be made with foreign cheeses that correspond to them in strength:

With English Cheeses.

Caerphilly: medium dry white wine, hock, dry sherry.

Cheddar : light claret, tawny port.

Cheshire : with red and white, light claret : with blue, tawny port or Oloroso sherry.

Double Gloucester: full claret, red Burgundy.

Lancashire: light dry red wine, medium dry sherry or ruby port.

Leicestershire: claret or Madeira.

Stilton: with white, ruby port; with blue, red Burgundy, tawny or vintage port.

Wensleydale (white and blue): as Stilton.

Wine Parties or wine tastings in general are subject to the same basic rules as meals; that is to say, the snacks or sandwiches served as the solid accompaniment follow the same rule according to their filling or main ingredient—dry white wine with fish, red wine with meat and cheese, etc.

The precise kind of wine that you are going to drink depends upon a number of factors—first, what wine, if any, has gone before it or will follow it (for this a general rule is white wine before red, lighter wine before heavier, young wine before old). Second, the kind of dish, whether rich or light, that is to accompany it (the plainer the dish, the younger the wine). Third, any personal predilections (you may have spent your last holiday in Italy, for example, and Italian wines are possibly your present favourites). Fourth, any particular reason you may have for choosing a certain wine (you may pride yourself on a certain national dish, in which case it would be reasonable to choose from the wines of the country of its origin). The factor of cost also arises. You do not want to throw away a fine wine on a dish that is beneath its merit, nor spoil a delicate dish by drowning it in a commonplace wine. Nor do you want to waste a fine wine on guests who cannot appreciate it. All these considerations have to be met in making your choice, and the ability to do this will only come to you from your own experience and from the taste in wine which is yours personally and only this experience can give.

CHOOSING WINE

There is no use blinking at the fact that drinking wine with one's meals is a luxury, but it need only be a small one; there are comparatively few of us ordinary people who can afford to drink wine with every meal we have. On the other hand, there are a very great many who enjoy entertaining their family and friends, and it is here that wine will give just that additional touch of luxury that puts the hall-mark on the simplest meal. So in this section I shall say nothing about years and nothing about the numbers or the x's with which the pundits are so ready to label the more expensive wines: I shall merely take as a mean average wines of different sorts and different nationalities and of different prices in a range bounded by half a guinea, which is as much as most of us are prepared to pay nowadays for an ordinary table wine. There are, of course, a few (and very excellent ones of their kind) for as little as seven shillings or so, and at the other end of the scale there are the really fine wines for those who understand them, wines which may rise as high as three pounds or so for a bottle of claret. To be able to appreciate wines like this takes a lifetime of experience, and this experience can only be gained by starting at the bottom, that is to say, with these young and inexpensive wines that are so easily accessible to-day.

But before I give some instances of the enormous range of cheap and good wines that are obtainable in this country, there is just one hint that I should like to give. Young people who have a natural inclination towards wine but no guidance on the subject have sometimes asked me how thay can begin to shape their opinion and taste. For at first sight the understanding of wine seems to be a very bewildering subject. My advice is quite simple. The human palate is naturally sweeter than dry, so start with a medium sweet white wine, preferably a French one, such as a Graves, as this will give you something with a well-known name to compare with, and proceed after this to other white wines of other countries and after this to the red wines, which very few young people who are not born in a wine-producing country will like at all without this preliminary experimentation. You will then, in time, be able to build up a kind of tasting chart of your own, and by using the comparison with the wine that you first started from, will be able to find your way about in the maze of the many wines at your command.

I thought it necessary to write this last paragraph because in choosing wine you can only rely on what you know from experience already or on comparison, because even if you ask the wine merchant to help you, as you certainly do, and he as certainly will, you can only tell him by such a comparison what it is that you like. But once you have done that and he has an idea of your taste, he can advise you and be able to say with some certainty whether such-and-such a wine would appeal to you.

And having set down these premises, let us glance at the various wines which are now obtainable in this country, none of these more than half a guinea a bottle.

The cheapest wines from France that you can buy to-day are the red wines from Bordeaux or, as we prefer to call them, the clarets. Looking at one well-known wine list alone, I find no less than fifteen different clarets up to the maximum price of half a guinea a bottle, the cheapest being what is designated as *vin ordinaire rouge*. This quite drinkable sort of wine is popular for wine parties and is a signpost in the drinking of wine in this country, since a number of merchants supply it not only in large (litre) bottles, but also in casks or glass jars. A word of warning may be whispered here, however. I have found that most of these young wines, when once opened, are not suitable for keeping beyond, say, two days.

White Bordeaux *ordinaire blanc* is supplied in the same way, and after the clarets, these white wines which have a fairly wide range from dry to sweet are the next cheapest. Normally the sweeter they are the more expensive they become, but it is still possible to get a *Sainte-Croix-du-Mont* or a *Barsac* within my limit. Of the medium-dry wines, which indeed might be a good one to start experimenting with as suggested above, is *Entre-deux-Mers*.

Red Burgundies offer a much smaller selection, and the white even smaller still. Of the red Macon, Beaune or Beaujolais, and if a named sort of the last happens to be a *Morgon*, *Fleurie* or *Juliénas*, we shall be in better luck. Of the white there is a *Bourgogne aligoté* within our range, as well as *Pouilly Fuissé* and an extremely pleasant *Petit Chablis*.

But by no means all French wines come from Burgundy or Bordeaux. I suppose one of the best-known French wines is the *Châteauneuf-du-Pape*, which comes from the valley of the Rhône, as well as another red wine *Hermitage*, which is also found as a white, and these all come in our range, though the first is only just inside.

After those of the Rhône the wines of the Loire have gained a good deal of popularity of recent years. These are mostly white, and might be compared roughly with white Burgundies. The drier kinds are *Muscadet*, *Vouvray*, dry *Saumur*, the fresh and delicious *Pouilly-sur-Loire* and *Pouilly Fumé* (not to be confused with *Pouilly Fuissé* from Burgundy), and the sweeter but very attractive *Côteaux du Layon*. A red Loire wine which many think has a flavour reminiscent of raspberries, is *Bourgeuil*, and there is a deepish pink wine from *Chinon*.

We are still in France, and moving southwards there are three wines worth looking for. These are *Château Minuty* (white, red and *rosé*), *Pélure d'Oignon* so called from its likeness in colour to the red skin of an onion, and the famous *Cassis* from near Marseilles. This last is a red, white or *rosé* wine and must not be confused with the liqueur Cassis that is made from blackcurrants. The last of the French wines in this category come from the Dordogne— the dry white *Château de Panisseau* and the much sweeter golden *Monbazillac* which would appeal to those who like a sweet light wine with their dessert.

Many of the names of wines that I have mentioned above will be familiar to those who have visited France, and though they will be glad to know that they can be obtained in this country, it will be as well to remember that wines tasted in the glamour and excitement of holiday-making may not seem quite the same under British skies. But apart from anything else, they will have their nostalgic value, and will of course fit in with the general scheme of wine self-education.

The best known of other wines than French are perhaps those of the Rhine and Moselle and of Alsace. The first, the Hocks, will all be found very young at our price, and this is perhaps unfair to wines that have such a wide and marvellous range of flavours, but *Niersteiner*, *Oppenheimer* and *Rüdesheimer* will be represented. Moselles are comparatively dear, too, but we shall find a *Moselblümchen*, a pleasant and unassuming wine, *Berncasteler* and an *Erdener* within our reach. Of the wines of Alsace, which gained a great deal of popularity during the war when Hocks and Moselles were difficult to obtain, you could start with the drier *Gentil* and the less dry *Sylvaner*, and proceed upwards, though you will thence probably be more attracted to the Moselles which these wines resemble.

Italy is the next country to demand our attention. *Chianti* of course is the popular name here to conjure with, but some will find other Italian wines just as and sometimes even more attractive: the cheap red and white Tuscan wines, the deliciously smooth *Soave*, a not quite so dry *Orvietano* and the pale gold *Orvieto seco*, if you want it with fish or white meat, *abbocato* if you want the sweeter kind. The strong red wines, *Barolo*, *Barbareso* and *Barbera* are often to be found in merchants' wine lists, and I strongly recommend you to look out for a much lighter and more delicious red wine, *Valpolicella*. Lastly, there are two wines from Sicily that I advise you to try, the white and the red *Corvo di Casteldaccio*, which are as good as any of the wines that come from the mainland itself.

The other European wines can only have a brief mention here. Portugal known to most of us by the sweet heavy wine that bears its name produces some excellent table wines of very modest price. Ask especially for *Campo Grande* and *Vila Real*, both of which are found red and white, and for the red and flowery *Periquita*, which should have a very wide appeal. Spanish wines, red or white, dry or sweet, are possibly better known than these, but I do not think myself that they possess the same qualities. Swiss wines have been coming into the market for some time lately, and these too will have a nostalgic as well as an intrinsic value to many. Among those to choose from are the white *Fendants* from the Valais and from Neuchâtel and the red *Dôle de Sion* which has an interesting flavour from the mountain vineyards. Hungary, too, is beginning to export more wines to us, and of those that I have recently tasted I should like to select a very dry *Mori Ezerjo*, a medium *Balatoni Furmint* and a sweeter *Balatoni Riesling* from the white, and the red and strangely named *Egri Bikaner*, which means bull's blood, of Eger, a light red-coloured wine with a highly individual flavour, which I think ought to be more popular in this country. There are also wines from Yugoslavia to be bought, *Riesling*, *Sylvaner* and *Sauvignon* white and a red wine *Prokupac*, while from far overseas Chile is sending us some remarkable wines, to quote three of them, a dry white *Steinwein*, a sweet *Sauvignon* and a robust and flavoursome red *Cabernet* which is most impressive.

If I have not mentioned before now the excellent wines that come to us from the Dominions it is because Australian and South African wines have been well known to us for many decades, and have mostly been described by the generic name of the European wines they most readily resemble, such as Burgundy, Hock, Sauternes, and so on and therefore need no further elucidation.

This is a considerable and (to some) surprising list of inexpensive table wines to choose from ! And the choice may be made more interesting by following not only the general rules of what to drink with what but also by exploring the byways in which one learns to suit a particular wine to a particular dish. It is here that one's ability to buy such a large variety of wines is of such assistance, for in these days when international cookery books are the vogue and the most unlikely tables are often ready to sport a dish first tasted on a holiday abroad, it is not only amusing but instructive to serve with it an appropriate wine from the same country. These are the kind of extra pleasures that even a small knowledge of wine can bring, knowledge which is by no means beyond the reach of those for whom intelligent wine-drinking is one of the major pleasures.

BUYING AND STORING WINE

Both these subjects can be dismissed quite quickly. The best way of buying wine, once you have more or less decided what you want, is to go to a good wine merchant. He is your friend, and will sell you only good wine; he is your mentor and will advise you if you ask him. A little individual knowledge can be gained in the recognition of the names of good shippers, of the names of Châteaux and in various other ways which can only be learned by experience. But the wine merchant wants to sell his wine as much as, if not more than, you want to buy it, and it is all to his advantage to see that you are well pleased.

As for storing, the days when people happily laid down bottles by the dozen are long since past. Most of us nowadays live, as far as wine is concerned (and often other things, too), from hand to mouth, and all that we are generally able to keep on hand, owing to lack of space and finances, is a few bottles of the wine we usually drink and perhaps a few bottles of better kinds for special entertaining. And, of course, accommodation for wine cellars is practically non-existent, under modern conditions, for the average family.

The main things to remember are that wine must be stored in the dark, in an even temperature round about 55 degrees Fahrenheit, and the bottles must lie on their side, slightly tilted down towards the cork, which must always be awash in the wine. (Spirits, by the way, should always be kept standing upright.) Many firms will supply a bottle-rack to accommodate small numbers of bottles, and a cupboard to suit the conditions outlined above can usually be found. One under the stairs is often as good as any, and the racks can be supplied specially to fit into these. But beware lest the hot-water pipe runs through the cupboard or the wall bounding it. Temperature, darkness and proper storage provision are the three essentials, and if you are thinking of storing fine old wines, they should not be kept in a place which is subject to vibration.

SERVING WINE

A great deal could be written on this subject, but the majority of my remarks would apply to the service of very fine wines, the question of de-canting and the theories of special glasses to be used for special purposes. As the wines with which we have to deal in the first instance are young ones, the need for decanting does not really arise, although if you do happen to possess a decanter the wine will look much better in it and show off its colour and brillance more than if it were in the bottle, and this applies to white wines as well as red.

The question of glasses is, however, of some importance, although there can be times when wine drunk out of a tumbler is better than no wine at all ! The best sort of glass to use for general purposes is what is known as a Bur-gundy glass, a large round glass with a stem, the bowl slightly curved in-wards at the rim. The purpose of this curve is to enable you to smell the wine while you are drinking it, for the senses of both taste and smell play their part in the enjoyment of all wine. When you pour out the first glasses, do not fill them more than two-thirds full, so that the olfactory sense can come at once into play. At refilling, a more copious pouring can be made, if wished. Do not use warm glasses with white wine, which should be served cold, or ice-cold glasses with a room-warm red wine. The glasses should be scrupulously clean and bright, and no cloth smelling of the kitchen or of scented detergents should be used in drying or polishing them. Nor should a hand recently washed in strong-smelling soap be allowed in the proximity of wine, least of all in touching a wine-glass at the rim (which is unforgivable in any case). The glass should always be held by the stem, unless one wishes to impart the hand's warmth to a red wine that needs a little fondling.

In serving wines care should be taken to present them at the right temperature. There are two simple rules here: white wines should always be cold, red wines nearly always at the temperature of the room in which they are to be drunk, though there are exceptions. These two rules are more important the finer the wines are, but for the purpose of the young wines that we have been considering, they can be departed from.

With regard to white wines, the sweeter the wine the colder it must be drunk, but it should never be below 45 degrees Fahrenheit, for violent cold will ruin its bouquet (which is the wine-lover's name for smell). Nowadays, the refrigerator is often used for chilling wines, and this is an excellent idea, provided you know how long a wine can remain within it. There is a tendency to ice Champagne too much; it is a great mistake, for this wine quickly loses its quality if it is too cold and, to my mind, it should not be chilled more than a dry white wine and sometimes, if it comes from a coldish cellar, not chilled at all.

Red wines, it is usually recommended, should be drunk at the room-temperature, that is to say, they should be *chambré*, as the French put it. This means that the bottle should be brought into the dining-room several hours before serving, perhaps all day if for dinner or overnight if for luncheon, and left there so as to assume the heat of the room. It is essential that the rise in temperature should be slow. Any sudden shock such as putting the bottle into hot water or wrapping it in a hot towel or even standing it (as some foolishly do) before a fire spells ruin to any wine. Clarets are always drunk thus room-warmed, but red Burgundies need rather less warming, and many say that they are best when served at cellar temperature. These are matters, again, for experience and personal taste.

I ought to add, though such a counsel would really seem unnecessary, that ice should never be put *into wine* (except in the case of certain cups, etc.).

By the way, port, rich sweet sherry and Madeira should also be drunk at room-temperature; a medium sherry can be drunk at cellar-temperature, while a really dry sherry or Madeira, drunk as an apéritif before the meal, should be served as cold as possible.

There is a third way, after glasses and temperature, in which red wines can be made to reach our palates at their best, especially if they are young ones, and that is by allowing them to 'breathe' before they are drunk. This is done by taking out the cork from the *chambré* bottle or the stopper from the decanter, and leaving it out for a specified time. This breathing gives the wine time to expand its flavours and attain a certain softness. You can easily find this out for yourself by treating a bottle of a moderate claret in this way, and comparing it with one which you have just brought from your cellar or from the wine merchants. There is a whole world of difference. The length of time for which this breathing should be allowed cannot be set down precisely. Some young wines can be improved by as much as six hours of it; I find on the average that a couple of hours will do. Heavy wines will stand more breathing than light ones: fine old wines require very little indeed, the older, the less. White wines can sometimes be allowed to breathe, too, for example, the heavier ones like Hock or Sauternes, but a quarter of an hour will do for this, and it must be done in a cool place though not in the refrigerator. Even some of the cheap dry white wines will sometimes benefit by breathing for half an hour. In some foreign wines there is a slightly sulphurous smell when the bottle is first opened, and this may be dispelled in this way before the wine is actually poured into the glasses.

Although it has taken all this to explain it, the question of the ordinary service of wine is not as complicated as it might appear. As I have said in the case of some of the cheaper wines these precautions are sometimes unnecessary, but you will find out for yourself that they are usually worth while and that the most modest of wines when properly and considerately treated, will occasionally provide you in its way with as much pleasure as something a good deal grander and more expensive.

Mixed Wine Drinks

I mentioned above that the exceptions in which ice could be put *into* wine could be found in those very pleasant mixed wine drinks so popular in summer-time at parties and other functions, which are known as cups, punches and so on. There are many hundreds of these, and many books which contain recipes for them, but I have been asked to add a few here, just to whet your interest, as it were, and here they are:

But first let me give you two very simple *hot drinks* of this kind, one made with red wine and the other with white, as well as one with port.

The first is **Mulled Wine** or **Vin Chaud.** Any red table wine can be used for this, and it is simply made. Pour a bottle of the wine into an absolutely clean saucepan, preferably of enamelled ware, and add a small piece of cinnamon stick, a single clove, a piece of lemon peel and enough sugar to sweeten it to your taste. Heat it up slowly, *being careful not to let it boil,* and just before boiling-point is reached draw the pan off the fire and strain the wine into heated glasses. Garnish each with a round of lemon.

Punch Marquise is made with Sauternes. Put a pint and three-quarters of it into a pan with seven ounces of sugar, a piece of lemon peel and two cloves. Heat it up until a white froth forms on the top of the wine, then take the pan from the fire, throw in a liqueurglassful of warmed brandy, and set it alight. When the flames have died down, remove the lemon peel and cloves, and serve the wine in glasses with rounds of lemon.

Of the drink called **Bishop**, Professor Saintsbury, who was a great wine connoisseur, wrote as follows:

'You take a bottle of that noble liquor (port) and put it in a saucepan, adding as much or as little water as you can reconcile to your taste and conscience, an orange cut in half (I believe some people squeeze it lightly) and plenty of cloves (you may stick them in the orange if you have a mind). Sugar or no sugar at discretion and with regard to the character of the wine. Put it on the fire, and as soon as it is warm and begins to steam, light it. The flames will be of an imposingly infernal colour, quite different from the light-blue flicker of spirits or of claret mulled. Before it has burned too long, pour it into a bowl, and drink it as hot as you like.'

Cold mixed wine drinks, of which the most popular are cups, have evolved from the very simplest mixtures:

Claret Lemonade (a pint of claret, six ounces of sugar, the juice of four lemons and a pint and a half of soda water).

Sherry and Lemon (a glass of medium sherry in a bottle of lemonade).

Port and Lemon (port similarly treated).

Black Velvet (half Guinness and half Champagne).

Rajah's Peg (a large glass of Champagne and a liqueurglassful of brandy), and as they evolved, so they became more elaborate.

Here are simple examples of cups made with Champagne, Claret, Hock, Moselle, Sauternes and Sherry.

Champagne Cup. One bottle of Champagne; one liqueurglassful of brandy; one liqueurglassful of Curaçao; a siphon of soda water, well iced. Decorate with different sorts of fruit and garnish with a sprig of fresh mint or borage.

Claret Cup. Stone and crush up a pint of black cherries and add the juice of three lemons and of one orange, and a breakfastcupful of castor sugar. Leave to stand for five or six hours, then strain and add a pint of claret and a quart of soda water.

Hock Cup. Mix a couple of liqueurglassfuls of Maraschino or Kirsch with one of Curaçao, sweeten with a dessertspoonful of sugar and fill up with a bottle of Hock. Decorate with slices of orange, add a small piece of cucumber peel and if you like, float a few mint leaves on top.

Moselle Cup. One bottle Moselle; one liqueurglassful of brandy; four or five thin slices of pineapple and the very thinly-cut peel of half a lemon. Sweeten and ice to taste, and lastly, add a bottle of soda water.

Sauternes Cup. See Hock Cup above, substituting Sauternes.

Sherry Cup. One bottle sherry; two bottles soda water; two bottles lemonade and liqueurglassful of Curaçao. Pour this into a wineglass and then fill it up with brandy. Ice well.

Lastly, an amusing **Peach Cup.** Prick a large, ripe, skinned peach all over with a silver fork, and put it into a pint of Champagne, or have ready a small peach prepared in the same way for each person, put each into a large goblet and fill up with iced Hock or Moselle.

*Two or three shades of lilac and pink peonies, blend with the gilded basket
in this graceful arrangement suitable for a buffet table*

CANAPES: *a varied assortment of cocktail canapé. Smoked salmon, shrimps, cheese, egg and sausages are used*

Ideas on Entertaining

BY KAY PENNETT

EVERY woman has her own ideas about entertaining. Every woman knows that the success of any party depends on the personality of the hostess. Much more important than etiquette, correct dress or even behaviour, certainly more important than lavish and expensive food, is that the hostess should be considerate of her guests and ensure that they should be at ease. Formality, among guests who are embarrassed by it, strict adherence to book etiquette with people who are a little unsure of the rules, ostentatious food served to those who live very simply, is not only unkind, it is a certain method of spoiling a party!

A good hostess has a mental list of her guests, and tries to arrange her party so that they will enjoy it—not *she*. To a hostess it ought not to matter whether or not she will enjoy her own party. Her only concern is that it should be enjoyed by her guests.

First she takes care to invite people whom she thinks will like each other. This is not quite as simple as it seems. She, herself, may quite easily enjoy the company of two people whom she knows would thoroughly dislike each other, perhaps because they hold completely different opinions on a number of subjects; perhaps because one is a dear fool and the other a wit. The reason does not matter. It is almost an instinct that warns a hostess that her two friends simply could not get on with each other. And because of that warning she takes care not to bring them together.

To the one party, then, she tries to bring together people who will take pleasure in each other's company. If she succeeds her party is well-started on the way to being a memorable one, so she takes a great deal of trouble selecting her guests.

A balanced mixed party, as many men as women, is more congenial. This is a harassing business! Often the best and most skilful hostess finds herself 'a man short.' Forty years ago this was considered a real catastrophe, but today it does not matter nearly as much. Indeed, I would always prefer to have an unbalanced party than drag in some slightly out-of-his-element soul, who, bewildered and embarrassed, tries so obviously and so heavily to get into the swing of things (and probably with his forced manner spoils the entire spirit of an evening!).

INVITATIONS

Having selected the guests, one has to invite them. Today, except for really big occasions, invitations are generally fairly informal. A phone call can, these days, be quite enough. Nevertheless, it must be quite clear. A guest likes to be quite sure that the invitation is a real one; it should not be so casual that the guest does not clearly understand that the hostess will be really pleased to see her, will know exactly when and where she is expected, and has some indication of the nature of the party she is attending so that she can know, within a little, what will be the most suitable clothes to wear.

There is an art of being a guest! Having received her invitation, a well-mannered guest lets her hostess know as quickly as possible whether or not she can come. Her acceptance (or otherwise) can be just as informal as the invitation and, indeed, to a great extent it is wise to couch one's reply in about the same degree as that of the invitation. For example, to give a formal, third-person reply to a casual postcard or phoned invitation can be downright rude!

The good hostess tries to remember personal tastes of her guests. Indeed, she notes all the little things that are easily forgotten and the lack of which may make a guest feel ill at ease. 'A' likes to have a biscuit in bed at night, 'B' cannot eat meat on Friday, 'C' is allergic to chrysanthemums and shakes the house with her sneezing if she sits in the same room with them! These idiosyncracies, remembered and unobtrusively looked after, make a guest know that his comfort and interests are of first consideration. Nothing makes him feel more quickly at ease and at home.

These remarks are general and apply to any sort of party however large or small. They are obvious, and yet, inexperienced housewives often overlook them. They are very important.

There are many parties—dinner parties, television parties, birthday parties, parties at the local, parties at the Ritz. Each is appropriate at its proper time and provided the guests are in the setting most congenial to them.

Suppose you, a housewife, reading this chapter, think of the sort of party you might give. It does not matter whether you live in a palace or a two-roomed cottage. It does not matter whether you have fourpence or £400 to spend. The spirit of your party can be the same and there are certain basic rules for it, whoever you may be inviting.

For what reason are you having your party? I am quite serious about this. There ought to be a reason for every party. Joan and I often give an *un*birth-day party. All our guests know that we're having a party because it is a good idea, and we feel we would like one and because it isn't our birthday. It may be somebody's celebration, or because you always have had a party on the first day of summer, or because the hens are laying well or because you have an anniversary. The actual reason does not matter, so long as your guests thoroughly understand that you want to be gay and there is a good excuse for festivity.

CHILDREN

Mary is eighteen months old. You must give her a party to celebrate her one-and-a-half years. Who shall you invite?

Mary's mother, obviously. That might be you or your next-door neighbour, and it doesn't matter very much. Who else? Mary is hardly old enough to have made a lot of bosom cronies yet. Who will you invite? Lots of other children eighteen months old? *And* their mothers? That might be a failure before you start. It could be much more fun to invite a lot of mothers, even one or two hoping-to-be-mothers, so that they can swap an anecdote or two, a knitting pattern or so, and probably, compare weights and measures. The babies will probably swap a squawk, anyway!

What about Mary and her contemporaries? Are they enjoying her party? Have you got everything pleasant and congenial for them? Are the facilities so organised that nappy-changing can be brisk and efficient. Have you a good supply of safety-pins, plenty of cushions, good spacious crawling room and all indigestible and uneatable objects put well out of the way? Are there milk, sugar, bibs, cotton wool and warm water in abundance?

Yes? Then Mary will have a good party.

Eunice is six-years-old. Her birthday was three months ago but you have decided to celebrate the fact that she is six and a quarter all but two days! Eunice is at school and has made friends. Indeed when you come to ask her, the entire school is her friend except for perhaps that horrid Polly who was her best friend yesterday but pulled her hair this morning.

Eunice has a mind of her own. You will require all your tact to ensure that she has her real friends to the party you give for her.

How are you going to entertain them? Children of that age dislike to feel they are 'being organised' and yet feel lost and woebegone if they are not. Plenty of pretty food, harmless, easy to eat and yet colourful and dainty, will help to break the ice and dispel the extraordinary shyness that unexpectedly attacks the most self-possessed toddler. Serve it early at the party. Have balloons and pretty Christmas decorations even if it is midsummer. Have crackers and a tiny toy – each toy *alike* so that there won't be silly squabbles. And have one or two simple, easy-to-understand games that they can all play (they will not all be exactly six and a quarter years old!). There is nearly always one little tot who will not, cannot, or is too shy to join in with the rest. Try to think of some simple little game he can play on his own. And don't give any of them a hard throwing game – they will wreck your house. Which reminds me that you will be well advised to clear valuable furniture and china out of their way.

It was Eunice's party. Not her mother's. And Eunice likes to be free of her mother sometimes. Incidentally Mother loves to be free of the Eunices of this world for a few hours, but make sure that the mothers know what time to collect their daughters – not too late. It is surprising how tired children get at a party.

James is somewhere round about twelve-years-old. You are having a party for him because the circus has come to town and James has never been to a circus. The circus is a great excitement in itself. Don't overdo it by taking too many of his friends; two, or three at the most are enough. At his age he knows which are his friends and he will brook no interference from you. You can either invite the offsprings of your friends and make it your party (when you are not really being a perfect hostess) or accept his friends and hope that they are yours as well!

No distractions during the circus, please! James has all his attention on the show and requires no additional amusement. But if, during the interval you light a cigarette, it is good manners to invite him to join you, though with the unspoken attitude "I believe you do not smoke?" He will feel adult and he will refuse the cigarette.

After the circus, ask him if he and his friends would care to have tea with you – and make sure it is a spread! They will have plenty to talk about. You can relax and enjoy your tea.

TEENAGERS

Elspeth is eighteen. She is feeling her feet among a lot of acquaintances all of whom she regards as being her friends. She is quite sure she is very sophisticated, she is a little out-spoken but, at heart, she is very unsure of herself and, as a defence against this strange world in which she finds herself, she acts with such self-assurance that she makes women twice her age feel uncomfortable in her company, old-fashioned, out-of-date and distinctly ill-at-ease.

She frequently has parties, although to those of us who are a little outside her world they are quite frighteningly casual affairs. Her greatest friend she meets with a nod and a grunt ; when she is enjoying herself most she looks most bored. Thus she has been since she was just turned sixteen – an odd mixture of untidy, almost slovenly, certainly careless, gaucherie and over-sensitive shyness.

You want to give her a party on her eighteenth birthday. Consultation, one-woman-to-another, asking her advice rather than making what you hope are helpful suggestions will find out who she wants to invite. (She will like to issue her own invitations.) Curiously enough, she will probably welcome the idea of a certain formality – invitations properly sent, place names at the dinner table. One or two touches like this will make her feel more sure of herself.

Give them the food she suggests. She may ask for a buffet, help-yourself side-board. She may like the idea of a several course dinner. But do it extra-well – her friends, and she, will love it. See they have music ; a gramophone is a must at a teenagers' party, with room to dance if they want to. And don't, if you value your name as a good hostess, try to persuade them to play games. Leave them alone ! But take my advice and insist that there is a definite finishing time for the party so that they all know when to go home.

THE HOUSEWIFE ENTERTAINS

Now let us suppose you want to entertain your contemporaries. Informal entertaining is most popular these days so we must deal with that first. There are the parties you have which are almost exclusively for women — mid-morning coffee and tea. These can be quite casual. Friends drop in, sometimes unexpectedly, and your duty is to ensure that no one of them feels 'out of it' and that they are talking away merrily. Apart from that you serve biscuits and plain type cakes with coffee in the morning and your prettiest and fanciest cakes, biscuits and sandwiches at the tea in the afternoon. Since your first consideration is always for the comfort of your guests, ensure that there are plenty of places where they can put their cup and saucer! Nothing is quite so wretched as that situation when one has a cup and saucer in one hand and a plate in the other, with no shelf or table near enough.

It is not usual to sit one's guests round a tea-table, except when children are present.

The housewife very rarely has much help in the home these days and the true domestic servant is hardly ever seen. When giving a luncheon or dinner party it will be almost certain that she will have to do all the work herself. There is no disgrace attached to such a state of affairs—it is the lot of every hostess to work, preparing for her party and clearing up afterwards. It is essential then, to plan so that things run smoothly. The mechanics, the method of making the party ' go,' the fact that she is probably thinking of several things at once, should not be too obvious. It is accepted that she may have to slip away to attend to the meal, but I think it is better not to say so, as she may make her guests feel they are being troublesome and a nuisance.

As the guests arrive, and according to how well she knows them and, indeed, to the time of year, she will give them an opportunity to take off heavy coats. Men look around vaguely for some place to park their hats and inevitable umbrellas. They will want to know if the car is all right in the road and whether they should remember to switch on their lights. Women, if they wear a hat, will probably keep it on at lunch time but give them the chance to remove it if they wish.

Take them all into the lounge, and unless there is a special programme they particularly want to see or hear do not have the television or radio switched on. They have come to talk to you and each other, not to sit looking at a little box. Ask if they are warm enough, or cool enough, make sure they all know each other and stay among them, helping the conversation along.

The weather as a topic of conversation is a bore unless it veers off quickly on to, say, gardening, sport or holidays. Talk about the things they want to talk about, and when they are chatting happily–be silent yourself. Give them a cocktail or a glass of good Sherry or Madeira, which is coming back into fashion, and relax while they enjoy themselves. Don't give much in the way of cocktail snacks, thus spoiling their appetites for the meal you have carefully prepared. A few stuffed olives, potato crisps, salted nuts, are plenty.

Now is the time when you can slip away, and if you have selected congenial friends for your party they will hardly notice your leaving. (Of course, if you have a modern Creda cooker with a timer your worries will hardly exist— you can forget the whole meal until you are ready to serve it!)

Try to be unruffled! Try to relax so that you, too, are enjoying the party. Plan your work before the party so that you have allowed yourself time to dress and look your best.

Be ready when your guests arrive, and if some are earlier than you expect, it is good manners not to let them know!

Whoever you are entertaining, however important your guests, however much you would like to impress them, it is not advisable to experiment with your cooking. Serve something that you have cooked at least once before and that you know will turn out a success! It is embarrassing for both hostess and guests if apologies have to be made for the food.

Decide on the menu well beforehand and consider the difficulties that might arise with last minute attention or with serving; you want food that is quickly dished up so that you are not hidden away in the kitchen for too long when you want to be with your friends.

Your table may be laid in advance, and these days it is considered perfectly correct if the first course, provided that it is a cold one and will not spoil, is already on the table. Place names are unusual at a small party held in your own house, but are not incorrect if you like to have them.

Your choice of menu will depend partly on the nature of your party. Obviously if it is a family-relation gathering, complete with children, the food you serve will be different from that you would select for a gathering of your husband's business friends and their wives.

In addition you will, of course, try to take into consideration the likes and dislikes of your guests.

It is when you are thinking about the menu, that you should remember the following points:

> The personal tastes of your guests
> The style of your party
> Choice of dishes that will not require much last minute cooking and attention
> Food that is fairly easily served

This last point is really quite important. It can create a lot of amusement, but nevertheless be a little ruffling, if you are wrestling with the carvers over a recalcitrant joint of meat! For my own part I prefer to select food that does not require carving at the table, for, however slickly you perform on it, it creates a gap in the smooth running of the meal. On the other hand many a family party is incomplete without the family joint, so that this point, again, depends somewhat on your guests.

Suppose you are having a summer evening party of adult friends. Summer is an easy time to entertain as you can serve some cold food. Suppose it is June and you want to put on a really splendid dinner party. A cold consommé, already served into individual dishes and placed at the table, would be a good start and you can forget about that course long before your guests arrive. Follow it by something that can be slipped quite easily on to a serving dish. How about asparagus? If you have tied this into bundles you will only have to lift it out of the saucepan, remove the string, pour melted butter over the tips and bring it to the table with the plates.

Do not let your guests help you. They will sit at the table, and you can continue talking as you take their consommé plates. Then slip away, bring in the asparagus, give each guest a hot plate and put the dish of asparagus by the lady who is the most important guest, who will help herself and pass the dish to her neighbour. If you have more than four guests it is perhaps easier to put each course in two serving dishes, so that the food rotates more quickly. You should serve yourself last, but don't make a very obvious business of this. If it is easier to serve yourself as the dish arrives in front of you and before one of your guests it does not matter very much, provided the whole atmosphere is relaxed and everyone is chatting happily, but certainly you should not start to eat until all your guests are served. You could follow this with cold meat, daintily carved in the kitchen and put ready on a serving dish, with a pretty salad; or you might like to have grilled steaks, all on the serving dish to be passed round the table. A cold pudding would be acceptable and this again can go round the table for the guests to help themselves.

In winter you will want to serve more hot food. I dish soups into individual, lidded, marmites, well before the party and keep them hot in the oven. I select a meat course that is easily served—tiny poussins so that each guest has one to himself—or cutlets altogether on the same dish—anything that I can put quickly on a serving dish in the kitchen and bring to the table to be passed round. Vegetables are chosen with the same idea in mind; carrots tossed in butter and put in some of the pretty, new ovenware can be covered and kept hot in the oven; so can peas, or indeed many vegetables coated with sauce. Some sauces must be made at the last minute, so try to have those which are very quickly made. On a cold winter's night something homely like steak and kidney pie can be very welcome, but it will be easier for you as a hostess if you make them in individual dishes. Serve a green salad, in individual side dishes; many people enjoy salad and it will add decoration to your table.

After the pudding I like to take my guests away from the table and serve coffee in another room—round the fire in winter, in the garden, perhaps, in summer—but this is another case where you may do as you wish. I do it because I can leave the last plates on the table and clear it later, but it is just as usual to remove the pudding or cheese plates and to serve coffee at the table.

If it is a real party, do not let your friends help you with the washing up, however earnestly they assure you that they would like to do so. Concentrate on their relaxation and forget the work you will have to cope with single-handed, later!

It ought not to be necessary to worry about providing entertainment for your guests. Nothing scares me more, nothing frightens shy people into their shells as much as determined efforts to 'make the party go' with games and charades! If you have done your job well and invited congenial people who will like each other's company they will chat together happily; and because someone is quieter than the rest, it does not necessarily mean he is not enjoying the evening. Your task is to watch, see that everybody has somebody to talk to and join anyone who is alone!

There are other parties. A comparatively new type is the television party, and it requires a new technique. Here, it is the task of a hostess, not to get her visitors talking, but to keep them quiet! To invite people to listen or look and then have such a clatter in your drawing room that they are unable to concentrate is, to say the least, rather unfortunate. It is always a puzzle to know what sort of refreshments to serve. Plates and cups can make a distracting noise, and I really think that a drink and cold snacks which can be held in the fingers are most suitable. If when the programme is over you can give them something more substantial, then do so.

Cocktail parties are easy as far as the drinks are concerned, but sometimes a hostess is puzzled what to give her guests to eat. At a true cocktail party the guests leave in time to go home for a meal, but sometimes the party lasts for an hour longer than one expected and one then feels that food should be provided. If it is a true cocktail party, or if your guests are staying to dinner afterwards, you only want to serve dishes of 'nibbles'—tiny cocktail biscuits, a few canapés and salted nuts. Perhaps you are having cocktails before a theatre followed by a late supper. In that case it would be considerate to make the cocktail snacks a little larger. Asparagus tips rolled in brown bread, some very dainty savoury sandwiches, tiny fingers of welsh-rarebit, small hot sausage rolls—all of these would be acceptable.

With the small party, run simply for the pleasure of meeting one's friends though with some slight reason for having it, the happiness of the guests is entirely in the hands of the hostess. A perfect hostess looks and behaves as though she is thoroughly enjoying her own party and is completely relaxed. In fact, she is working very hard. She has slogged away to make everything perfect before they come, and yet she has found time to dress and look her best. She knows that the minute they leave she must put on a large apron and work hard to set her house to rights again, but while they are there, she gives her guests her full attention, talking when necessary, but watching to see that other people are enjoying themselves and *listening* to them.

WEDDINGS

However informal her household, however casual her parties, there are some gatherings where a hostess must study etiquette. Perhaps the most important of these is the wedding party.

The bride's parents invite the guests to the marriage of their daughter. Friends of the bridegroom, including his relations are invited by the bride's parents. This formal invitation to the wedding ceremony includes an invitation to the reception to be held afterwards.

The reception is therefore given by the bride's parents who act as the host and hostess. It is essential that they and the bride and groom arrive at the place of reception before their guests and immediately followed by the bridegroom's parents. It is the job of the best man and the ushers to ensure that this order takes place and that the guests are conveyed from the church to the reception at the proper time.

The bride and groom usually receive the guests who then go on to meet their parents. It is *not* correct to congratulate the bride who should be wished every happiness. The groom is the one to receive congratulations.

The refreshments can take the form of a buffet, which is much more usual these days, but some people prefer to serve a formal meal. During the reception drinks are served continuously—sherry or cocktails.

The bride cuts the cake (one cut only), with the assistance of the groom, after the buffet and the cake is then removed for cutting before handing round to the guests. A glass of champagne is usually served to everybody while the cut cake is being handed round.

At this stage the speeches take place. How long they last and what form they take depends on custom in your particular circle, but they must take the following order. First, either the bride's father or a very old friend of her family proposes the toast of the bride and groom. This is replied to by the groom, who also proposes the toast of the bridesmaids. The best man replies on behalf of the bridesmaids and reads the telegrams and messages of goodwill.

Sometimes, if the father of the bride has not spoken first he likes to conclude the proceedings with a short speech, but this is not strictly necessary.

Other speeches are sometimes given but those above must be made in their correct order. Any other speakers therefore follow the best man, but precede the bride's father.

The guests will appreciate it if the bride and groom circulate among them at this stage, saying a few words to each before having to change for going away.

The engaged couple should acknowledge and thank friends for presents as they receive them—never at the reception.

This wedding reception party is the really important formal occasion. Deviation from what is accepted as strictly correct can lead to real confusion.

All other parties—wedding anniversaries, Christenings (where the formal part of the proceedings takes place in the church anyway), engagement parties, twenty-first birthdays—all these can be as informal or as formal as you like to make them and these days there are no strict unbreakable rules.

To sum up, I would say that with all parties there is only one unbreakable rule and that is that your guests—not you, but your guests—are entertained.

A hostess has a right to know whether or not she has succeeded in keeping this one rule! There is an art in being a guest. Apart from showing at the time that the party is being enjoyed, the perfect guest sends her hostess a letter of thanks and appreciation!

Table Decoration

BY CONSTANCE SPRY

THERE are few women today who do not regard flowers as an essential part of the decoration of the table; certainly for special occasions; generally for as many days in the year as can possibly be managed.

The great Miss Gertrude Jekyll, to whom women interested in flowers and gardens probably owe more than to any other single person, was born in 1843 and died in her ninetieth year in 1932. In a book on flower decoration written in 1907 she says that she remembers when flowers first began to be used for this purpose. In those days, and indeed for many years, it was the duty of the head gardener in a big house to arrange the table flowers, and many and magnificent were the schemes they devised. Among my books is an early encyclopaedia of cookery which illustrates some of the more ambitious efforts then in vogue; there is a description and instructions for the making of a shallow lake containing fish into which a fountain flows, the whole surrounded by flowers, and you are also told how to contrive matters so that palm trees seem to be growing through the table. Another book written by the gardener to a ducal estate depicts intricate patterns of leaves and flowers laid flat on the surface of the table and so planned that each dish of fruit or sweetmeats is encircled in a continuous and complicated design. There is no doubt about it that table decoration was taken seriously in those spacious days.

What a gamut of fashions we have gone through in the succeeding years! One early table piece was something called an epergne, which rose in tiers of ornament bearing little swinging baskets for sweetmeats, dishes to hold fruits, trumpet vases and what-nots, but however it was made, of silver or glass, when filled it constituted a high and concealing barrier. In those days there was considerable etiquette about conversation at dinner, so it did not matter that you could not see your *vis-à-vis* because you were not expected to exchange banter across the table.

Gradually head gardeners of the calibre of those days became rare; flowers for the table on the other hand grew increasingly popular, and so 'doing the flowers' often devolved on the daughter of the house. What a diversity of 'rages' we ran through! I remember that silver 'gates' with hollow posts to take the water for sweet peas and fern were much affected for local shows; silver trumpet vases figured largely in the brides' wedding presents and silver rose bowls graced the centres of our tables. 'Rucked' velvet, satin, brocade and fancy work were the materials used for the elaborate and essential table centres.

After this there was the 'rage' which included the highly popular black 'floating' bowl and the ubiquitous posy bowl.

186

Now I would say our taste has become broader and more discriminating and many beautiful objects, not all of them originally intended to hold flowers, are pressed into service for this purpose, often with very good and artistic results.

For years now women have had great opportunities to express their individuality and taste in all matters concerning the décor of the house; they have cast off the strong ties of convention that restricted their mothers and grandmothers, and particularly through the medium of flowers they have found an outlet for their artistic ability.

There are certain guiding principles which affect all forms of flower decoration, and it might be worth considering some of these in relation to the table.

SUITABILITY TO PURPOSE AND OCCASION

Applied to flowers for the table this calls for little comment; obviously those intended for luncheon are planned on simpler lines than those for a dinner table, and the importance of the occasion will also be taken into consideration. But I want to emphasise that simplicity or otherwise is not a matter of the rarity or value, in financial terms, of the flower chosen, it is the way these are put together or their relationship with the other objects that defines the 'simplicity' or the 'grandeur.' A basket or bowl of red garden roses on a wine-coloured linencloth might be perfect for a luncheon party, but a most exotic dinner party table can also be contrived with garden roses. For one that I find charming on a hot night we use a soft celadon green cloth with long sprays of pale full-blown yellow roses as a centrepiece. Candle bowls are fitted in a pair of two-arm candlesticks and in these there is another touch of yellow from a smaller rose, which carries the colour theme attractively to a higher level.

For parties for children, for the tables at a dance for young things, suitably gay effects are to be achieved with garden and wild flowers; for example a wide sun hat, fitted with a cake tin in the crown, tied around with ribbons and filled with poppies and corn is charming as a simple decoration; children are intrigued with a 'maypole' of flowers with ribbons spreading to each place ending in a little posy; and it does not matter whether the flowers be daisies, chrysanthemums, rambler roses, or whatever is in the garden; it is the idea which pleases.

Before leaving this aspect of 'suitability to purpose' I would like to mention one unusual table decoration which illustrates the point in perhaps an extreme way. The occasion was a supper party for 20 people; the only suitable place the large kitchen, the only table well-scrubbed deal. Of flowers there were plenty but they seemed to lack a *raison d'être* for this setting. On a simple tray of woven grass we made a 'still life' of the most decorative vegetables and fruits the garden could produce; we included bunches of tomatoes, green globe artichokes, sprays of ripe berries and purple plums and added the dark brown of an imported coconut; the whole had a sculptured look that seemed right on the large and heavy table. Even the prettiest basket of sweet peas, or the loveliest bowl of roses would, I feel, have failed here in their suitability to purpose.

187

RELATIONSHIP TO BACKGROUND
AND OTHER ASSOCIATED OBJECTS

No flower decoration for whatever purpose will be entirely satisfying if it bears no relationship to its background. If, in addition to a sympathetic setting the arrangement can by reason of colour or form be related to some other decorative object, the general effect is enhanced. This is fairly obvious when one considers flowers for general decoration, less so perhaps when it comes to table flowers. Nevertheless, even here it has importance. The hostess who insisted that her dinner party flowers must be designed to emphasize the colour of her curtains was a little off beat, for the only individual whose place at table allowed him to enjoy this was her husband who faced the curtains, and this had not been her primary consideration. It is the table itself that is the cynosure of all eyes, and for all practical purposes it is the table surface or the table cloth that constitutes the 'setting.'

Let us consider some surfaces and some cloths; a really beautiful dark polished table is an enviable possession enhancing, as it does, any beautiful thing set upon it. It adds also the beauty of reflection if flowers are arranged with this intention. White or pale-tinted flowers in particular show well on such a surface and when gleaming silver is added you may have the apotheosis of elegance.

I have a table of lesser quality which nevertheless produces not dissimilar effects; originally of bleached wood, I have had it 'marbled' a rich dark green and a piece of plate glass has been cut to fit the top. On this massed white roses, in particular an old-fashioned one called Blanc Double de Coubert, the 'muslin rose', looks exquisite. So does a posy of lilies of the valley, surrounded by a frill of their own leaves, set in a brandy glass, the stems slightly magnified by the clear globe of water. Water lilies, too, suit it. If these are required to remain open until a late hour, a teaspoon of melted wax must be poured into the middle of each flower; the process spoils in some degree their exquisite centres though this is only to be observed on near view. Dark red roses with dark green china; pale yellow daffodils and gayer china in turn look good on this surface.

This particular table although of no great value seems to reject, for it has dignity, any vases of too pretty-pretty a nature and it just won't have a posy bowl. I suppose really I like it best when I can go down to a certain bush of old roses, wine-purple in colour, and of these make a long low arrangement on its quiet surface, this has a restrained, velvet look of considerable richness. Before I leave this table I must mention the other ornaments which I find can be used to enhance the general effect. Two pieces of white decorative china. Flowers and figures are sometimes used to flank a central arrangement of pale flowers, they give an added high light. A pair of green china birds look good with the purple roses and with many other things, too.

I think that the darkly reflecting surface of this table looks particularly lovely when it is adorned by an oval garland at its centre. Later in connection with roses used I will describe it in more detail but for the moment it suffices to say that we use small sprigs and buds of crab apple, wild pear or of hawthorn and that when these are laid closely together in a slender and well graduated way it looks as though the centre of the table were garlanded with Dresden china. The space within the oval may hold a candelabrum or centrepiece of decorative china.

But whatever type of table one may possess it is by the use of tablecloths that one can ring the greatest number of changes. It is possible, without embarking on any undue extravagance, to have the prettiest possible collection of cloths to suit the flowers of each season of the year and if I may be allowed, I should like to describe those, made at home, which over a period of time have been collected and which add considerably to the general gaiety of everyday life as well as to party days.

It is a long time ago that I escaped from the tyranny of large double damask cloths; once, soon after I had a home of my own, I was faced with having to launder one myself because the laundry, always a long-term affair in a remote country place, had not come home. An old-fashioned kitchener, an old-fashioned iron, imperfect acquaintance with the ways of starch combined for my undoing; the cloth, like a stiff shirt-front in patches, tiredly limp in others, presented in the end an allover grey aspect. This was depressing and I vowed then and there not to be caught like that again. From then onward I have made easily washed cloths of all sorts and kinds, to suit the flowers, the occasion and the setting; for the most part the expenditure has been of time rather than of money; needlework for a winter's evening or for a summer holiday.

The simplest of them all are those made of coloured hessian; one of russet brown, one of wine-colour and another of yellow each edged with crochet of thick cotton. You may think hessian sounds a little rustic and coarse for the table, but it looks very good in the garden, on a porch or in the kitchen. On the brown I put simple wicker baskets filled with such flowers as kingcups and wallflowers; in the autumn berries and coloured leaves are equally pretty. The cloth of wine colour looks at its best when I can arrange in some simple bowl, perhaps of rough earthenware or tin-lined wood, a mass of rose, pink and claret coloured outdoor chrysanthemums or the brilliant French willow herb from burnt over patches of woodland. The yellow is useful in spring with masses of wild or garden daffodils and with baskets of tulips. I also have several table coverings made of the extremely pretty glass cloths that have recently come into the shops; these may be joined together by a simple overcast stitch or more decoratively with a linen tape laid over the edges and secured with herringbone stitch in cotton to match the predominant colour in the design. One such cloth has a design of roses bold enough to take a basket of mixed garden flowers; another has pink, blue and yellow stripes, very clean looking and charming with sweet peas.

For dinner parties there are several home-made cloths on which I can ring the changes; perhaps my favourite is the celadon green satin, mentioned earlier, the surface is soft rather than shiny and a rectangle at the centre is outlined by let-in bands of the reverse side of the satin. Believe me, this does not look overbright and is a lovely setting for pale yellow or pale pink flowers. Another is of inexpensive pink washing silk; I have had it for a long time and it has a familiar acquaintance with the wash tub; each year as rose-time comes round I find occasion to use it, decorated with a thick oval garland of pink full-blown garden roses it really looks like a party, yet never was party effect achieved with less expense. The full blown heads only of the roses are picked, no wood, no buds are wasted; the heads are floated all day in a bowl of water and then, shortly before dinner are removed and dried. By then I have cut out from thick paper the shape of the oval I want and have laid it on the table; inside this encirclement may stand candlesticks or central ornaments or the space may even be just left unadorned. The edges of the paper are concealed with a fringe of rose leaves and then the roses are laid on the paper. Towards the middle of each side of the oval the garland thickens and it is allowed to diminish a little at the ends. You may regard this as a somewhat extravagant use of flowers; in point of fact, it is far from being wasteful; only the heads are taken and after the party they may be picked up and put in floating bowls for use in the sitting-room. Another flower used in this way, too, is the hollyhock; we take the heads of double flowers in shades of soft pink down to the darkest to be found and graduate the colours in a similar garland.

In winter when flowers are scarce it is possible to add to the colour of the table by the use of cloths embroidered in somewhat rough and ready fashion with coloured tape or prussia bind.

It is best to take material of loose weave; a thick needle with a very large eye, called a pile needle, is required and a small needlework frame. The easiest method is to draw or trace for yourself a simple motif; perhaps the head of a marguerite or a spray of oats. The material, already joined to the size required, is spread out so that you can plan and decide the amount and the position of the ornament you wish. I generally pin small bits of paper at irregular intervals over the surface; when I am satisfied that I have enough and that the spacing is satisfactory, I mark the spots with a tacking thread. If then a close guide for the stitching is required the design may be transferred by means of carbon paper. You will find that after very little practice no pre-cise guide is wanted, for by the nature of the materials used no fine effects are possible or needed, the whole affair should look casual as though the little bunches had just been scattered at random over the surface. It is as well in the interests of lightness to use something in the nature of 'lazy-daisy' stitch; that is to say, keeping short stitches at the back whenever possible. Plain heads of white marguerites on a navy ground make a smart luncheon cloth, but one must buy dye-proof fabric so that the colour will not run in the wash. This cloth is edged with white cotton fringe; another of ears of corn on a yellow ground is finished with a wide hem.

A gift from Paris has re-awakened in me an interest in the once popular art of stencilling with washable colours on thin fabric. This gift was a cloth of white Swiss muslin, delicately stencilled all over with a design of lilac and roses with napkins to match. As the surface of my table is dark I put a sheet under this so that the colours may be well seen. When the first of the garden's pink roses and the last pale lilac are in bloom together I use them with this cloth and find it one of the most enchanting summer decorations. I would not tantalize you by telling about it except that you may so easily make one for yourself; you can buy quite a variety of stencils, washable paints are easy to get and the work is quickly done. We have a new one at the moment which has a pattern of green ivy leaves that will look well with any flowers in season.

Before leaving the matter of table cloths I would like to mention some party tricks; tarlatan, though not really practical for the wash tub, is inexpensive and can be used with good effect. Once for a very special occasion at a beautiful villa in Versailles we used a different tarlatan over a white base for each small supper table and this gave a delicate rainbow air to the room; at the centre of each table was a low mass of roses to match the cloth.

For a children's party we made a cloth of white tarlatan on which a design of cherries and leaves is applied; the cherries cut out in red satin ribbon were stuck to the cloth with Copydex, the leaves painted with washable paint. By mischance, after a while, this cloth found its way to the wash and while it has no longer its pristine crispness the cherries and the leaves are still there and we can still use it. A small white chip basket tied with scarlet ribbons and filled with ripe cherries is then put in front of every place for each child's delectation.

I should like now to describe to you some tables that over the years have remained in memory in spite of the diversity of decoration that I have been privileged to see: I remember in particular the simple arrangements we used to plan for a great London hostess before the war. Her house was of the most sophisticated, her table appointments beautiful. She had the cleverness that induced her to accept among much that was rare and costly the most simple flowers. She had a range of pale-tinted table cloths: spring green lawn, a primrose yellow, shell pink muslin, pale blue organdy, on which we planned a succession of luncheon party tables. I remember in particular putting wild daffodils on the pale green cloth, they were arranged in little baskets which were set about the table with a misleadingly casual air and they looked dewily fresh from the country. I rather think that her guests carried them away, which after all added to the success of the party.

Some times we used childish bunches of double pink daisies and forget-me-nots in low vases, and whenever we could pick enough we were encouraged to introduce the bright little fruits of wild strawberries. I remember, too, filling shells with trails of nasturtiums in colours of yellow and pale brown. Such decorations as these in the midst of elegant surroundings had a touch of sophistication. They were planned for very special, even royal, occasions and I think they made considerable impact on many of her visitors who were only just emerging from an era when carnations and fern, orchids and florists' roses were the flowers primarily considered suitable for such high occasions.

At night for dinner parties, the table took on a different aspect, and I remember a combination of shell pink camellias with some jade ornaments that was quite breathtaking.

For a city banquet we were allowed to use the wonderful silver gilt cups and bowls that were the property of a rich company; then the more exotic flowers came into their own, and yellow arums and tropical leaves echoed the grandeur of the rest of the *mise en scène*.

On another occasion we wanted to use a magnificent gold candelabrum at a moment when candles were not required. Each candleholder was fitted with a pointed posy of small flowers and the arrangements seemed to crown the table with colour. This set a fashion so that we now have bowls made which fit into a candlestick and hold both candles and flowers.

Now to come to a much simpler theme; have you ever found yourself called upon to decorate very narrow tables such as are used for accommodating a large number of people at a conference or similar assembly? And have you at the same time been told that only the smallest possible sum of money was available for the purpose? Many of us have. The least satisfactory use of the funds available is to buy a few florists' flowers and to use them in trumpet vases somewhat sparsely down the tables; this can be invidious and does not create a maximum of decorative effect. One plan which can be found both attractive and economical, particularly with spring flowers, I may be allowed to describe here. The day before the decoration is needed as many as possible simple flowers are collected; primroses, snowdrops, wild daffodils and so forth and all are allowed to remain overnight in deep water in a cool place. Then, to protect the table cloths, strips of paper of suitable width, and of any chosen length, are cut; on these a couch of moss, just damp, but not wet, is laid. The flowers, arranged in small bunches with an appropriate leaf or two, are then set about in the mossy bed. This has the effect of a tapestry of flowers. In the dampness they will keep fresh for the duration of the party. If required for use over several days small vases to contain water can be concealed in the moss.

A few small points still remain for discussion; they concern the height suitable for table flowers; the type of vases which may be used, the mechanics of fixing flowers in at the angle required and last of all, the proper preliminary and continued treatment that will help them to last.

For the home it is generally considered that low arrangements are best for the centre of the table, and in the interests of general conversation the idea is practical and sensible; but it is also restrictive and is apt to lead to a plethora of puddings and close-set posies. For a small party of three or five it is pleasant now and then to have the flowers not at the centre but towards one end of the table; this permits of change to a tolerably high arrangement. For large parties, tall flower arrangements are found convenient and indeed for the long tables for a banquet are, in the interests of effect, generally required. For buffet tables tall flowers are essential if the result of your efforts is not to be concealed at a very early stage of the proceedings. When a number of low arrangements are called for we often resort to bread tins, these may be painted in an unobtrusive colour although more often than not in such types of arrangement the container is quite concealed by overhanging flowers. It is as well to test new tins to see that they are, in fact, watertight.

I have mentioned the value of baskets to hold flowers and I have always in mind woven baskets of simple materials in good shapes rather than gilded florists' baskets. I very much like to use a tazza for the centre of my own table; provided this is not too high it enables one to have graceful down-falling curves of flowers which do not preclude a proper view of the table. I will confess to you that recently I have begun to arrange table flowers for special occasions in two and even in three tiers, almost going back decades in fashion; I find that provided the arrangement is light and well spaced the effect is not

A MEAL FOR ONE: *veal fillet, broad beans,*
new potatoes and salad

Steak and kidney pudding

too concealing and it is a most pleasant change from the low theme we have enjoyed for a very long time. For some occasions I have used a fruit comport with a second higher vase set inside it but now a simpler affair of three diminishing bowls is being manufactured for this purpose.

There are one or two practical points that may be found useful; it is inadvisable to pick or to buy flowers and to arrange them straight away in a warm room, most flowers greatly benefit from being given a night in deep water before being arranged. The tips of woody stems should be hammered and those of softer ones split to about an inch. Difficult subjects such as hellebores (Christmas and Lenten roses), bluebells, petunias and others can be made to last if, after picking, and before being plunged for the night in water up to their necks, the extreme tips of the stems are held in a saucepan of boiling water for a few seconds. Short-stemmed flowers must have their heads protected from steam by means of a cloth or soft paper. This is also good treatment for flowers that have wilted.

I use warm water in vases and fill up with this, too. It is most important to replenish the water in the vases but it is not necessary or advisable to change this at frequent intervals; flowers do not like to be disturbed and overhandled. Care must be taken that no overhanging leaf is acting as a siphon for the water.

There are various types of holders for flowers, one known as a pin-holder is popular, but perhaps the best all-round one is crumpled up two-inch mesh wire netting which may be allowed to stand above the rim. For open bowls this may be kept in place by bending 'ears' of the netting at intervals over the edge of the bowl; on the other hand, a piece of string passed right over both bowl and netting will serve, and if after arranging the string is not completely hidden it may be cut away for the intertwining stems of the flowers will remain safely in place.

In conclusion, it is to be remembered that in any flower arrangement you are in effect painting a picture with living materials and it is important that there shall be no blemish, no view of the holder, no sign of dirty water or green sediment although this is less likely to be a problem in low table arrangements than in higher vases of flowers. It is well, too, to remember that however beautiful the flowers, however delightful the colours, no arrangement will really please unless the lines of the whole are graceful.

Laundry Work

BY MARGUERITE PATTEN

THE MODERN washday becomes daily more and more mechanised and more and more efficient. Mechanisation means the introduction of washing machines and—the latest help to the housewife—the Creda Debonair Spin Dryer. Efficiency means the use of modern washing products, particularly of soapless detergents. Of these, my choice is Daz—a blue-mild and supremely efficient washing product, both for washing by hand and for use in a washing machine. But in order to get the very best out of your equipment and washing powder you need to know exactly how to use both of them! This is not because modern washing equipment like a washing machine or a spin dryer is difficult to use. There are, however, certain general principles about operating this labour-saving equipment which enable the wash to be done in the right way and in the right sequence. Only then is it possible for the equipment to operate at its maximum efficiency.

Before a spin dryer is put on to the market it is tested and re-tested. During the testing certain general principles about loading the dryer are evolved. The correct quantity of clothes to be dried is worked out. If the manufacturers say that a spin dryer will dry six pounds of clothes it is advisable to regard this as the maximum as overloading could cause damage to the fabrics. The same principle applies to the use of a washing machine—overloading will give an inefficient wash and should, therefore, be avoided.

A Creda Debonair Spin Dryer is like a good housewife—a little care and understanding works wonders, if it is to work hard and at its maximum efficiency.

In this chapter the aim is to give an idea of how to use washing machines and spin dryers to their best advantage—the right sequence in which to wash the clothes, the right sequence in which to spin dry, either for the machine, or for washing by hand.

The great increase in the sales of washing equipment, both washing machines and wash boilers, means that more and more women are doing not only a part, but all of their washing at home. This makes a Debonair a necessity as a part of the mechanical wash, for the articles must be dried quickly to save the time and effort of hanging them to dry.

The laundry problem will, therefore, be covered under several headings, the main ones being: Before Washing (things to do before you start); How to Wash (including recognising the different fabrics); How to Dry (getting the best out of a Debonair); and, a few notes on ironing and stain removal.

194

HOW TO WASH

Things to Do Before Washing

Sorting. Sorting used to be simple in the old days. There were only three different types of material—cotton, silk and wool. Sorting the family wash is not such a simple matter to-day. The introduction of man-made fibres and fabrics has introduced many new types of materials. There is nylon which has the feel of silk, cotton which seems like satin, and tweeds which are made of cotton, though they look and feel like wool. Sometimes a material may be a blend of two or more different types of fibre—natural and synthetic —such as terylene and wool, nylon and cotton and other variations.

So the first thing to do is to find out what sort of material a garment is made from. The best idea is to find this out when buying the garment or the material. Once the *type* of material is recognised, then it is a simple matter to sort out the various categories of washing which are not so very different after all from the old three categories. Therefore, the first stage of the wash is to *know your fabric.*

Categories of Fabrics

Strong fabrics. This is usually the main part of the family wash, and includes all whites and fast-coloured linens and cottons. Terylenes and nylons fall into this category (but not terylenes mixed with wool, for in the case of blended fabrics the weakest fabric takes precedence over the stronger). Strong fabrics include sheets, towels, all linen (tablecloths, table napkins), shirts (whether cotton or terylene—but not rayon), cotton aprons, most of the children's clothes, and the kitchen linen (tea towels, oven cloths, etc.).

Delicate fabrics. These include all silk garments, rayons, and cottons or other materials with special finishes (everglaze, permanently-pleated materials and drip-dry materials). Delicate underwear with permanent pleating, children's party dresses, and non-fast coloureds all come under this heading. But never forget that non-fast coloureds must *always* be washed by themselves.

Woollen fabrics (knitted and woven). These will include heavy knitwear, lightweight woollen materials and lightweight woollen sweaters, cardigans and underwear. Orlon and Acrilan are both man-made fabrics which should be washed as wool.

When a garment is bought, it may carry a tag with washing instructions, or perhaps the words 'Wash as Wool' or 'Wash as Cotton'. In that case it is a simple matter to follow the instructions given. But if it is not certain exactly what type of material the dress or blouse is made from, then it is best to err on the side of caution, using *warm* suds only and delicate treatment until it is quite certain how the material should be washed.

Pre-washing Treatment

Before the washing is put into the washing machine, or the wash boiler, or even before it is washed by hand, there are a few pre-washing jobs which should be attended to:

Don't forget to empty *all* the pockets of shirts, trousers, jeans, etc. It is so easy to spoil the entire wash with a piece of sticky rock in a jumper pocket, a crayon left in a school blouse, or even father's tobacco ash in his week-end shirt breast-pocket.

Don't forget to mend torn clothes before the washing is done. This applies particularly to machine washing, because the weight of the water going through the garment may cause small holes to become larger ones.

Colour testing is *very* important, especially if the garment is a strong colour. The greatest offenders in this category are blacks, strong bright blues and reds. They all have a tendency to be 'loose' dyes and it is always better to wash them alone. Other garments to watch carefully are coloured woollies. When woollens are dyed the fixative of the dye is acid in character. Nearly all washing products are alkaline and this has the effect of gradually neutralising the acid. After a number of washes the acid dye of the woollen garment may, in its turn, become 'loose'. So treat woollen garments very carefully, especially if the colours are bright.

It is quite simple to colour-test any garment, and this should be done before it is washed. Dip a small piece of the garment to be washed in sudsy water of the temperature recommended for washing the garment, then squeeze the fabric in a white towel or piece of plain white cloth. If the cloth is stained, then the colour is not fast. With woollens (especially the more delicate ones) it is a good plan to wet a small corner of the garment (in some place where it will not show) in the solution and then to press it with a warm iron between two pieces of white material. Again, if the cloth is stained the colour is not fast.

Once it is certain that a garment or material is non-fast coloured, it should be washed, rinsed and 'Debonaired' absolutely alone.

Badly stained whites (especially baby's nappies) should be pre-soaked before washing. The new plastic buckets are especially suitable for this job.

Loading and Timing the Washing for the Machine Wash

When the washing machine or wash boiler is being loaded, the main point to remember is that the garments must have enough water to enable them to move freely while they are being washed. The maximum load of a washing machine or wash boiler can vary considerably, but a good principle to remember is that it is better to put in fewer clothes than the washing machine manufacturer recommends, if the wash is to be really clean.

If the washing machine is overloaded, free movement, which is so necessary to get the washing load clean, will not be possible and the clothes will not be completely penetrated by the sudsy water.

The manufacturers' notices about loading a washing machine or wash boiler are always carefully worked out and tested, and if the instructions say '6 lbs. of dry washing' they mean just that. Another two or three garments popped in may mean that the whole wash is not its sparkling best.

Stain Removal

Bad stains, as distinct from ordinary dirt, should be removed *before* the garments are put into the washing machine, or in the case of hand washing before they are put into soak. Successful stain removal will depend very much on the recognition of the stain and the right treatment will vary accordingly, so this subject will be dealt with under the special section of 'Removing Those Stains', page 205.

Washing Method

Once the weekly wash has been sorted into the categories of strong fabrics, delicate fabrics and woollies, the next step is to decide on the right way to wash them. Each different fabric will need a different method, although many different fabrics can be washed together if the correct sorting has been done.

Machine Washing

Fill the tub to the correct water line with very hot water, start the machine running, and then sprinkle in the right amount of washing powder.

When the machine has made a good lather, add the load of whites gradually, starting with those which are cleanest. The average washing time recommended is five minutes. Once the first load is washed, the washing machine should be switched off, and the sudsy water removed from the clothes by putting them through the spin dryer.

If it is intended to boil any articles they can be separated at this stage and if the washing machine *boils* as well as washes, these things can be put aside until the washing is done. Other garments can be put straight into the sink for rinsing.

Lastly, put in heavily soiled articles, which will include kitchen tea towels, overalls, etc. Many people like to boil these as well as washing them because it has the effect of sterilising them. Then rinse them in the sink.

Washing by hand

Soak for half an hour in cold water. If necessary, clothes and linen can be soaked for up to four hours, but an overnight soak may have the effect of re-depositing dirt on to the fabric, and so do more harm than good. Don't forget that garments and linen should never be soaked in a wash boiler. A porcelain sink, a polythene bucket or an enamel bowl are all good receptacles for soaking, but don't use enamel utensils if they are rusty as this might mark the washing.

Stubborn marks which occur on the collars and cuffs of blouses should be rubbed with a little extra suds before the washing process begins.

Use water as hot as your hands can bear, and rub and squeeze soiled parts in the lather.

Rinse twice, first in hot water and then in cold.

Boiling Water is used for

Heavily stained towels, sheets and pillowcases, household linens, table-cloths, table napkins, baby's napkins. All these items will benefit from a weekly boil, both from the point of view of getting them cleaner and also from the fact that boiling sterilises the article. The latter fact is an important one to remember when you are dealing with kitchen linen and with all baby's napkins and towels. It is very important that these should not only be clean, but sterilised; and to keep soiled materials sterilised an occasional boil is the simplest way.

Articles for boiling can be added to lukewarm water containing either soap or a soapless detergent and then brought slowly to the boil and boiled for ten minutes. This should be done in the washing machine if possible, in a wash boiler or an enamel pail.

Once the garments have been boiled, they can be picked out with washing tongs and rinsed twice in warm water.

Hot Water is used for

Table linen, bed linen, personal garments (these will include handkerchiefs), coloured cottons and linens. Other types of material which can take hot water are knitted and fleecy cottons. These can be washed in a hot soapy water like coloured cottons.

Flannelette. This is a cotton material and can be washed in hot water, just like coloured cotton.

Nylon and Terylene and Tricel. When these materials are unblended with other fibres they can be washed in hot water in just the same way as coloured cottons and linens. But they should *never* be boiled. Points to remember about hand-washing nylon articles are:

Wash very frequently *before* the garment becomes heavily soiled.

White and fast colours can be pre-soaked for half an hour in a hand-hot solution of soap or soapless detergent.

Wash in fresh water with just enough washing product to make a good lather. Do not twist or hand wring. Machine wringing is safe when you have a wringer with rubber rollers under a light tension, but it is better even in this case to fold the material in a towel, and better still to put it in a spin dryer where the fabric can come to no harm.

Rinse nylon garments twice in hot water.

Nylon and Cotton. This can be washed exactly the same way as 100% nylon or Terylene.

Warm Water is used for

Woollens, Silks, Rayons.

Woollens. (This will include Orlons, Acrilan and other woven wool-like garments.) Most people prefer to wash woollens by hand although many washing machine manufacturers state that woollens can be washed for one minute in the machine in a warm solution of water and detergent, and a washing machine is invaluable for woollen blankets. One general principle to bear in mind concerning the washing of woollens is that they should not be allowed to become too dirty. Regular washing keeps them soft and pliable.

White Woollens. Make a good solution of detergent and warm water and squeeze the suds gently through the articles, making sure not to rub or twist. Rinse immediately in warm water.

Coloured Woollens. The method for washing these is exactly the same as for white woollens, but do colour-test the garment before each wash. Speed is a great help in keeping woollies their bright best, so wash them quickly and wash them separately. If colours are inclined to run the garment can be rolled in a piece of old cotton or linen before it is put through the Debonair—this will avoid the colour staining other garments.

Silks. Silk is, like wool, a natural fibre and will be best washed in warm water. Don't forget to colour-test before it is washed, and rinse twice after washing.

Rayon. Washing rayon is very much like washing silk, but a point to remember is that nearly all rayon loses its strength when it is wet, so it should be handled gently, and supported when it is washed and only squeezed—not wrung by hand. Rayon regains its strength when dry. Spin drying is the best way to remove moisture after washing. The washing solution used should be a mild one.

Mixtures. Terylene and Wool, Rayon and Cotton. In both these cases the material should be washed by the method required for the weakest fibre—that is, in warm water as for wool or rayon.

Cool Water is used for

Every garment which is not fast coloured, whether it is of wool, cotton, silk, rayon or even nylon. Non-fast coloureds must be washed alone. Chief offenders amongst colours which run are reds and blacks, whether they are plain colours or part of a pattern.

Wash non-fast coloureds separately very carefully in a cool detergent solution and then rinse twice in cool water.

Things to Wash by Hand

Most of the more delicate things should be washed by hand—fine silk or rayon underclothes, any garments which contain lace or net or delicate trimmings, knitted silks, fine woollen garments such as angora and cashmere, and the frailer chiffons and nets.

All these materials should be washed in warm water and rinsed twice in water of exactly the same temperature as that used for washing.

Baby's Wash

It is very important for a baby's health that his clothes should be well washed, rinsed, ironed and aired. If they are washed frequently they will also last longer. Dresses and woollies should be washed by hand according to the material, i.e., woollies and rayons need warm water, while little nylon dresses and cotton vests can take hot water.

Nappies. This is the biggest of the daily washing jobs for baby. They must be washed and boiled frequently. Both dirty and wet nappies should be rinsed quickly and left to soak in detergent solution.

After soaking wash by hand or in the machine in a hot detergent solution. Rinse very thoroughly. This is particularly important with nappies and the great advantage of a spin dryer is that it helps to extract the suds if you put the nappies in it *before* rinsing as well as afterwards.

To keep nappies spotlessly white, they should be boiled twice a week, either in a washing machine or wash boiler or else in an enamel pail.

Toys. All baby toys should be kept clean—sooner or later he will want to suck them, and it is very important that they should be spotless. Toys which are not specifically stated to be washable can be sponged with warm suds. Washable toys can be treated like woollen garments, that is, washed in warm suds and rinsed twice in warm water. Spin them. They will come to no harm in a Debonair, and more soil will be removed as you extract the water.

Fabrics with a finish

Some of the newest materials whether they are cottons or nylons, are specially treated to give them some extra type of finish. Most of these garments and materials have washing instructions attached to them when they are bought, but there are a few general rules which can be followed in washing these new materials.

Everglaze, Satinised Cotton, Embossed fabrics. These materials should never be bleached, rubbed or twisted as this may destroy the finish.

Seersuckers, Waffle Cottons, etc. These are not strictly finishes but a type of weave and they can be washed as cotton, in hot water.

Non-iron and minimum-iron clothes. Many of these can be washed in exactly the same way as cotton, but they should be well rinsed and *never* starched. Do not put through a wringer for this puts creases into non-iron cottons. They can, however, be put into the Creda Debonair (see page 203).

Crease-resistant cottons. Like Everglaze these materials must not be boiled or wrung. They should be washed in warm suds and well rinsed. They can be put into the Debonair (see page 203).

Durable pleating. There is strictly speaking no absolutely 'permanent' pleating, but pleated skirts and dresses can be washed many times with success. Wash this pleating gently in warm water and Daz, dunking the pleats in and out of the water. Don't rub or twist the pleating. Rinse twice and then 'strain' off the water by pulling it down towards the hem. Don't put pleated skirts and dresses through the wringer, but to avoid troublesome 'drips' put into the Debonair for 15 seconds only (see page 204).

Foundation Garments

Foundation garments, suspender belts and many brassières which contain rubber should be washed frequently. Clothes which are worn next to the body can easily be damaged by perspiration, and frequent washing not only keeps them in shape but preserves them and lengthens their life. It is possible to wash foundation garments by hand or in the machine. The main thing to remember is that heavy foundation garments go into the heavy wash, while the more delicate ones are washed in the same way as any other delicate undies.

Don't forget to do up any zips, hooks, or tapes before you start to wash them. Heavy garments will take hot water and finer things will need warm water—always, of course, with a good solution of washing powder. Rinse twice.

Swimsuits. Many swimsuits contain rubber, or rubberised fibres and they should be washed exactly like foundation garments. If the swimsuits are made of wool, they should be washed in warm water, while cotton swimsuits can take hot water. As a general rule, it is a good idea to wash most swimsuits in warm water to protect any rubberised parts. Coloured swimsuits should be colour-tested before they are washed, and in most cases should be washed by themselves. Rinse twice in warm water. Like foundation garments, swimsuits will keep their shape better and wear longer if they are washed frequently. This applies especially to suits which are worn in swimming pools. The disinfecting chlorine in the water may tend to discolour swimsuits and should be washed out.

THE WAY TO QUICK DRYING

Many women now have washing machines—some have automatic ironers —but between washing and ironing, there is the tiresome problem of drying. The Creda Debonair Spin Dryer is the answer to this tedious business ! It is small, compact, portable and safe. It will get your wet washing ready to iron in just four minutes. This means that the double job of washing and drying can be a one-morning task, saving time, labour—and clothes because when they are washed so quickly and safely you need fewer of them !

Although many people still say that the sun is the best drying agent, there are a great many modern fabrics which are damaged by being hung in the sun. Even old fashioned cottons fade by exposure to the sun so that, although for the strong old fashioned white linen it might have been a blessing, for modern fabrics a modern method of drying is not only quicker but more satisfactory. Furthermore, if you remove the water by extraction rather than by evaporation, the clothes are cleaner.

The Creda Debonair dries garments quickly and yet there is no strain on the fabric. Buttons and fasteners are not pulled off. The reason is that the moisture is extracted from the clothes by centrifugal force. They remain motionless in the rotating inner drum and are not therefore subjected to stretching or pulling. It is perfectly safe to dry any type of materials from thick blankets to fragile nylons in this easy way.

The Creda Debonair will take 6 lbs. (dry weight) of clothes. Six pounds is the quantity of clothes which will fit into the average washing machine, and it is certainly more than you would put into a basin or sink at one time. Six pounds of clothes means very little to the average woman, so here are the weights of a few of the usual things to be found in the average wash:

Single blanket	2 to 3 lbs.
Double blanket	4 to 5 lbs.
Single sheet	1 to 1½ lbs.
Double sheet	2 to 2½ lbs.
Pillow case	4 to 8 ozs.
Bolster case	8 ozs.
Tea tablecloth	8 ozs.
Dinner tablecloth	12 to 16 ozs.
Hand towel	4 to 8 ozs.
Man's shirt	8 ozs.
Woollen vest	11 ozs.
Silk blouse	3 ozs.
Pyjamas	12 to 16 ozs.
Overall	8 to 10 ozs.

Cotton vest	4 to 6 ozs.
Underwear	4 to 8 ozs.
Children's dresses	4 ozs.
Rayon slip	4 ozs.
Nightgown	4 to 8 ozs.
Housedress	8 to 12 ozs.
Handkerchiefs (six)	3 ozs.

The correct method of loading is to fill the Debonair with dripping wet clothes, *pressing* them down into the cylinder but not exerting too much pressure. Ensure that there are no ribbons or ends that could 'fly' over the top of the inner perforated drum, as this can cause tearing. Two inches from the top should be used as a rough guide line to a full load.

What is Dry ?

Dry enough to iron, is naturally the correct answer, but this is not as simple as it seems. When clothes are hung to dry, the water evaporates unevenly where there are several thicknesses of material, as with a hem, or when a garment is lined, the thick parts hold more water which, of course, takes longer to evaporate. The only solution is to hang the garment until it is bone-dry, and then 'damp it down' so that the moisture is spread evenly.

With the Debonair the water is extracted by centrifugal force. Each garment has the right degree of dampness, evenly spread over the whole fabric. Experiment will show that this is just right for ironing; the iron will slip easily over the fabric without any effort or excess steam.

How to Dry

Nylon. Drying nylon nighties, blouses and shirts used to present a problem, as it is often impossible to wring the water out of them with wringing, either by hand or a mechanical wringer. Very often a shirt which had already been through the wringer would, after being hung up, start to form a large pool on the kitchen or bathroom floor. These nylon garments now take four minutes in the Debonair, and they will be almost bone-dry. Drip-dry fabrics are perhaps better dealt with if enough water is left in the garment to pull out the creases, and it is recommended that you spin them for only 7 to 10 seconds. They will still be wet, wet enough to dry smooth without ironing, but there will not be enough water in them to cause puddles on the floor.

Nylon stockings. These should be tied in a flour bag. Although the inside of the Debonair is quite smooth and safe for stockings, it is easier and quicker to keep them together. Once the stockings are taken out of the bag, they can be hung to dry for a minute or two to get them back into shape, and then put away. Quick drying of stockings is a great saving of time and labour, not to mention the fact that this banishes the usual bathroom decoration—dripping stockings.

White and Fast-coloured Linens and Cottons

Good rinsing is the secret of getting these fabrics really bright and sparkling.

When the linen has been washed or boiled, it is a good plan, instead of putting it into the sink, to take it out of the sink or washing machine, hot or boiling, and put it into the Debonair. In this way the water (and incidentally the dirt and soap) is extracted immediately which is a great help to handling it. In the case of garments or household linen which has been taken straight from the boil, don't forget that the water which comes out of the Debonair will also be boiling, and add a little cold water to the pail before moving it.

The linen which remains in the Debonair will still be very hot, and it is a good plan to push it back into the bottom of the cylinder with the wash tongs, and slowly pour over it a jug of cold water. (Make sure, of course, that the pail is put back into position before this is done.) The Debonair is started again and after a couple of minutes the machine can be stopped and the cool linen taken out and put to rinse in the sink. Once the rinsing is finished they should be put dripping wet into the Debonair for the final 4-minute spin before ironing.

The excess water will immediately drain off, so again make sure to replace the bucket or pail. Close and turn the handle to lock the lid and switch on the Debonair. Some linen will only require one rinsing, but if it is thought necessary you can repeat the rinsing and drying process.

Woollens

Woollen fabrics, whether they are knitted or woven, will usually keep their shape when they are dried in the Debonair. It is water which is bad for wool and causes shrinking and felting, and the weight of the water drags knitted garments out of shape. Therefore, the more quickly woollen garments can be dried, the more chance there is of keeping them in shape during the life of the garment.

Three or four minutes in the Debonair is enough for most light knitted or woven woollen garments. Although they will not be absolutely dry when they come out of the dryer, they will have had the bulk of the water removed. They can be hung on the line immediately, and will be perfectly safe as they will no longer contain enough water to pull them out of shape.

Blankets

Blankets hold an immense amount of water and consequently drying by evaporation can take several days. However if they are put in the Debonair for four minutes, they will only require a short airing before they are put away !

Wash the blanket, put it through the Debonair to remove the suds and water, rinse it in the sink and put it again, dripping wet, into the Debonair. Don't forget that nearly a pailful of water will drain away before the Debonair is switched on. Empty this, and then put the pail back, and close and lock the lid to switch on. Another half pail of water will then be spun out of each blanket.

The blankets will not be completely dry, but most of the water will have gone, and a short hanging in a warm place will make them dry enough to shake out, fold and put away. (In the case of blankets with silk edges a quick iron to finish these adds a professional touch.)

Wool handled in this way is easier and quicker to deal with when the water is extracted quickly.

Synthetic Fabrics

Non-iron Cottons. These will need a little special handling. The usual instructions for non-iron cotton blouses or dresses is to 'hang to drip-dry'. The idea behind this is that the weight of the water in the fabric pulls it into place, and therefore, these garments need not be ironed. In the case of these specially treated fabrics, put them into the Debonair for 10 *seconds*. Take them out while still damp and then hang the blouse or dress on a plastic hanger in the air to dry in the usual way.

Pleated Terylene Skirts. Once these have been washed and rinsed, they can be dried very satisfactorily in the Debonair following this method. Make sure to put the skirt into the machine so that it is lying in a circle at the bottom of the cylinder and the waistband meets the hem.

In this way the skirt will not be folded across the pleats. Switch on the Debonair and in 15 seconds nearly all the water will have been extracted.

Rayons and Silks. After four minutes in the Debonair, these will be ready to iron.

Taking care of your Washing Machine and Debonair Spin Dryer

When the washing and drying is done, don't forget to wipe out the tubs of both your spin dryer and washing machine, and also wipe over the outside with a damp cloth. Always release pressure on your wringer rollers, pour clear water over them and if the rollers cannot be actually separated put a piece of clean white linen between them.

Ironing

A Hot Iron for

White Cottons and Linens. Iron when damp with a hot iron until quite dry. For a glossy finish, iron on the right side and on the wrong side for a matt finish.

Embroidery should be pressed first on the right side and then on the wrong. Don't press folds over firmly—this applies especially to starched articles. It is a good idea to change the way of folding from time to time. This will help the life of the linen.

Coloured Cottons and Linen. Starch and iron in the same way as white cottons. But don't forget that rough or dark materials should be ironed on the wrong side. Make sure that non-fast colours are thoroughly aired—otherwise they may run after ironing.

Organdie and Cotton Voile. Cotton voile should be ironed while evenly damp, on the wrong side. But organdie should be rolled in a damp towel after the final rinsing to remove excess moisture. It is then ironed on the right side while still very damp. This will produce a smooth crisp finish and starching will seldom be necessary.

Trubenised Collars. Iron damp with a hot iron.

A Warm Iron for

Silks. Most types of silk, should be slightly but evenly damp for ironing. If they do get too dry, they should not be sprinkled with water, but rolled in a damp cloth for a little time. Light coloured silks should be pressed on the right side and dark colours on the wrong side. Don't forget that tussore and shantung should be quite dry before they are ironed, otherwise the finished result may be patchy.

The folds of any silk should not be ironed.

A Cool Iron for

Rayons. These should be ironed when slightly but evenly damp. In the same way as silk, if they become too dry they should be rolled in a damp towel. Never iron the seams of rayon. Most rayons should be pressed on the wrong side, except in the case of those with a lustrous or satin finish.

Crêpe Suède should be ironed when quite dry.

Many rayon garments will carry ironing instructions and they should be carefully followed. Two points to remember are to keep the iron moving and not to press too heavily.

Rayons should be folded without pressing and aired thoroughly before being put away.

Thin Knitted Fabrics. Press with a cool iron when almost dry.

Nylons. Some of these will need no ironing at all, but if nylon is ironed, it should be with a cool iron when the fabric is dry.

When the label says, NON-IRON.

Sometimes it means exactly that—seersuckers, whether they are nylon or cotton should never be ironed, it spoils the effect although it will return when the material is damped down. Many materials are 'minimum iron' and this will mean that they will just need a finishing touch with a cool iron. When ironing most man-made fibres it is better to err on the safe side and use a cool iron.

Removing those Stains

There are a few general principles to remember when removing stains.

(1) The quicker it is dealt with, the better.

(2) The simplest way first. A cold water soak.

(3) If a stain remover is used, try it first where it doesn't show.

(4) Always rinse after treating with any stain remover. Bleach should never be allowed to dry into the fabric.

(5) *Test* frail materials before trying to remove the stain.

(6) Don't forget that some stains—like lipstick, are really two stains, colour and grease.

(7) Keep all chemicals out of the way of children—preferably locked up.

Tea, Coffee, Fruit, Beer and Wine Stains

All these are vegetable stains. If the stains are fresh, soak them immediately in cold water and then rinse.

If the stains are old or 'set': When the stained fabric is the type that can be boiled, spread a little Borax on it and pour boiling water through it. Rinse, put into hot Daz solution and bring to the boil. Boil for 10 minutes.

When the fabric cannot be boiled, steep in warm Borax solution (1 oz. to 1 pint), rinse, and wash in the method suitable to the fabric.

Fruit and wine stains should be covered with salt immediately, if possible, to prevent the spreading of the stain.

Butter, Cooking Fat, Wax, Cod Liver Oil, Lipstick

All these are grease stains. The first thing to do is to scrape off as much of the grease as possible. When the fabric can be boiled, boil it for 10 minutes. If it cannot be boiled, then use a grease solvent such as carbon tetrachloride, rinse and wash in warm water. There are also many proprietary kinds of grease solvent or eucalyptus may be used. If the grease is mixed with colour matter (lipstick) or dirt, the stain may need longer treatment, and it should be cleaned with carbon tetrachloride near an open window. Never inhale the fumes.

Iron Mould or Rust

If the fabric can be boiled, immerse in a solution of 1 tablespoonful tartaric acid to 1 pint of water. Boil till the stain is removed. Afterwards rinse in a solution of 1 teaspoonful bicarbonate of soda to 1 pint of water.

With white cottons or linens, stretch the stain over a bowl, sprinkle with salts of lemon crystals and pour on boiling water. Rinse very thoroughly and then boil for 10 minutes.

When the fabric cannot be boiled, treat the stain with fresh lemon juice. Then rinse and wash in warm suds.

Another method for fabrics which cannot be boiled is to make a solution of salts of lemon, using 1 teaspoonful to 1 pint of boiling water. When still hot, dip the stain in and out several times. Rinse thoroughly and then wash in warm, sudsy water.

Very delicate fabrics can be treated in this way, but the action of the salts of lemon should be immediately counteracted by soaking in a weak solution of Borax.

Ink—Blue or Black

If the stains are fresh, soak them in sour milk or rub with lemon juice and salt. Rinse well and wash in sudsy water.

If the ink stains are old, they should be treated in the same way as iron mould or rust stains.

Ink from Ball Point Pens

Most of these inks can be removed with methylated spirit. Or there is a special ball point pen ink remover which is effective. Some types of this ink can be removed with acetone, but this should never be used on acetate rayon. Whichever method is used, these stains must be washed afterwards.

Egg or Blood Stains

Soak in cold water and salt, and then finish by a five-minute soak in detergent solution, afterwards wash accordingly as stated on the material.

Grass Stains

Remove the marks with methylated spirit. Some very bad stains may need a soaking in the spirit, but usually a rubbing will be enough. The garment can afterwards be washed in detergent solution, according to the fabric. Don't forget that white flannels should not be soaked unless it is absolutely necessary.

Dyes and Discoloration

If a thorough washing does not remove these stains, then bleaching is the only answer, and this cannot be done at all on coloured fabrics.

BLEACHING WHITE MATERIALS

Linen and Cotton

Soak in methylated spirit and ammonia (5 drops of ammonia to 1 eggcupful of methylated spirit).

Silk and Wool

Use 10 vol. hydrogen peroxide to which is added a few drops of ammonia. (This can also be used for linen and cotton materials.)

Rayon

Use bleaching powder (1 oz. to 1 quart of water). Another bleach which can be used is sodium hypochlorite but in this case the material should not be soaked for more than 20 minutes.

Taking a Pride in One's Home

BY JOAN WHITGIFT

WHAT makes a home? A dwelling can be wealthy and spacious, or shabby and tiny. That does not seem to matter. It can be spotlessly clean or not so spotless; it can be a two-roomed flat or a twenty-roomed house, in a slum or a park; it can be a caravan or a cottage—any of these may or may not be a home. In any of them there may be something lacking, a quality that is indefinable but makes the family restless and a visitor ill at ease; but if, on the other hand, it is there, if the character is in the house, then that house becomes a home!

In these days of do-it-yourself, of little fortune and expensive living, it would be idle to define a home as a place of rest! We work hard, even at our hobbies, and as for the housewife, she will probably be running, single-handed, a house that contains enough work for three women, and be doing a full- or part-time paid job as well. To suggest that a house becomes a home because it is a place of relaxation is futile. Nor does its character, reflected by the tastes and idiosyncrasies of the family, entirely make it a home. One will fill his house with books, another has flowers or beautiful furniture, another takes pride in delicious food, perfectly served—but none has necessarily a home.

The occupants of a house that misses being a home are, and I am always sorry for them, aware that they have not caught the right spirit. They are constantly striving to 'make it right'. It can easily be detected—a feeling of tension, an over-anxiety to please, an apologetic attitude or sometimes a too-obvious complacency, makes the visitor feel that he would not be less uncomfortable in an hotel. (Come to that, some hotels can have the feeling of a home while others make you conscious that you are merely paying to stay there!)

I believe that the answer lies in orderliness, and by this I do not mean that only the well-organized and tidy house is a home; even untidiness can be orderly! In a house where the whole family, especially the children, untidy as they may be, know they have a sure place where there is no uncertainty and they can be confident and relaxed, *there* they will feel at home.

This is what every housewife endeavours to give. She seeks a feeling of order for her family, and she calls it 'taking a pride in her home'.

Children are often such self-contained creatures, so full of their own lives —the school, their friends, their own secret games—that the importance to them of orderliness in their home lives is sometimes overlooked. It can be quite startling to see their consternation, even fear, when something unusual comes into the routine. After years of opening the door to them as they come in from school, one afternoon their mother is not there. The simple explana-

Vegetable soup, roast beef, Yorkshire pudding, pineapple upside-down cake

PUDDINGS: *raisin batter, steamed puddings,
lemon meringue pie and fruit flan*

tion, that she has been delayed whilst shopping or has gone to tea with a friend, does not occur to them. Mother has gone! And you can see panic coming to faces of any age from five to fifteen.

A family likes to feel that there is a routine, that whatever happens outside, in the home nothing unexpected will occur inside to give any feeling of insecurity.

On the other hand, all families are composed of individuals with a very proper independent spirit, and a housewife needs all her tact if they are not to have a feeling of being organized and regimented. She has to be unobtrusive in her organizing. She must manage the home—not the family.

To a housewife, the most important room is probably the kitchen. This is her workshop, the place where she arranges the whole spirit of her house. To her family, however, the important place is the living-room. Here they eat, play, watch television, do their homework, entertain and work at their hobbies.

The housewife has work to do when the remainder of the family is at rest, and although it is more than likely that everybody will be willing to help, one will wash up while another peels the potatoes, there are many jobs that only she can do to her satisfaction. It may be cooking, or ironing, or polishing the silver: only she may do it. Most of these jobs are got out of the way during the day when she has the house to herself, but some of them, such as preparing a meal, must be done as they are needed during the time when the family is relaxed. One of the problems of housework is to do this work on time, so that routine is not upset and the house in an upheaval, and without disturbing the peace of the home. A housewife can slip from the living-room and slog away on her own, but no affectionate family can really rest if one member is getting hot and tired while she waits on them. She can interrupt their relaxation by demanding help—and feel guilty at doing so. Or she can fit the essential work into the family's plans for the day so that no one is put to any inconvenience when giving a hand with the chores.

A modern idea is to bring the family living-room into the kitchen, and sometimes this works well, especially where there are very young children. But the average kitchen is small, too small even for work, and there is little room for the family to sit at table or a television set. Good housewives try therefore to plan the evening and week-end work very carefully so that they can leave the kitchen and join the company in another room.

I believe that it is very important for the family to know the exact times of meals, so that they, too, know when they must be home, and at what time they will all be free. Of course, the time table can be altered to allow for special events, but if they know, for example, that Sunday lunch is at 1 p.m. and will be on the table at that time to the minute, they, too, will be punctual. They will know that by the time they have enjoyed their food and helped with the clearing away they can be free by, perhaps, 2.30 p.m. Some of the happiest families have a quite rigid time table and schedule of work. Even the toddler can be given a job, which he knows must be done before the whole family can relax together—and because he, too, is occupied, he is the happier for it.

This routine can best be established and most easily carried out if the kitchen has been well-planned and if it contains modern, labour-saving equipment. Much has already been said about modern kitchen equipment and I only want to point out here that a good work-room, well-stocked with useful appliances, while it will not in itself make a home, will go a very long way towards helping a housewife maintain a smooth-running, unflustered routine. It will bring orderliness into her family and less time will be spent alone in the kitchen.

A woman thinks of the kitchen as her personal domain, and while of course it is used by the whole family, she has an idea that this room is her particular possession. Her tools are placed where she could lay hands on them in the dark, and if each one is not put back in its particular place she feels at a loss, and for a moment irritated that someone has been interfering! Probably she keeps her cookery and other reference books here, where they are always at hand. Here she plans her day's work, thinks out the next menu, makes her shopping lists and experiments with her cooking. For this reason, the kitchen usually reflects the personality of the housewife alone, whereas every other room in the house will bear the stamp of the entire family.

Take the living-room. It shows the character of all its users. The furniture is polished, and there are flowers in a bowl; there is a sewing box in one corner. On the mantelshelf there is a pipe-rack, and a tray of spills. There is a small writing desk, somewhat splodged with ink, and with a deep cut in the wooden surface where an attempt has been made to carve initials. There is a high-chair, a television set, and, pushed well into the corner, an old arm-chair with a spaniel asleep in it. Other furniture is there, too, of course, but the things I have mentioned show that the room belongs to a family with two children and a dog. The room may be large or small, the contents shabby or shining new—it does not matter. Four people and a dog are at home in it. It belongs to them.

Each bedroom in the house becomes the property of its occupant. The housewife may furnish it and keep it clean, but she will not erase the marks of the one whose room it is. It may carry a very obvious touch, such as books or writing materials, or be a hobby workroom, with sewing machine or fret-saw. From these one knows the owner at a glance, though in many cases the personality is less obvious. The position of a chair near the window may mark an enthusiastic needle-woman, a couple of unexpected pictures will reveal the hobby of one, while a single trophy shows the sporting aspirations of another.

It would be foolish indeed for the housewife to attempt to exclude the personality of her family. It is frequently attempted, nevertheless, and it sometimes succeeds. Like a vacuum cleaner, some housewives pass through every room in the house removing every trace of the occupants, and leaving the new-cleaned furniture, all character eradicated, shining, spotless and completely without personality. Unfortunately, these are the women who are said most frequently to be taking a pride in their homes. In fact, I would define them as those who are merely proud. They take pride, not in their homes but in what they estimate to be their own efficiency. And to live in their houses must be misery!

To me, a garden is most revealing. You can look over a wall and tell just what sort of people live in the house. You can tell if they have children, if they keep pets, whether they have decided that the garden must be a playground or a garden first, whether they are leisurely, if they like good food, whether they are tidy, if they are ambitious, if they are affectionate—all from the appearance of their garden. Do they grow vegetables and herbs for cooking? Is there a swing for the children? Do they mow the lawn in unbroken green lines and cut the edges so that they are straight and sharp? Is there a set of paving-stones for the greater comfort of the housewife in wet weather? Is there a greenhouse all trimly and newly painted? Do they keep chickens and does the fence sag in the corner?

The answer to such questions will tell you a great deal and if you are sufficiently discerning it will even say whether or not the house is a home. An untidy garden, the grass worn bare, does not necessarily speak of neglect. It may merely mean that the owners have subjugated their own pleasures in order to give a very necessary playing area for their children.

Which is precisely what makes a home! Unless a house is easy, comfortable, and happy for the people who live in it, it will never really be a home.

The essentials in a home can be listed very quickly. Food, a place to store it, somewhere to cook it (a Creda cooker, of course), and somewhere to eat it; water and some means of getting it hot, warmth in winter and air in summer, a bed to sleep in and a place to keep one's clothes—these are the essentials. It is interesting to note that what you and I regard as the absolute minimum of necessity is a great deal more than many people possess. There are still houses in this country that have no water and one has not far to look abroad before one finds whole areas of unfortunates who never have enough to eat. If we have the essentials listed here, we can count ourselves lucky.

Once you have these essentials you are on your own! What else you get, what else you want to get when you can afford it, is up to you, but I believe most women would agree that this next list of mine is not unreasonable.

Less essential, but still essential. A housewife needs light—windows in the proper place, and electricity at strategic positions so that she can see to work at all times. All her efforts are directed towards the well-being and health of her family and to attain this, she must ensure that food and clothes and her house are clean. Not only, then, does she need to see, she needs a good sink with hot and fresh cold water. She needs dust-excluded cupboards, and a really cold food store so that food does not become contaminated. Because she must keep everything clean, the method of heating her home must be dustless, the methods of collecting dust and soil that settles in her house must be efficient.

Most women want to give their dwelling that feeling of home. Most women will agree with me that to have a sense of orderliness, to allow the house to keep its character, to be able to give their families a feeling of restfulness by relaxing with them, some help is imperative. We have already agreed that if the housewife spends all her waking hours on making her house efficient, the home is gone.

Electricity can save her many hours in the week and will do an enormous amount of work for her. To give one or two small examples, the week's home laundry can, with the help of electricity, be washed, dried, ironed and put away in a single morning. Food can be put in the oven, ready prepared for a meal, as long as fourteen hours before it is wanted, so that the housewife can plan her menus at a time when she does not need to join the family. A simple vacuum cleaner will save her hours of scattering damp tea leaves and brushing and sweeping. Polishers will brighten up a parquet floor in a few minutes, while a refrigerator will allow her to shop when it suits her, instead of hurrying out just before she needs the food. Electric heating will supply her with warmth when and where she wants it, and save stoking and lighting the fire with all the inevitable dusting and cleaning that follows in its train.

I do not agree with those people who think that a housewife has labour-saving equipment primarily to save labour. The saving of her time and work is an incidental to the much more important matter of making an orderly home for her family. Even the study of their health and proper feeding, while imperative, is valueless unless they are comfortable, happy and relaxed; and they cannot be at real rest unless she is relaxing with them. The housewife saves her time and labour so that she can be with her family. Thus, and only thus, will she have a healthy and a happy home.

It is for this reason that the housewife views with envy every labour-saving product she comes across. Fair game for every salesman with any kitchen gadget, greedy for anything that promises her a few more minutes with her family, she is sometimes deceived into buying worthless or badly-designed tools. Fortunately she is no fool, and while she may be persuaded to squander a few shillings on some minor appliances, she will think carefully and seek expert advice before she spends pounds.

Every woman, having acquired the essentials, has a mental list of the equipment she will have as soon as she can afford it. She puts it in order of preference and saves up to buy it when she can. Among the essentials she will already have water-heating, a Creda cooker, a refrigerator, a Debonair and a vacuum cleaner, but her 'saving-up-for' list will almost certainly have near the top of it an electric mixer, a floor polisher, a washing machine and a dish-washer—all things, you note, that will allow her to spend more time with her family.

GOING AWAY

Order tends to break down at holiday time. This is partly due to the extra work of preparation and packing, but is mostly the fault of the children who get so excited that it becomes almost impossible to keep them under control. Indeed, many a start for a holiday has its share of tears, and it is not surprising if some housewives get flustered at the noise and turmoil that suddenly boils in their homes.

Whether or not she is the sort of woman who writes tidy lists of clothes to be taken and jobs to be done is a matter of personality, but every wise house-wife certainly has a very clear idea of the work that lies in front of her before she can close the house for a holiday. If the laundering and mending has been attended to regularly throughout the year, one would imagine that there would be little else to do but pack the appropriate clothes, but it never quite seems to work out! Even supposing everything is clean, some clothes that are only worn on holiday are no longer suitable. Probably the children have grown out of them and at the last minute they have to be replaced.

Whatever way one is travelling, I think it is advisable to pack everything possible into suitcases. I remember seeing a rather forlorn and very hot family party on a railway station, their arms full of clothes, spades and buckets hanging on bits of string. Their car had obviously failed them and they were completing the journey by train—and very difficult they were finding it. Whenever they moved they seemed to drop something.

It is also a good idea to label each piece of luggage so that it can be clearly identified, and an added precaution is to paste another addressed label inside the lid of the suitcase in case the outer one should be torn off.

What clothes you take with you depends on the sort of holiday you have planned, but when there are children in the party it is as well to remember that they are happiest when they have no worry. It is very frustrating for a small boy if he has some beautiful, climbable rocks before him and his best shoes on his feet. A little girl may enjoy wearing a dainty dress, but she has no wish to be dainty when she might be building sand-castles. Old clothes, comfortable to wear and quick to wash and dry, are what children like best on holiday; then nobody worries if they get them grubby.

I always ensure against wet weather by taking raincoats, and some kind of amusement in case, one day, it should be really too wet to go out. Again, this is particularly important for children. A summer shower will not hurt them provided they are clad for it, but have some new, amusing game that they can play under cover in case it should be necessary. Children like being out in the rain, however, and as most mothers regard the summer holiday as belonging to them first (and they are right for they will remember it all their lives) they will take them out whenever possible, despite the weather. As long as they are warm the children will love it. With children in the party, warm clothes and raincoats are essential for everybody, so do not, because the weather has been fine up to the time of your going away, 'chance it' and take only summery, fine-day clothes.

Ensure that all lights and heating circuits are switched off before you leave. Switch off the refrigerator, empty it and leave the door open. Turn off the water at the main. Make arrangements well in advance so that the family pets will be properly cared for by kindly people, otherwise you will be fretting or feel they are fretting for you while you are away. Switch off the control unit of the cooker and make sure that you have not left any food in the oven. Throw away flowers and empty the vases and bowls.

As for the garden—if you take a pride in it, it is sure to be looking its best while you are not there to see it. It always does! And it is certain to look slightly woebegone when you come back, with dead flower heads awaiting the secateurs and weeds bobbing up in the rose bed. If you had perfect weather for your holiday, it probably looks parched, the lawn turning brown, leaves looking dusty, but, whatever the weather, your first weekend back is sure to be a very busy one tidying the garden to its usual appearance. Before you leave, you can guard against some disasters by staking and tying all tall plants. They say that one should cut the flowers in bud and give them away so that one does not come back to a wilderness of plants gone to seed, but I have never been able to bring myself to do that. If you love your garden, you cannot cut flowers before they bloom even when you know that you will not be there to see them.

It is advisable not to advertise the fact that your house is empty. Close and lock the windows, but do not draw the curtains. Do not forget a window, by the way. An open window, even a very small one which you might think quite impossible to get through, can prove big enough for a really resourceful thief, and there is a legal difference between walking (or crawling) into an open house and breaking in, and apparently a big difference if the thief is caught. Many would-be thieves will hesitate to force a way into a closed house but would slip through an open pantry window without a second thought.

Do not leave notes on the doorstep for the tradesmen. Other people can read them as well as they. Give money and valuables to the bank or somebody you know, for safe keeping. And never, never leave the front door key in a really clever secret hide. It will be the first place the thief will look in. They have that sort of brain. Leave the key and your holiday address with a nearby friend, and, for added precaution, tell the local police how long you will be away. The police are too busy to keep a special guard on your house and it would be unreasonable to expect it, but the bobby on his beat will give a second glance as he passes, and if your nearby friend reports something suspicious, they will come the more quickly.

Take a final glance into every room, register in your mind that everything is switched off, everything is closed or opened as it should be, close the front door behind you—and forget it! Do not, I beg of you, be one of those housewives who worry all through a fortnight's holiday, wondering whether they *did* switch off that fire in the bedroom!

If the housewife is calm and unflustered during the preparation and journey, so will be her family. Remember that travelling and excitement will tire the children very quickly. On a train or car journey, I have come to the conclusion that it is well-nigh impossible to persuade youngsters to take an interest in a game or a book. It is easier and less exhausting to find a new game that has a particular appeal for this one day of the year—how many airfields shall we pass, how many times shall we see the sea, how many miles nearer are we in this last hour? And I speak with real feeling when I suggest that every mother should insist that her children, however excited, are obedient, and do not make themselves a nuisance to other travellers. They should be given food at normal eating hours during their travel and plenty to drink, but they must not have sticky lollipops and other things that might prove troublesome in a railway carriage.

To a happy family, home-coming is as pleasant and exhilarating as going away.

THE CONVALESCENT

Looking after a convalescent is another of the unusual jobs that, I hope, only come to a housewife occasionally. As a rule, the really very ill are looked after professionally and in these cases the housewife can do very little beyond concealing her anxiety from the rest of the family. The convalescent is a very different matter. He is probably entirely dependent on the housewife, who has to divide her attention with some skill. If she devotes her whole time to the sickroom she neglects the remainder of the household and causes discontent. If she neglects the sickroom for the rest of the family the convalescent will be unhappy. If she brings them all together she may either spread the sickness or over-excite the invalid and make him worse.

Adults in her family will understand if she appears to be engrossed by the convalescent. It is, once again, the children who will make difficulties; and, if she is wise, she will try to devote at any rate some part of every day to them, if only long enough to assure them that everything will go back to normal as soon as the invalid is well again.

The convalescent needs a lot of attention for he is quite helplessly dependent on other people. At this stage, when he is recovering from an illness, he needs nourishing food, plenty of sleep, and a quiet house. These the housewife will endeavour to give him, but because the brain does not accept rest as quickly as the body, he will also need something to pass the long hours when he is not actually sleeping. When he is bored he asks for something—anything to get someone to come to see him. If he has something interesting to do he is less likely to be constantly calling for attention. A good book may keep him happy for hours, but he will probably want to read more than one at a time and he should have a good stock to choose from. He may like to do puzzles or to play patience. In any case, it will make him feel more restful if everything that he might want is close at hand.

The room should be warm but not overheated; he must have air but should not be in a draught. His bed must be made frequently, and the sheets and pillowcases must be fresh and clean.

The advice of a doctor should be taken about his food, but as a general rule, by the time he is convalescent he may eat anything he wants. If he is weak after a long illness he will have to be tempted with small, frequent dainties. Indeed, as soon as he asks for more substantial fare, the housewife can tell herself that he is well on the road to recovery.

Never give a convalescent large helpings until he asks for them. Do not ask him what he fancies to eat; his appetite is gone and he probably does not fancy anything. Give him a taste of what you think might prove appetizing—and give him really only a taste, so that he will decide that it is less bother to eat than to argue.

These tiny tastes should be served very frequently and they should be varied enough to make him look forward to the next one if only for the sheer pleasure of seeing what you have thought of this time. For the same reason, the tray should be pretty, the cloth smooth and spotless. A tiny jar with one or two fresh flowers helps, and the flowers should be different each time so that there is variety as well as daintiness.

Many a housewife, who serves normal meals quite brilliantly, experiences great difficulty in providing food that will stimulate the convalescent appetite. The most important rules are to vary the food, and to supply a little very often. This entails extra work, but provided there are a sufficient number of simple ideas and small dishes, at least some of the anxiety is gone.

The patient is almost sure to need plenty to drink, but a large jug by his bedside so that he can help himself is not the best way to persuade him, and in any case it is better for him if the drink is varied and, above all, fresh. Orange or lemon juice, hot milk, a cup of unsalted marmite, or beef tea—these should come to him at frequent intervals during the day, always in clean receptacles and only enough at each serving for him to drink at once.

Eggs are nourishing and, unless otherwise instructed, should be included in the diet. A tiny piece of toast with a scrambled egg on it, garnished with a very small piece of parsley; a plain omelette; a one-egg baked omelette in a small dish—all these can go up to him during the day and, provided they only consist of a couple of mouthfuls, will be enjoyed.

Cooked cheese and salads are not easily digested and should be avoided unless the patient asks for them (always try to give him any food he requests) but fish and some meat is nourishing and easily eaten. Do not give him a dollop of boiled cod with a plain white sauce. It looks ugly and unappetising. If you must give him cod, cook it, leave it to cool, flake it into small pieces and put a little of it in a baked omelette, but try to find some fish that would be more interesting. A single fillet of sole, the quarter of a whole fish, skinned, coated in brown raspings and grilled is an improvement, although it is advisable not to be lavish with butter when you are cooking it. Butter is good for the convalescent, but too much fat is inadvisable and deep-fried foods should, on the whole, be avoided. A pleasant way to serve fish is to mix an egg in a short half pint of milk, put it in a small pie dish with two rolled, skinned fillets of sole. Bake it in a very slow oven (200°F.) until set, and serve in the dish in which it is cooked.

Steamed salmon served hot with a couple of new potatoes can make an occasional treat, but do not garnish with cucumber, which is indigestible. Salmon is perhaps the only oily fish that should be given him as herrings and mackerel would probably require a stronger digestion. All white fish, but not shell-fish, is suitable.

Small pieces of the white meat of chicken can be steamed and served in a white sauce containing chopped mushroom. A poussin, split in half, grilled slowly, and laid on a bed of peas in a coloured dish may tempt him, while the remaining half can be kept in the refrigerator and served later as a fricassée. Sometimes a patient may like the thought of a piece of stewed steak; if he does, cut the steak into three or four one-inch cubes, coat them in seasoned flour and put them in a casserole. Then pour over them enough white stock to cover, cover the casserole and put it in an oven, cooking at 300°F. for about $1\frac{1}{4}$ hours, by which time the liquid will have thickened. Serve the steak with a little of the liquid with a few creamed potatoes and a grilled tomato.

Milk is nearly always good for the convalescent, but it must be made interesting. A milk jelly, or a junket in a white blob on a white plate looks pallid and insipid, but try making a milk jelly in an egg-cup and a prune mould in a saucer. Turn the prunes on to a plate (a coloured one if you have it) and then put the milk jelly on top and the dish immediately acquires some character. A blancmange may be no more nutritive because it is coloured, but it will appeal better to the appetite, and it is very little more trouble to make it of two colours. All jellies, and any food containing gelatine are of good nutritional value.

Vegetables and fruit are good. They are nourishing and, being colourful, they look appetising. Small pieces of steamed veal or lean ham mixed into a purée of spinach and served on toast and garnished with creamed potatoes, is much more imaginative than a spoonful of each side by side on a plate. A slice of liver is dull, but if you roll it in seasoned flour, stew it in a little stock, chop it in the stock when it is cooked and serve in a border of rice, garnished with asparagus tips, the same meal becomes exciting.

Cornflour and arrowroot custards are said to be excellent food for the convalescent. Make them slightly on the thin side, separate the yolk of an egg and whisk it into the custard. Let it cool, and whisk the egg white until it is stiff, folding it in. Then bake the custard for 15 minutes at 400°F. The difference in flavour and appearance is remarkable.

A little attention to details such as these will help the patient to regain his enthusiasm for food. And as soon as he begins to take an interest, the housewife knows that he is getting better.

*　　*　　*

The foregoing chapter is on the subject of taking a pride in one's home. The real pride of any housewife lies in her ability to tackle any job, however unexpected, however exacting, so that her house is not disorganized. Her house contains as many good tools as she can afford, all chosen to help her make the family comfortable and happy, with her enjoying their company.

The housewife is nurse, nursemaid, cook, cleaner, laundress—all these and many more.

The house is not a home until she is also a sympathetic companion to every member of her family.

Index